MALCOLM GOOD was born, brought up and went to school in Edinburgh. From school he worked in financial services, leaving in 1996 to complete a full time Masters of Business Administration at the University of Edinburgh. He is also professionally qualified in banking, marketing and project management. On leaving university, Malcolm worked as a management consultant, mainly abroad, including projects in Malaysia, Spain, Turkey and the United States of America. He returned to Edinburgh in the early 2000s, working in financial services and also part-time as an art dealer. In 2007 he left paid employment in order to complete *Self-Help for the 21st Century*. He enjoys sport, particularly watching football, and is interested in art, business, history, politics and people.

Self-Help for the 21st Century

MALCOLM GOOD

Luath Press Limited

EDINBURGH

www.luath.co.uk

First published 2008

ISBN (10): 1-906307-58-X

ISBN (13): 978-1-906307-58-5

The paper used in this book is recyclable. It is made
from low chlorine pulps produced in a low energy,
low emission manner from renewable forests.

The author's right to be identified as author of this book
under the Copyright, Designs and Patents Act 1988 has
been asserted.

Published by Luath Press
Printed and bound by CPI Antony Rowe, Chippenham
Designed by Tom Bee
Typeset in 9.5 point Quadraat by 3btype.com

Self-Help for the 21st Century

PAGE

Acknowledgements 7

Introduction 9

Historical context 11
By David McClay,
Senior Curator of the John Murray Archive, National Library of Scotland

I **Ambition** 'you can do it, anyone can do it' 15

II **Upbringing** 'we are all victims of being part of groups' 37

III **Learning** 'grain of the brain' 68

IV **Help and advice** 'what do you think?' 88

V **Opportunity** 'the talent or skills to cash in' 107

VI **Confidence** 'one of the keys to progression' 131

VII **Perseverance** 'just to keep going is often the supreme act of courage' 142

VIII **Structured approach**
'the most methodical man in Scotland' 160

IX **People skills** 'as good as any qualification on a piece of paper' 175

X **Leadership** 'at the top of the mountains, not in the valleys' 190

XI **Respect** 'it is not how you behave in the company of kings' 200

Biographies of the contributors 210

Cover image: *Portrait of Samuel Smiles* by Calum Colvin

Acknowledgements

I was introduced to Samuel Smiles' *Self-Help* by David McClay of the National Library of Scotland. More precisely, David was showing me a letter written to publisher John Murray in which Charles Darwin outlines a proposal for a scientific book, *On the Origin of Species*. The letter gives 12 chapter headings in roman numerals and, for example, Charles Darwin writes 'IV. Natural Selection (important; parts rather abstruse)'. Fascinated, I asked David 'what book was a big seller of the time?'. The reply was '*Self-Help* by Samuel Smiles', which was published by John Murray on the same day it published *On the Origin of Species*. So my interest started. David, thank you for writing the historical context for this book.

To Calum Colvin, I very much appreciate you allowing me to use your *Portrait of Samuel Smiles* as the cover image for this book, thank you. Calum created this portrait for *Heroes, Nineteenth Century Self-Help Role Models*, a joint exhibition between the National Library of Scotland and the Scottish National Portrait Gallery, which explores the influence of *Self-Help* and Samuel Smiles. The exhibition opened at the Scottish National Portrait Gallery in May 2008.

Without the assistance of many people this book would never have been completed. Thank you to my friends for their support and to those who helped arrange the meetings I had. In particular, I very much appreciate the time, effort and encouragement of Angela Audretsch, Tom Bee, Mary Blackford, Brenda-Gillian, Niall Brennan, Sally Cowburn, Leila Cruickshank, Fiona Cummings, Duncan Finlayson, Caroline Flynn, Alix Fraser, Alex Good, Ann Good, Susan Johnston, Jacqui Kane, Lorraine Lockley, Chani McBain, Gavin MacDougall, Karen Moss, Senga Nicol, Marlene Olsen, Wilma Shalliday, Caroline Smith and Doreen Waterland. Also, thanks to Leigh Campbell, Mark Mulhern and Derek Smith for reading and providing comment on early drafts of this book, your suggestions were extremely helpful in challenging me to improve my writing.

To Michael Atiyah, Chay Blyth, Calum Colvin, Eileen Crofton, John Crofton, Tam Dalyell, Tom Devine, Norman Drummond, Tom Farmer, Alan Finlayson, Brian Gill, Evelyn Glennie, Ron Hamilton, Robin Harper, Irvine Laidlaw, Jonathan Long, Margo MacDonald, Sheila McLean, George Mathewson, Kenneth Murray, Noreen Murray, George Robertson, Lewis Robertson, Jackie Stewart and William Stewart: thank you very much for your time, recommendations, voicing your opinions and encouraging me with this project.

By speaking with the contributors to *Self-Help for the 21st Century*, and thinking about what they have said and done, I learnt about them and their approach. But also, I have learnt about myself.

Introduction

'If you have genius, industry will improve it; if you have none, industry will supply its place': a quote that Samuel Smiles uses in *Self-Help*, which was published in 1859, to illustrate his overriding message that anyone can achieve through hard work and perseverance.

Reading *Self-Help* fired my imagination and intrigued me enough to ask 'what would be a modern interpretation of *Self-Help*?'. The best way I thought to answer that question was to talk with people that Samuel Smiles might have been interested in speaking with if he was alive today. Samuel Smiles was a Scot, who was born in Haddington, so I further defined the question by thinking in terms of Scots or those with a strong Scottish association. In addition, I added the proviso that each contributor had to be over the age of 40, as I took the view that someone with more experience of life would have greater insight than a younger person. Having set the criteria, I sent a few speculative letters to people that I consider to be prominent figures in their field requesting a meeting to discuss the topics raised in *Self-Help*. Although I approached the resultant interviews without a hypothesis and with no thoughts of writing a book, it was just something that I found interesting. However, I was encouraged by the very positive response I received, with recommendations to meet other people and the suggestion that I should publish a paper. And so it went on, contacting and interviewing people from across a range of disciplines. From a further recommendation, I contacted Luath Press, which showed interest in publishing a book based on my interviews. Suddenly I had deadlines and my focus turned from interviews to writing as I worked on presenting the material I had gathered.

No doubt, other people will have different views about who I should have included in this book. However, while I may not have contacted someone that I perhaps should have considered, a number of the people that I did contact preferred not to participate. Thus, this should not be viewed as some type of 'representative view', but rather, more simply, a presentation of the details of the interviews I held. What was said by the contributors forms the chapters of

Self-Help for the 21st Century and a summary of what was said is provided at the end of each chapter. A biography is given for each contributor at the end, and the book starts with a historical context that considers Samuel Smiles and *Self-Help*.

It was rewarding for me to speak with the contributors to *Self-Help for the 21st Century* and I have found their opinions very thought provoking in challenging and developing my thinking in relation to the concept of 'self-help'. I hope you enjoy reading their views.

Malcolm Good
May 2008

Historical Context

The idea for *Self-Help for the 21st Century* came from reading *Self-Help* by Samuel Smiles. This section is written by David McClay, Senior Curator of the John Murray Archive at the National Library of Scotland, who gives a historical perspective on *Self-Help* and Samuel Smiles.

'A book that defined an era'

> 'There are few books in history which have reflected the spirit of their age more faithfully and successfully than Samuel Smiles' *Self-Help*'.
>
> Asa Briggs, Historian

Self-Help: with Illustrations of Character, Conduct and Perseverance by Samuel Smiles (1812–1904) was published by John Murray in 1859. It was one of the most successful non-fiction books of the century and was an immediate bestseller; 20,000 copies were sold within a year and over 250,000 copies by the end of the century. Compare this with another of Murray's books published the very same day; Charles Darwin's *On the Origin of the Species*, which by the author's death in 1882 had sold 18,000 copies.

The title page of the first edition of *On the Origin of Species*, and a page from the account books of John Murray, showing the royalties paid to Charles Darwin and Samuel Smiles between 1868 and 1874. *Reproduced by kind permission of the Trustees of the National Library of Scotland.*

Self-Help was even more successful internationally, selling millions of copies. Although, much to Smiles' annoyance a lack of effective international copyright laws saw his work extensively 'pirated', particularly in the United States of America where a dozen publishers had combined sales that outsold the official Murray edition several times over. *Self-Help* was also translated into over 40 languages. This included the principal languages of Europe and nine language editions in India, including editions in Pali, Canarese and Tamil. In addition, the Korean, Chinese and Japanese editions are still in print today.

The international success of his works encouraged Smiles to travel. He particularly enjoyed his visits to Italy, where *Self-Help* was a phenomenal success, being reprinted over 60 times in 40 years. In Italy, he was introduced to Queen Margherita, the Prime Minister Benedetto Cairoli and patriotic national hero Giuseppe Garibaldi, who all admired his works.

Self-Help presented biographical sketches, anecdotes and quotes from a wide range of people who, for Smiles, displayed the necessary qualities of character to inspire working men. The principal quality and virtue Smiles wished to promote was perseverance; the determination to overcome adversity and obstacles. His message was that success in life depended not on genius or intellect but on 'the energetic use of simple means and ordinary qualities, with which nearly all human individuals have been endowed'.

Smiles displayed something of these qualities himself. Born in Haddington, Scotland, his father owned a modest general store. Whilst not poor, his parents had to work hard and do without to provide an education for their 11 children. His early education was solid, if undistinguished; in his *Autobiography* he recollected the words of one of his schoolmasters: 'Smiles! you will never be fit for anything but sweeping the streets of your native borough'. Despite this low opinion, Smiles managed to progress to Edinburgh University to study medicine.

However, he struggled to make his way as a surgeon and general practitioner in Haddington, where work was scarce and not well paid. He moved on to edit the reformist *Leeds Times*, but this was also poorly paid. He eventually became a company secretary, firstly to the Leeds and Thirsk Railway, then the South Eastern Railway and afterwards the National Provident Institution. In his evenings he campaigned for parliamentary, social and educational reform through lecturing and writing.

It was his interest in the railway engineer George Stephenson that produced his first real literary success; *The Life of George Stephenson* (1857). Encouraged by this, Smiles dusted off a previously rejected manuscript. It was the accumulated notes he had used for speaking to working men's associations and consisted of quotes and anecdotes of Smiles' heroes, whom he thought suitable role models for his audience. Perhaps unsurprisingly, the publisher Routledge had been dismissive of this cobbled together work and had rejected it four years earlier. However, the publishing house of John Murray saw little risk in publishing the work as Smiles himself was to cover all costs, with Murray receiving a modest 10 per cent of the sales income to cover his involvement. This book was *Self-Help*.

The success of *The Life of George Stephenson* and *Self-Help* brought Smiles a lucrative career as the biographer of the day. He favoured biographies of the new heroes of the Victorian age: the engineer, industrialist and manufacturer, particularly if they had achieved success through hard work and had overcome adversity and obstacles. The most notable of these biographies was his multi-volume *Lives of the Engineers* (1861–62). Also, more instructional and inspirational books in the *Self-Help* style followed with *Character* (1871), *Thrift* (1875), *Duty* (1880) and *Life and Labour* (1887).

Despite this literary success Smiles continued to work, with his writing being confined to evenings. He only retired from his company employments in 1871, at the age of 59, following a debilitating stroke. Having recovered from his stroke, which involved him relearning how to read and write, he continued to write and be published into old age. His final work *Josiah Wedgwood* was published in 1894 when he was 82. His energetic literary output consisted of 25 books and hundreds of articles, essays and pamphlets.

His books, particularly *Self-Help*, sold solidly throughout the 19th century. This was despite Smiles' insistence on maintaining a relatively high price for the book, against the advice of his publisher John Murray. Following his death, *Self-Help* continued to sell reasonably well for many years, although this may be largely attributed to the reduced price. The book received some criticism, particularly from socialists because of his emphasis on individual achievement. The manuscript for *Conduct*, Smiles' proposed last instalment in the *Self-Help* series, was burned in 1896 on the advice of John Murray.

Few, if any, would claim any great literary merit for *Self-Help*. It has a repetitive, almost relentless form, and lacks structure. Even his children dismissed it as a collection of scraps. Nor was Smiles the first to coin the phrase 'self-help', and he was not the first or only author to write inspirational or instructional advice. He was, however, one of the most successful in that genre and *Self-Help* deserves to be considered not only as a bestseller but also as a book that defined an era.

CHAPTER I

Ambition

'You can do it, anyone can do it'

What is ambition?
How is ambition progressed?
What drives and motivates ambition?

This section considers these questions to better understand what ambition means to people, what drives them on to achieve their ambitions and what additional motivations shape their approach. Chapter II then looks at the influences on upbringing to see how that may encourage or inhibit ambition and the fulfillment of potential.

'Charm of near horizons'

Ambition defined

Ambition tends to concentrate on the near term and is thought to evolve with people as their needs change, their learning increases and their perspectives alter. This is something physician John Crofton, who is best known for developing and instigating the protocols that cure tuberculosis, refers to as the 'charm of near horizons'. Sir John explains his approach when saying 'I have been mainly involved with trying to cope with the day-to-day problems that I face', concentrating on 'the more immediate short-term ends which seem practicable, achievable, moral and rewarding'. That does not mean that long-term goals are completely ignored as from 'time to time' Sir John turns his attention to ambitions associated with medicine's immediate concern of saving lives, 'such as relieving poverty, more closely at home, more remotely internationally'. The approach of concentrating on day-to-day activities, but with an eye on the future, is also given by former teacher and first parliamentary representative of the Green Party, Robin Harper, who recommends 'think ahead but do everything that needs to be done today'.

Evolving ambition informed by a concentration on the near term is perhaps also demonstrated in the approach of scientist William Stewart. This started in his childhood when, no doubt like many other young Scots, his first ambition was to play football for Scotland. On realising that he was not going to make the grade as a footballer, Sir William wanted to be a joiner. That ambition faltered when his father witnessed him wielding a hammer and advised that his vocation in life probably lay elsewhere. With both of these ideas consigned to history, Sir William had 'no real ambition' as a youngster except to do well in whatever he faced, whatever was immediately in front of him. This gave him the aspiration to do well in his Higher examinations at Dunoon Grammar School. Good Higher results enabled him to attend Glasgow University where he started out with the ambition of completing his degree course. That soon gave way to the ambition of a degree with honours, which was replaced by the ambition of gaining a 1st. With his 1st Class Honours Degree realised, Sir William saw the next step as a Doctorate. After attaining his Doctorate he wanted a job, then a good job, a Fellowship of the Royal Society, and so on until this ongoing incremental ambition led Sir William into senior and influential positions, such as Chief Executive of the Agricultural and Food Research Council, Chief Scientific Advisor to the United Kingdom Government and President of the Royal Society of Edinburgh.

Changing ambition, particularly in formative years, can be seen in former Deputy Leader of the Scottish National Party and the only current independent member of the Scottish Parliament, Margo MacDonald. Her childhood ambitions were as diverse as wanting to be the world's best netball player, the world's fastest swimmer, to sing at the New York Opera House, to become a successful psychiatrist and to be a successful advocate. She eventually decided to mix sport with teaching and attended Dunfermline College, where she graduated with a Diploma in Physical Education that resulted in her taking up a teaching post in 1963. Businessman Tom Farmer, who founded Kwik-Fit and grew it into the world's largest auto-care company, thinks evolving ambition is linked to needs within what he calls the 'cycle of life', where someone's ambitions change depending on the priorities that they have as they move from adolescence into adult life, such as buying a home, getting married, or starting a family.

In a similar vein, artist Calum Colvin, whose 'constructed photography' hangs in some of the foremost galleries in the world, sums up his approach to ambition when saying 'ambition will mean different things to different people, with that being dependent on what is important to them and their attitude at any given time'. Professor Colvin is another who focuses on what is in front of him, rather than following any long-term career ambition, as he prefers to concentrate on making his next picture better than his last one. Likewise, engineer and the inventor of daily disposable contact lenses, Ron Hamilton believes strongly in incremental improvement. This is demonstrated in his ongoing pursuit of enhancements to contact lens design, production, distribution and customer care. Businessman and three-time Formula One Motor Racing World Champion, Jackie Stewart, also sees improvement as incremental and comments that 'you don't go from kindergarten to university'. Such ongoing improvement in approach and attitude is something which Church of Scotland minister, motivational coach, former army chaplain and former headmaster, Norman Drummond believes people aspire to on a daily basis. Brian Gill, the Lord Justice Clerk and Scotland's second most senior judge, feels that people are always developing as they try to build on their strengths and reduce their weaknesses. Lord Gill believes that by retaining a clear sense of purpose, development will be supported. Also, Sheila McLean, who is a university Professor and advisor to government and world bodies on law and ethics in medicine, does not see herself as making a 'conscious drive to get to the top' but rather aspiring to be the best that she can be through working hard.

Scientist Noreen Murray, whose groundbreaking work on genetic engineering and DNA is fundamental to the research and understanding of molecular biology, is matter of fact in her summation of ongoing development or evolving ambition when stating that 'I just grew into things', as her knowledge increased and perceptions changed. Such a pragmatic approach may be seen in Tom Farmer's career. On leaving school, a failed eye test thwarted his ambition to follow his brother into the Merchant Navy. Instead, he joined a tyre distributor as a store boy where, rather than any long-term plan, his ambition was to become a van driver. That ambition was fuelled by the incentive of learning to drive, obtaining his own transport and gaining the trust of his employer. This more immediate view of ambition continued when he started his own business, as Sir Tom was not thinking about creating a global auto-care company. No, his ambition was to earn £15 per week; £5 to pay his rent, £5 for housekeeping and £5 left over for his own enjoyment.

George Mathewson notes that, when reviewing his career, it may look like he had put in place a programme of progression to achieve the long-term ambition of becoming Chief Executive of a FTSE 100 company. In fact, the opposite is true. Sir George has never had any great ambitions or career plans and he prefers to focus on the short-term. Sir George is perhaps best known for his work as Chairman and Chief Executive of the Royal Bank of Scotland Group and as Chairman of the Council that advises the Scottish Government on economic matters. Such short-term evolving ambition means that words such as 'aspiration' and 'ongoing improvement' are bracketed with 'ambition'. Indeed, theologian, philosopher, former headmaster and leading thinker on the education of children, Jonathan Long describes ambition as a 'boo word', meaning that it is often viewed as having negative connotations. He goes on to say, that should not be the case. Some people, such as Tam Dalyell, a Labour Member of Parliament for over 40 years, do not see themselves as ambitious at all, although he does respect ambition where someone is trying to achieve something as opposed to be somebody.

Even ambitions which could be considered as long-term can evolve. For example, internationally acclaimed musician, Evelyn Glennie's ambition has changed from being the best percussionist in the world, to being the best soloist, then the best musician and, presently, the best communicator that she can be. That ambition shifted as her perspective altered through achievement, learning and self-evaluation.

'I'll show you'

Drivers of ambition

A complex mixture of emotions and influences is thought to drive forward incremental ambition and improvement. It is considered that principal amongst those are an innate ambition, anxiety, encouragement and criticism.

'Continually raise the bar'

Innate

Innate ambition is described as an inbuilt drive that Tom Farmer suspects certain people, such as media mogul Rupert Murdoch, have, which pushes them to the top regardless of the area they work in. This may be true of Ron Hamilton, who surmises that even if he had lacked a formal education, his innate or natural ambition would have enabled him to have a successful career. It is that natural inbuilt ambition which ensures his quest to 'continually raise the bar' is never far away.

Maverick yachtsman Chay Blyth, who was the first person to circumnavigate the globe non-stop solo westwards, refers to an innate ambition that comes to the fore when he is faced with a challenge as he simply 'wants to do the thing'. This is also the case with internationally recognised mathematician Michael Atiyah, whose work in developing and solving complex problems is driven by the natural enjoyment he takes from the science that he encounters. Jackie Stewart sees an innate 'compulsion and necessity to achieve' in those who 'come from money' and were born with a 'silver spoon' but have a desire to achieve in their own right. This, he thinks, comes from an internal need for them to prove themselves rather than from any necessity to earn money.

A prominent feature of innate ambition is given as an ability and willingness to challenge yourself to improve. This is part of the make up of businessman Irvine Laidlaw, who founded the Institute of International Research and built it into the largest conference and event company in the world, as he is 'never satisfied with my own efforts'. Likewise, William Stewart advises that you should challenge yourself and those around you to do better than before and 'never duck a challenge'. Calum Colvin is another who challenges himself to improve. He describes himself as his 'own harshest critic' and knows intuitively if his work is good enough against his own demanding standards. Professor Colvin believes that if he stops striving to make his next picture his best then 'it is time to give up'.

'Fear of failure'

Anxiety

John Crofton advises that 'studies have shown that it is a mixture of anxiety and hard work which drive people forward', with Calum Colvin, Norman Drummond, Brian Gill, Jackie Stewart and Margo MacDonald all giving anxiety as core to their ongoing improvement and progression. Professor Colvin has a 'deep seated fear of doing something wrong', which manifests itself in his need for perfection in the art that he creates. A 'fear of failure and of letting people down' pushes Reverend Drummond from one challenge to the next and limits his ability to stop and take credit for achievements, and Lord Gill has a continual 'fear of not reaching my own standards'. He goes on to describe these standards as 'exacting'. This feeling of anxiety is also seen with Sir Jackie, who, even when he is on a high, starts to consider what could go wrong and 'can this continue?'. As he is never wholly comfortable with what is happening, Sir Jackie continually thinks about what improvements can be made or how new ideas and applications can be developed. The anxieties caused by childhood insecurities help drive forward Margo MacDonald's ambition to improve and she tries to be better than, or at least as good as, other people.

A desire to improve and succeed, driven by anxiety, is central to prominent academic, historian and writer of a number of critically acclaimed works on the history of Scotland and her people, Tom Devine. Professor Devine gives the 'profound sense of anxiety' he felt when his favoured university rejected his entrance application, as the catalyst that continues to shape his approach to improvement. At that time Scottish universities had an admission policy, based on 'The Attestation of Fitness', which required excellent examination grades across English, science and mathematics, regardless of the eventual subject to be studied. Professor Devine did well in his school examinations. These included geography, which he had been advised was a 'mathematical' subject, and he even bagged the school geography prize. However, his first choice of university advised Professor Devine that geography was not in fact classed in the 'mathematical' category. The advice he had been given was bogus and, with no other qualifications that fell into the mathematical grouping, his application was rejected. Oxford University was less dogmatic in its interpretation of school examination scores and he was offered a place to study there. Unfortunately, due to family issues, he felt unable to leave home at that time and he was eventually glad to accept a place at the recently constituted University of Strathclyde. The University of Strathclyde was formed in 1964 when the Scottish College of Commerce and the Royal College of Science and Technology amalgamated. The anxiety caused by that rejection continues, to a degree, to this day and was no doubt a force in Professor Devine achieving his 'naive ambition of writing a rounded, scholarly and successful history of the Scottish ethos' on the publication of *The Scottish Nation* in 1999.

'Cultivated my motivation'

Encouragement

Words such as 'you can' are considered by Norman Drummond to be of great importance in encouraging ambition and the fulfillment of potential. In particular, he believes that the encouragement given to a young person can have a positive impact way beyond reasonable expectations. In a similar sense, Irvine Laidlaw gives credit to someone on a job well done or the positive aspects of work completed. However, he also discusses, identifies and then implements improvements because he believes that 'positive encouragement' coupled with an appropriate challenge is the key to development and is essential for good mentoring.

The encouragement of his manager, Eric Kennedy, is something that molecular biologist Kenneth Murray feels he was lucky to have when working in his mid-teens as a technician with Boots the Chemist in Nottingham. Sir Kenneth eventually went on to conduct pioneering work on DNA, which included creating a vaccine against viral hepatitis B. In a similar way, Tom Farmer cites family and friends who celebrated his accomplishments with him and who have always been there to encourage him if he was down. Sir Tom credits much of his success to this caring and supportive environment, something he considers himself fortunate to have. A positive environment was also a key part of Noreen Murray's childhood, to the point that she feels that encouragement at home and the example set by her father 'cultivated my motivation'.

'Ridiculed, abused and humiliated'

Criticism

Jackie Stewart advises that the severe criticism he suffered of being 'ridiculed, abused and humiliated' at school due to his 'inability to read and write an essay', something he describes as 'basic for most people', was the catalyst to 'do well in something'. Sir Jackie now feels that his, at the time, unrecognised dyslexia meant that he was 'starting behind everyone else'. Thus, from the age of 12 to 14, he began to look for that 'something' as he wondered 'what to do?'.

Criticism can also be a spur to further improvement. Evelyn Glennie gives the example of when a contributor to Internet site YouTube concluded that somebody who is deaf can never be a 'proper musician'. Even though that comment attracted a torrent of opposing opinions, she used it as a stimulus to improve because she wanted to show that the contributor was wrong. Having said that, Dame Evelyn believes that strong challenges 'can make or break someone's interest'. Therefore, she encourages each individual to challenge themselves to improve by taking an approach that has been thought through and works for them. Another who is affected by the comment of others is Calum Colvin. He cannot recall the '98 per cent' of reviews of his work which were positive but can recollect, almost word for word, the 'two per cent' which were negative. Professor Colvin is motivated by those negative reviews to improve, his attitude being 'I'll show you'.

'Pay back time'

Motivations

The key impetus for improvement is thought to come from the drivers of ambition. However, other motivations are described as providing an outlet for that ambition. These include service through duty and responsibility, monetary reward, wealth creation and financial distribution. Rather than drive improvement, these motivations are thought to shape a particular style of approach and inform career choices.

'Not trying to save the world'

Service

Service is most often described in terms of, as Evelyn Glennie puts it, 'duty to the individual' because it is 'people that you connect with'. Serving others through personal accountability is something Jonathan Long regards as an implicit part of common humanity and 'fundamental to the universe'. He describes this as being 'on the side of right', where hope and faith form part of a bigger picture. This theme is taken up by Brian Gill. He contends that to be successful in life people need to have hope, take chances, require the assistance of others and most importantly, take the opportunity to help other people. Lord Gill considers that self-improvement is important, but he thinks the purpose of it all, the bigger picture, is to assist other people. He believes that putting the needs of others before your own needs gives meaning to life and that if he has not made sacrifices 'then I have failed as a person'. In addition, he thinks that those who concentrate on 'their own aggrandisement are doomed' and concludes by saying that service, as opposed to an egocentric approach, is the 'normal imperative in life'. Norman Drummond sees life as a calling in which he follows 'the man from Nazareth' and he places particular emphasis on the parable of the Good Samaritan. He is 'happiest when serving' and believes that this desire to serve was instilled in him by his parents. Reverend Drummond promotes compassion towards his fellow human beings, through the 'open-hearted' service of others, and he believes that you can see acts of kindness 'hourly, if you are looking for them'.

A practical approach to serving others is relayed by Tom Farmer. He believes that Mother Teresa was 'not trying to save the world' but was focused on helping one person. Once she had helped that person, she would then assist the next individual, then the next and so on. By adopting this incremental approach, and encouraging others to do likewise, she hoped to make a real difference to a large number of people.

This feeling of service to the individual saw Robin Harper volunteer to work on the Children's Panel and he describes his ambition as 'to be useful'. Alan Finlayson was concerned about child welfare from an early stage in his life. In particular, he is interested in the circumstances of upbringing and how that may be influenced by custody disputes. This led to him becoming the first Reporter to the Children's Panel for the City of Edinburgh in 1970. The Children's Panel is part of the Children's Hearing System and was established to take responsibility for deciding the appropriate assistance or response to youngsters, under the age of 16, who were either at risk or had committed a crime. Prior to this appointment, he worked as a solicitor in legal practice and more recently he was a Sheriff. He is now a Child Law Consultant providing advice to government and the courts. William Stewart lent direct assistance to a family of Vietnamese boat people, something he describes as 'very difficult' due to the language barriers and ingrained ideals. This meant that he found more common ground with the children, rather than with their parents, as they proved more open minded to new ideas. A concentration on the individual is also given in an example by John Crofton. His team had noticed the natural intelligence of a deaf and dumb homeless man who had 'desperately bad TB' and they stimulated his interests by encouraging him to play board games with the other patients. After the man was cured of his tuberculosis, thanks to the Church of Scotland, he was found a position as a gardener. Sir John calls this his 'greatest triumph'.

Generally, service is viewed as to an individual. However, on occasion, it is also given in terms of to a country. For instance, Chay Blyth expresses his time in the Army, which he describes as 'fabulous', as having 'served my country'. Although Sir Chay says that his motivation for joining the Parachute Regiment was 'adventure'. In his youth, Robin Harper was a member of the sea cadets and wanted to serve his country through joining the navy. However, he now thinks that duty or service is 'far deeper and broader' and considers it in terms of serving a wider society or the global environment. Sheila McLean does have the 'grandiose aim' of making things better for society as a whole, but in doing so recognises there are implications for 'real people'. This means that she believes in being considerate towards others, as she feels that ultimately, responsibility is to individual people. Michael Atiyah is motivated by serving society, something which he thinks came from his father, Edward, who was a writer and broadcaster. His father became such a 'disciple of Gandhi' that he considered going to follow him until his wife (Sir Michael's mother, Jean) convinced him otherwise. From that influence, Sir Michael sees himself in some ways as an 'idealist' which, he thinks, makes some people consider him to be 'unrealistic'. However, this means that he wishes to serve and contribute to society, and it has prompted him to take on the Presidencies of the Pugwash Conference, the Royal Society and the Royal Society of Edinburgh. Founded in 1957 by Bertrand Russell and Joseph Rotblat in Pugwash, Nova Scotia, the Pugwash Conference on Science and World Affairs works towards the resolution and reduction of armed conflict and threats to global security, in particular from nuclear weapons. The Royal Society is the United Kingdom's national academy of science and it supports scientific research and contributes to scientific policy making. The Royal Society of Edinburgh is an independent and non-political educational charity, which works for the public benefit in Scotland. As he has got older, Sir Michael's desire to contribute to society has increased and he thinks that people tend to be more selfish in conducting their own research and building a career when they are younger.

Kenneth Murray and Noreen Murray feel that service is in their thinking, but in the subconscious. However, that thinking was perhaps more obvious when they created the Darwin Trust of Edinburgh, Noreen Murray advising that they wished to help the 'very positive' approach that Edinburgh University had to molecular biology, and Sir Kenneth saying that they 'thought the Trust would be significantly useful' in developing students and research. Sir Kenneth adds that he also recalled hearing the phrase 'pay back time' being used by American university alumni. It was with that phrase in mind that they both decided to concentrate on their research in the United Kingdom, as having had the benefit of receiving their education there, they felt that they should 'pay back our responsibility to the British taxpayer'.

Service is considered to be closely linked to responsibility, with that perhaps giving a duty of care. For example, due to a higher public profile and the potential to influence other people, Tom Farmer believes that with financial wealth comes responsibility. Within that, he includes 'having to behave' in order to set a good example. Brian Gill adds to this thinking when suggesting that the prosperous, either in financial wealth or knowledge, should make sacrifices for the benefit of other people. A sense of responsibility is remarked on by Norman Drummond, who was brought up in a family that believed in 'social justice' and felt a responsibility to everyone in the local community. In particular, a responsibility to the employees of the family-owned Denholm Group, which has interests in shipping, seafood, logistics, industrial and oilfield services. Industrialist, administrator, first Chief Executive of the Scottish Development Agency and company recovery specialist, Lewis Robertson took a similar responsibility towards those working for the companies in which he had an executive role. Both Reverend Drummond and Sir Lewis had high levels of responsibility from an early age and feel that responsibility is something you just live with, as Sir Lewis puts it, 'doing what you have to do'.

In his roles as Secretary of State for Defence and Secretary General of NATO,

George Robertson has had direct responsibility for large numbers of people. For example, in the shadow cabinet he was responsible for three full-time and one part-time member of staff but 'overnight' gained direct responsibility for 343,000 people when he was appointed Secretary of State for Defence in 1997. However, he considers that his previous role of Shadow Secretary of State for Scotland (1993–97) was, in many ways, 'tougher' than when he was in actual Government. He advises that this was due to the Labour Party controlling 20 out of 29 Scottish Councils at a time when the Conservative Government had polled only 11 per cent of the vote in Scotland. Lord Robertson argues that this gave the Labour Party responsibility to the electorate, but not the power to meet those responsibilities. In addition, when shadowing Government, Lord Robertson had to be a 'jack of all trades' and speak on a huge variety of topics, in contrast to the more defined role he held in Government.

A responsibility to others may manifest itself in a desire to spread knowledge, and most of the contributors have lectured or taught in a formal setting. This is considered 'important' by Evelyn Glennie, who teaches primary school teachers how to teach music to their pupils. Her concentration on the teacher, rather than the pupil, helps to ensure that the lesson is not lost as it can be re-used by the teacher. In addition, Dame Evelyn does not take her normal fee, but instead uses that money for the benefit of the pupils by, for example, purchasing new musical instruments for the school. Tom Devine 'feels a responsibility' to educate by speaking about Scotland in an unbiased fashion. He thinks that Scotland often tends to have a 'Burns' supper school of history' of notorious subtitles about 'disasters of Darien, Culloden and Highland Clearances', or veers towards the other end of the scale and stresses its own self-importance. Professor Devine goes on to describe Scotland's 'collective amnesia' on its involvement in Empire and the 'chip on the shoulder' that can suggest Scotland was colonised and is a victim, 'try telling that to the Aboriginal people in Australia'. He believes that schools should take up the responsibility to teach a balanced view of Scottish History, by showing its relationship to Britain and its place in the wider world. Calum Colvin also feels a responsibility to educate, both through his art and his teaching. This comes from his desire to explore visually aspects of Scottish culture and history, in order to comment on the human condition and other people's perspectives of Scotland.

Taking responsibility is something that Noreen Murray advises that she is usually willing to do. However, when taking responsibility Evelyn Glennie believes that you cannot meet all expectations or be responsible to everyone because 'that would be too much'. For example, when performing, Dame Evelyn is perhaps educating an audience, but she does not see that as her responsibility. In carrying out his work, George Robertson does not worry about the weight of responsibility as, if you do, he thinks you could end up 'worrying about worrying', and William Stewart makes light of the pressure of responsibility that comes with the positions that he has undertaken when saying 'you should go and watch Dundee United!'.

'False illusion of success'

Money

Tom Farmer states that the primary reason people work is for money. He thinks that often secondary to that is the pleasure that people take from their job. Although he does add that practical considerations, such as travel time to and from work, are also important. Sir Tom used money to recognise and motivate employees by introducing a system of profit share to the work place. A similar approach was taken by Irvine Laidlaw when paying 'balloon bonuses', large amounts of money to staff that had attained a prescribed high level of performance. Sir Tom makes no apology for making money and, as he wants both him and his family to enjoy it, he is 'not just going to give it away'. Although, those comments should be balanced against his philanthropic work, which was recognised when he was awarded the Carnegie Medal of Philanthropy in 2005.

For Jackie Stewart money is not an objective in itself, but rather a by-product of doing well, and Margo MacDonald advises that money is not a motivator for her. However, she does not 'despise having it' and considers herself lucky that she now has enough money not to worry about it. Similarly, money was not an objective for Alan Finlayson when he took on the role of Reporter to the Children's Panel as his 'income halved'. Neither is it the main motivation for George Mathewson, although he does see money as an indicator of how well someone is doing. Sir George advises that he was the 'lowest paid CEO in the FTSE 100' and that he could have earned more money, for example, in investment banking. Sir George does though believe that pay is related to the job being done, and he argues that high Chief Executive Officer remuneration is due to few people being capable of carrying out that role.

Sheila McLean is concerned that increasingly people seem to want to be 'rich and famous' and gain 'obscene amounts of money' by 'humiliating' themselves in public, and she wonders 'what happened to wanting to be a doctor?'. However, an escalation in income is not viewed by Jonathan Long as equal to a corresponding increase in contentment. Indeed, Dr Long believes that chasing material gain can 'beguile us' and feeds an 'affluenza', which may have negative impacts through giving a 'false illusion of success'. Noreen Murray notes that people often seem more concerned by financial rewards, especially when they are near the end of their university degree. She sees this in science students who, she thinks, may gain and contribute more through following a career in science but are seduced by higher salary jobs such as city financiers. Norman Drummond notes that people can be happy with very little financial wealth and sees examples around the world, from Bedouin tribes to those in the United Kingdom who are happy to forego materialism. Calum Colvin does not believe art to be the most financially rewarding career and he is not money orientated, while Chay Blyth sees himself as ambitious, but not in a materialistic way. Sir Chay does not consider money to be a motivator in his personal or career choices and he describes people, ecology, environment and nature as the important things. However, he does add that money is perhaps more of an issue 'for the man on the Ford factory line'. Like Sir Chay, Robin Harper is not driven by money and states that he would not have become a teacher if he was. Although he does wonder if money would have been more in his thinking if he had married earlier or had children to support.

Evelyn Glennie takes a practical stance when saying that money influences decisions, such as what instruments to play and where to hold concerts. In addition, she believes that over the years she has been involved in the music industry it has changed due to the influence of money. In particular, Dame Evelyn sees some musicians receiving financial reward early in their careers which, she argues, may make them feel good but can 'spoil people', especially if it comes too easily or at a point prior to their talent being fully developed. Dame Evelyn does not view success in financial terms, but considers success to be about knowing yourself and being able to give something to others.

'Tremendous feeling to do something'

Wealth creation and distribution

Setting up and growing private enterprise is viewed by George Mathewson as a service in itself because it creates jobs and wealth. Ron Hamilton refers to himself as a 'wealth creator' and Irvine Laidlaw advises that if existing wealth was simply redistributed, it would only make a small difference to people's lives and it would lack the positive impact or sustainability of new wealth creation. Jackie Stewart describes wealth creation and distribution as a natural process, where jobs are created and living standards improved as people make and spend money. Sir Jackie considers that paying people for work is an effective means of distributing wealth and gives the example of employing a driver, 'a racing driver having someone drive him about, why are you doing that?'. He points out that by having a driver he is able to work in the car, which 'makes me more effective', and that both his direct employees and those people he contracts on a temporary basis earn money to support their lifestyles and families. He adds that these people will then spend their earnings and may even employ other people. Thus, Sir Jackie dislikes and thinks 'ridiculous' the extreme discontent or bitterness that he feels some people have against those who are monetarily better off.

In creating wealth, Tom Devine considers that a measured and sustainable increase in economic growth is best. In particular, where there is a balance between keeping up with the competition, meeting individual expectations and keeping gross materialism in check. Professor Devine thinks the state has a strong role to play in this and, as an example, he points to the state intervention that stimulated economic growth in the period following the Second World War. Professor Devine also advises that other small population countries, such as Austria, Denmark, Norway and Switzerland, have bigger state sectors and larger GDP growth than Scotland. This desire to increase overall wealth is highlighted by William Stewart when saying that in addition to health, education and security, people want to improve their standard of living; 'so a country's innovative capacity coupled to ways of exploiting that to national advantage via trade and industrial competitiveness in the harsh global economy of the 21st century is hugely important'.

Sheila McLean believes that 'obscene levels of earning', which are not based on an overall contribution to society and where people gain vast amounts of money that 'they cannot possibly need', is bad for wealth distribution and is likely to generate antipathy in certain sectors of the community. In certain instances she would 'cap salaried earnings' because she can see no justification for the likes of 'huge city bonuses' or the amounts paid 'for kicking a ball around'. She does though have a respect for those that have earned large amounts of money through their own hard work, have made a positive contribution to society and are using their money for the benefit of others. Professor McLean names Bill Gates, who founded computer business Microsoft, and Tom Hunter, who founded retailer Sports Division and who is now head of Private Equity Partnership West Coast Capital, as examples of these people.

Jonathan Long believes that there is a positive philanthropic focus in Scotland. Irvine Laidlaw describes this as a 'tremendous feeling to do something' which, although he does not know why, 'above all countries' is something he sees in Scotland. Jackie Stewart mentions that all the wealthy people he knows make donations to charities and good causes, and Ron Hamilton believes that he should have the discretion to spend his earnings as he sees fit, which he illustrates by saying 'another penny on income tax and I'm off'. He feels that his judgment on how to redistribute his money is as good as anyone else's and he chooses to do this by investing in new companies and, at a charitable level, by giving through the Church. When deciding how to distribute his financial wealth Lord Laidlaw applies the same rigours of business to his charitable work. For example, he finds out what benefit people are receiving and if he deems that charity 'is not giving a proper return on my money, it will not receive any more money from me'. In a similar vein, when making a donation, Evelyn Glennie 'must know' where it is going and how it will be used. For instance, every second year Dame Evelyn gives a concert at her local church and the money raised is split equally between two charities that she knows will use the funds for practical benefit. Getting the best return on its investment was the criterion used by the World Bank when it gave financial support to help implement the protocol against tuberculosis that John Crofton had developed. Karel Styblo, working with the International Union against Tuberculosis, had shown that this treatment and method of control was practicable even in very poor countries in East Africa. An investigation later by the World Bank demonstrated how tremendously cost effective this could be. As a result, the World Bank funded the World Health Organisation to greatly increase its international efforts in tuberculosis.

Calum Colvin rings a 'cynical note' on the relative nature of some charitable donations. Professor Colvin wonders whether an unemployed person donating £10 is, in relative terms, more generous than the multimillionaire giving thousands? He does though admire the 'super rich' who follow Andrew Carnegie's ambition to die penniless. Professor Colvin goes on to describe himself as having been 'more idealistic' in this area in the past.

Robin Harper considers that he was only 'incidentally' involved in wealth creation when he was working as a teacher, in so far as he was educating pupils to allow them to participate in society. For him, wealth generation is not the main part of human activity and he emphasises a need to curtail the excesses he thinks that can bring, such as 'trashing the planet' or 'shooting others with machine guns'. Alan Finlayson sums up his view when saying that he is 'not interested in creating a wealthier country but in creating a better society'.

'There has never been a better time'

Fulfilling ambition

It is suggested, particularly in Scotland, that there is unlikely to have been a better time than the present for people to fulfill their ambitions and potential if, as William Stewart says, 'you have drive, resilience and enthusiasm'. Calum Colvin thinks it depends on how 'up for it' you are, and Kenneth Murray also strikes a positive note when saying that if you really want to do something then you will.

An improved ability to achieve ambition is thought by Irvine Laidlaw to be, in part, due to what he sees as a definite movement in the United Kingdom towards a society based on merit. In the 1960s, when studying at the University of Leeds, he felt that ambition and the fulfillment of potential were stifled by the class system, which he feels was more prevalent then than today. Lord Laidlaw compares the present position in the United Kingdom to the lack of a strong class structure which he encountered in the United States of America in the 1970s. He found that merit-based approach refreshing and really got the feeling that anyone could make it, anyone could achieve their ambitions. That is not to say that he considers everything to be perfect today, far from it, as he sees great difficulties for those who are brought up in deprivation. Chay Blyth has heard opinions that are based on perceived class differences because the 'moment you use a knife and fork you are pigeon-holed'. However, he believes that people from Scotland and Ireland are more likely to be taken on merit as, he thinks, those from other parts of the British Isles cannot so readily place them into a class structure.

When considering the climate to fulfill ambition in Scotland, Tom Devine concludes that 'there has never been a better time'. Professor Devine quotes the 2001 Census and Scottish Attitudes Survey, which shows that a third of all Scottish males in employment have risen above their parents in social class. He sees that as part of the evidence that, over the last 25 years, Scotland has been transformed from perhaps the most strongly working class society in Western Europe to a middle class structure, where manufacturing has given way to a knowledge and service-based economy. Professor Devine ventures that this change supports opportunity for individuals and their families. Or as Irvine Laidlaw says, 'you can do it, anyone can do it'.

However, the influences that someone receives during their upbringing are described as determining the ability to develop and fulfill ambition or potential, as George Robertson states: 'how you are brought up in the early part of your life is crucial'.

Ambition: Summary

'You can do it, anyone can do it'

Ambition may be defined as simply trying to do your best at any given time whilst continually looking to improve. This concentration on the short-term and doing well in the next immediate thing may result in evolving ambition and incremental improvement, which is thought to alter in line with changing needs and perspectives in both professional and personal life. It is considered that principal amongst the drivers that push people forward are an innate or natural drive, where people challenge themselves to improve; a fear of not reaching certain standards; the encouragement received from other people; and criticism, where someone tries to prove that the critic is wrong. Even though one of these drivers may be prevalent, a combination of all four can play a part.

Service, responsibility to others, money, and a desire to create and distribute wealth are given as motivations that can determine career choices and shape ambitions, or how potential is satisfied. Service is usually described in terms of to an individual, although it is also given as to humanity or society and, on occasion, to a country. As opposed to taking a selfish view, there is a belief that service is the more natural human approach, even if that service is not necessarily always at the forefront of someone's mind. The responsibility that people take for their actions and how that affects other people, such as colleagues and employees, is considered to be closely related to service. However, it is thought that an individual cannot be responsible for everything or to everybody and should not be weighed down by the worry of responsibility. Money is described as a form of recognition and may be viewed as a measure of how well someone is doing or as an indication of someone's value to their employer. Having said that, greatly increasing income is not necessarily thought to correlate to the same increase in personal satisfaction. Nonetheless, wealth creation is viewed as a service and is seen as a sustainable way of producing and redistributing wealth, rather than by making straight-forward donations. Where donations or investments are made, whether by an individual, corporation or world body, the best return is sought.

There is a view that there has never been a better time to fulfill ambition or potential, in part due to a society that is perhaps moving increasingly towards rewarding merit. However, that view is tempered by a recognition that the circumstances of upbringing can influence how ambition is developed and potential realised.

Upbringing

'We are all victims of being part of groups'

What are the main influences on children during upbringing?
Can an appropriate attitude be adopted?
What part does intellect or talent play?

This section discusses the influences on early life, especially the individuals with whom children have regular contact, such as parents and teachers. In addition, the influences of wider society, including religious beliefs and the local community, are considered. Intellect and talent are also discussed, as is the part that personality and attitude play. This then leads into Chapter III, Learning, which starts with *Attitude to learning*.

The influence of peers is thought to become more prominent in later adolescence and is discussed under *Like-minded people* in Chapter IV, Help and Advice.

'The connection between merit and life is a myth'

Main influences

Ambition and the ability to fulfil potential can be inhibited by barriers that are described as inherent in society. Whether these barriers are broken down or reinforced is thought to depend on the influences received during upbringing.

'Dictated by the circumstances'

Structural barriers

Tom Devine affirms that economic, cultural and spiritual 'structural barriers' can lock people into poor economic circumstances, low ambitions and destructive lifestyles. The scale of those barriers being dependent on the circumstances that someone is born into and the influences on them as they grow up, as

John Crofton states, 'the starting point in life is hugely influential'. It is these barriers that Brian Gill thinks cause the 'tragedy of lost opportunity', where people are 'destined to fail', and he wonders 'how many people with undiscovered talent are lurking in neglected areas of society?'. Likewise, Irvine Laidlaw believes that talent is going to waste and he thinks that Scotland is no different from any other country in that regard. In some British cities he thinks that a lack of ambition is linked to a decline in heavy industry that has seen jobs become less obvious, more dispersed and maybe lower paid. Sheila McLean believes that such employment prospects, which she links to a decline in manufacturing and increase in the service sector, result in people not gaining the same fulfillment from 'making things and seeing output'. Professor McLean thinks that this can add to the barriers in society, including poor health, and exacerbate a 'defeatism' in young people that leads to some of them becoming 'out of control'. She is concerned that this could cause a reduction in overall standards and, she thinks, requires the Government to show 'gumption, will and intellect' in order to define and then address those issues. Professor Devine refers to these difficulties as the 'blight of major cities', where no city in the developed world yet knows how to rectify the position of significant numbers of people being left out of an overall ever increasing prosperity.

Robin Harper believes that life chances are 'dictated by the circumstances' someone is born into and not by their innate possibilities, although George Mathewson does think that there is a link between the value of someone's contribution and how well they do in life. However, Sir George warns, that does not mean people will fulfill their potential or get the success their efforts deserve. This is something that Tom Devine takes a stronger line on when saying 'the connection between merit and life is a myth'.

Brian Gill observes that those from a 'more privileged' background tend to have a better understanding of how society works and he argues that society 'punishes' those from difficult circumstances due to the prevailing system working against them. Sir George feels that this is not a deliberate exclusion by society but rather an inevitable part of opportunity being created and taken by others. Another slant to this view is given by Calum Colvin who asserts that certain groups in society do not get an 'even break' due to a system of 'political self-interest'.

The difficulties in this area are acknowledged by Kenneth Murray who likes to think that if there is a sufficient incentive to 'go for it' then you will succeed regardless of your background. Nevertheless, he recognises the influence of upbringing and considers this to be an exceptionally difficult area. Similarly, Michael Atiyah describes this as a 'difficult question' and widens the thinking by saying that 'if you are born into poverty in Africa, it will be very difficult'. Tam Dalyell also sees this as a difficult area and, due to circumstances varying so much in upbringing, 'no general rule can be applied'. Likewise, George Mathewson appreciates that there is no easy answer and mentions that, while some may disagree, every conceivable solution has been tried in the United States of America with limited success. However, he does think that simply throwing money at such issues is not the answer. Brian Gill does think that the present system, where the state provides a social security net, is far more favourable than the often little checked free market ideals that were prevalent in the Victorian society in which Samuel Smiles lived.

Robin Harper contends that a large proportion of the young men in Polmont Young Offenders Institution, which incarcerates young adults who have committed offences punishable with a prison term in Scotland, have been through a cycle that started with an extended period of 'appalling deprivation'. This, he thinks, leads some youngsters into criminal activity and, often after being taken into care, the prison system. In some of these cases, he sees 'poverty, violence, abuse and drunkenness' prevalent in families over a number of generations, exacerbated by some care homes being 'dreadful places' where children suffered further abuse.

How to remove the barriers that society can create is seen as a difficult question but, as Irvine Laidlaw points out, a lack of ambition can be determined in upbringing. This is something Margo MacDonald agrees with, and she advises that the ability to fulfill potential will depend upon the environment someone is brought up in. Influences on that environment are believed to come from teachers, other adult role models and the wider community. However, the greatest influence on children is generally thought to come from their parents.

'The prime educator of values and attitudes'

Parents

Tam Dalyell, Norman Drummond and John Crofton all view parents as the biggest influence on a child's future. Sir John quotes a study that was conducted in the United States of America, which tracked those with high intellect to try and explain why some people seemed to underachieve in relation to their capacity for understanding and reasoning. The conclusion was parental influence. Sir John does though think that parental influence switches at about secondary school age to peers and to fashion. Sheila McLean advises that children tend to repeat the behaviour of their parents, something Reverend Drummond observed when he was enjoying a coffee at a bookshop in Edinburgh. He noticed two families, each consisting of a father, mother and their baby. One child was calm and at ease but the other child was very irritable which, he noted, mimicked the approach and behaviour of the adults. Reverend Drummond considers himself fortunate in having 'tremendously strong parents' and for being recognised within his family for what he was and what he achieved. He gained a keen sense of social responsibility from his parents and that permeates much of his work and informs his opinion that you should 'surround children with positivity'. In a similar fashion, William Stewart received 'terrific support from my parents', and Ron Hamilton gained his ethos from his family, particularly his father. This identification with his family was accentuated, at the age of 14, when the family moved from Bellshill to Glasgow and he was thrown back on his relatives, as his friends changed.

The link between parents and an incremental ambition fostered in childhood is perhaps seen in Noreen Murray. She regards her father as a tremendous influence in stimulating her interests; academically, socially, environmentally and in sport. This was not dented by her father, a school teacher, taking the cane to her and fellow pupils when they were caught breaking the rule of no running in the school corridors, only one day after a serious accident in a corridor. She took the attitude that she had broken the rule and should accept the punishment. Chay Blyth also thinks that parents are the key influencers of children. His mother came from a 'reasonably well-off family' but on becoming pregnant to a soldier her parents disapproved to the extent that they flung her out of the family home. Thus, his own home environment was 'working class' but this experience, he thinks, influenced his mother to encourage him to 'get up a rung'. Similarly, Margo MacDonald was encouraged to 'aim high' by her mother. This was despite coming from a 'broken home which can give insecurities' as she was 'not approved of' as a child, except by her mother.

Parental influence was important in defining Kenneth Murray's choice of career. His father was a coalminer who moved the family to Nottingham when work dried up in Sir Kenneth's native Yorkshire. Subsequently, on suffering an accident at work, which made it impossible to continue as a miner, his father 'was fortunate' to get a job above ground before leaving to become the local school janitor. Encouraged by his father not to follow him down the pits, Sir Kenneth gained a job as a laboratory technician with Boots the Chemist at age 16 and thus started his career in chemistry and eventually molecular biology.

The ambitions that children develop are thought to be linked to parental aspirations, which may be seen in an emphasis being placed on education. To illustrate this, Sheila McLean advises that her parents always assumed that both she and her brother would attend university, and that the family would work out some way of affording it. Alan Finlayson's parents were also determined that both he and his brother should have a university education. Both his parents were the first in their family to go to university and his mother benefited from the generosity of four siblings who 'clubbed together' to pay for her university studies. His maternal grandmother had died when his mother was very young and, with his grandfather spending most of his money 'on drink', she was brought up by her oldest sister. However, his older brother was a 'rebel' and took up an apprenticeship with a baker while, in contrast, he never thought about doing anything other than what was expected of him and following the career path 'set by my parents'. This parental influence continued to shape his career as the work that his mother and father did, as career school teachers and as volunteers for the Royal Society of the Prevention of Cruelty to Children, 'rubbed off on me'. For example, he mentions that when he left an established legal practice to take up the new role in the Children's Hearing System his mother voiced her surprise, and perhaps disappointment, to which he replied 'don't blame me, blame yourself and your husband'. Parental influence is also given by Irvine Laidlaw, who describes being 'pushed' rather than encouraged by his parents, particularly by his somewhat 'strict mother', something he now views as 'tough love'.

Respect for education was witnessed by Tom Devine in the 'working class housing estate' where he grew up. Professor Devine's grandfather was a steelworker who made great sacrifices in order to send his son to university from which Professor Devine's father went on to become a teacher. Such was the respect in the local community for education that Professor Devine remembers seeing men in their 40s and 50s saluting his father in the street. This esteem for learning led his father and his circle to view the attainment of a university chair as the highest accolade. While Professor Devine does not believe that thinking was a direct influence on him reaching his present position, he does see his exposure to this respect for learning as a great advantage. Brian Gill's parents made sacrifices to support his education. Lord Gill came from anything but a financially wealthy background, one where both his parents had left school at an early age in order to work. Furthermore, during the great depression his father was made unemployed and had to fall back on his musical talent to earn a living. His parents realised what they had missed by not having the opportunity of a fuller education and made huge sacrifices to allow Lord Gill to gain the best education that they could provide, something he is still very much appreciative of. George Mathewson grew up with a similar respect for education, something he worries society is losing. When at school he could think of nothing worse than a teacher contacting his parents to discuss bad behaviour, as Sir George would have been fearful of his parent's reaction. Now though he suggests some parents are just as likely to tell the teacher to 'f-off' as to take action to improve their child's behaviour. Sir George emphasises that if you 'cannot read, write or add up' then you will have the huge handicap of not being able to communicate effectively which may lead to 'cultural poverty'.

Chay Blyth believes that communication, developed from learning vocabulary in childhood, gives opportunity in life. He considers that language should be practised from a young age through 'useless conversation', something he did with his daughter and her friends to improve their vocabulary and communication skills. John Crofton sums up his view of the link between parental influence and education when saying that he sees adverse parenting, rooted in poverty, resulting in a lack of development of normal behaviours in children. Sir John describes this as a cycle that starts with parents not talking to their children. This, he thinks, can result in children having limited vocabulary, which can result in difficulties in primary schooling, potentially causing truancy and illiteracy, which may result in crime, which is 'all too sadly evident in our prisons'. Children can then experience similar difficulties to those that their parents experienced, which can inhibit their ability to pass on more positive influences to future generations.

Alan Finlayson is concerned by the 'unacceptable behaviour' he sees in some young people which, he thinks, may be down to many children not having a consistent family background. To illustrate that, he gives the example of some primary schools where 'under 10 per cent of pupils are living with the same two parents in primary seven as they were in primary one'. It is because of failings in parenting and the barriers caused by society that Brian Gill believes people often end up in court. Due to that mixture of upbringing and circumstance, Lord Gill does not see it as the individual's own fault if he or she has committed a crime and believes that while the court cannot overlook the offence, it can consider circumstances when passing its verdict. Lord Gill explains that the lack of a positive parental or adult role model is prevalent in 'chaotic family backgrounds', which he thinks is in part 'due to the lost concept of the family unit as the natural unit of society'. Lord Gill maintains that there is no adequate substitute for good parenting because parents are 'the prime educator of values and attitudes'.

'Draw out the interest and inner part of each individual'

Role models

Sheila McLean emphasises the positive influences that children can gain from good adult role models, and Tom Farmer views 'good teachers and the influence of decent people when growing up' as the mainstay of a positive environment. Sir Tom reiterates that the circumstances you are born into and the environment that you live in have a huge bearing on how potential is fulfilled. Alan Finlayson appeared in court at different times as defence solicitor for seven members of one family, one of whom he shared the same date of birth with and who went on to become 'a very serious criminal'. He wonders if 'the cots had been swapped' when they were born, whether he would have led a life of crime? However, he points out that two members of that family took a different route, which he thinks came from the positive influence of someone outside of the family, perhaps a teacher, who assisted them to think differently. Norman Drummond believes that it is crucial for children to have the presence and positive influence of a 'consistent recognisable adult', especially parents but also teachers and others. For example, Reverend Drummond was advised by one of his school teachers that 'if we work hard we can go to Cambridge'. This was one of the first occasions that somebody had shown such faith and belief in him, and it helped to give him the confidence to aim for and attain a place at Cambridge University to study law. John Ferguson, a teacher at Dunoon Grammar School, enthused William Stewart's interest in biology and gave him encouragement and advice on his university studies. It was John Ferguson who told Sir William that he would succeed if he chose to 'work rather than spend time playing snooker'. Evelyn Glennie points to her experience at school where the Headmaster of Ellon Academy, Mr Slater, was able to 'draw out the interest and inner part of each individual'. Alongside that, and the encouragement she received from her school music teachers, Dame Evelyn cites the inspiration gained from James Blades. She met James Blades when still at school and she refers to his welcome advice at crucial times in her career, describing him in her autobiography *Good Vibrations* as 'one of the world's great percussionists'.

A number of teachers and writers have had a marked effect on Tom Devine. In particular, he names T.C. Smout, who wrote *A History of the Scottish People*, which was published in 1969, the year after Professor Devine graduated from Strathclyde University. *A History of the Scottish People* provides a social history of Scotland from 1560 to 1830 and was described by the *Sunday Times* as 'by far the most stimulating, the most instructive and the most readable account of Scotch history'. This work still resonated with Professor Devine when he wrote *The Scottish Nation*, which the *Herald* described as 'one of the most significant Scottish books of the century'.

In addition to parents, teachers and other adult role models, the wider community in which someone is brought up is thought to play a part. That includes the influence of religion.

'Faith, hope and love. But the greatest of them all is love'

Religion

Religion can have a significant influence on approach or thinking, even for those people that do not have strong religious beliefs. For example, Chay Blyth does not consider himself to be very religious in his thinking, but he does pray every day he is at sea because it 'only takes a minute and you just never know'. Indeed, he describes his voyages as having a big slice of help from 'up above' and wrote in his logbook when navigating the globe nonstop westwards, 'to atheists I say go sailing single-handed for a few weeks'. Others, who are not religiously minded, refer to the influence of religion in their upbringing. For example, Kenneth Murray gained encouragement from both his family and church life when growing up, and he admires Christian values such as those seen in the parable of the Good Samaritan. However, Sir Kenneth does not subscribe to a faith as he considers it 'too demanding to sign up'. William Stewart advises that he was brought up in a committed 'Christian household', something he considers positive, and Tom Devine describes himself as increasingly drawn to the religion of his birth. Alan Finlayson's parents attended church but were 'not committed Christians', and he considers Christian sentiment to be positive. He also mentions the parable of the Good Samaritan and doing unto others as you would like done unto you. He goes on to describe trying to live by 'Christian values' even although he does not go to church.

Michael Atiyah refers back to the mid-19th century when Samuel Smiles wrote *Self-Help* and notes that a lot of scholars were religious and often worked to further 'the glory of God', something he sees as a function of that time. Sir Michael does agree with certain Christian values, such as 'help thy neighbour', but he does not believe in the resurrection, considers elements of religion as superstition and does not 'call on God' in times of trouble. In addition, Sir Michael thinks that there is a loosening in religious dogma and sees beliefs stretching towards the agnostic, even in Church leaders. For Irvine Laidlaw religion has pluses but also minuses and, despite his parents going to church, he takes a strong secular stance and describes himself as an 'atheist'. John Crofton's father was brought up in a strongly low church Protestant family in Dublin and Sir John relates the story of how his father was not allowed to play with his toys on a Sunday, unless he used them to build churches. These views came from an Anglo-Irish Protestant background, which traces the family roots to Cumbria. Sir John's forefathers had to flee England during the reign of Bloody Mary (who reigned from 1553 to 1558) but returned under Elizabeth (who reigned from 1558 to 1603) and Sir John's ancestor proceeded to Ireland in Essex's army in the mid-16th century. Even with these keen influences, Sir John is not a believer and, in particular, he disagrees with those that argue against Darwin's theory of evolution.

Sheila McLean was brought up to be 'secular' in her religious beliefs and she thinks that strong faith can curtail the rational thought and debate that she considers to be hugely important in decision making. Professor McLean considers it 'almost impossible' to debate something with people who have a strong belief or faith as, she thinks, they can be rigid in their views and closed to logical argument. In particular, she is concerned if religious faith influences government policy and she gives the United States of America under President George Bush and the United Kingdom when Tony Blair was Prime Minister as examples of where that may have happened. She notes that Tony Blair would sometimes give his reason for taking a course of action, 'whether invading Iraq or something else', as that he believed he was doing the right thing rather than offering any rational basis for the decision. For this reason she argues that religion has no part to play in government. Furthermore, she is concerned that religious beliefs could take a 'stranglehold' due to people being 'frightened to criticise' someone if their beliefs come from a religious faith. As an example of this, Professor McLean contends that there was a 'much less muted response' than there would have been in previous years to the Sudanese Government imprisoning a United Kingdom citizen, Gillian Gibbons, over the naming of a classroom teddy bear in December 2007.

Evelyn Glennie sees herself as spiritual rather than following any particular religion. During her childhood she became increasingly religiously minded and avidly read a copy of the bible that was given to her whilst at Ellon Academy. Dame Evelyn has since reconsidered her position and her religious beliefs have lessened over time, although her respect for religion remains undiminished. These beliefs are still part of her and she is sure that they will be reappraised again at some future date. Margo MacDonald is religiously minded but she 'does not like organised religion'. However, she 'wouldn't be without either the Catholic or Reformed Churches' because she sees their influence as positive, believing that what the Church leaders say is 'likely to be right' and if it is 'not able to be proven it will not cause much harm'. Similarly, Robin Harper considers that the Episcopal Church, of which he is a member, gives good general advice. He describes it as a relatively broad Church, even if he does sometimes question that when he hears some of the Archbishop of Canterbury's pronouncements. He adds that he would 'rather be in than out'.

Lewis Robertson describes himself as a 'church-going Christian' who believes in traditional values. This traditional view is shown in his preference for the *Scottish Book of Common Prayer*, adopted by the Scottish Episcopal Church in 1929, as opposed to more contemporary versions. He has held appointments on numerous Church committees and councils including membership of the Provincial Synod from 1963 to 1982, and Director of Scottish Episcopal Church Nominees Ltd since 1990. Sir Lewis thinks the Church should, and he hopes does, have an influence on him. For Tom Farmer the Church and religious beliefs 'helps to give you a conscience', something he considers to be of great value.

Jonathan Long came into contact with the Church of England in his early 20s, his brother encouraging him to go along because of the girls that they might meet! He felt the message that was preached was 'credible' and he involved himself in Church youth work. Dr Long went on to be ordained into the Church of England and he also undertook research into the moral and spiritual development of children at the Oxford University Department of Educational Studies. While his faith has become more eclectic, particularly through his interest in Eastern philosophy and religion, he feels it helps to keep him 'rooted' through the Church being an institution that provides community support. This means that rather than preaching his Christianity he tries to live by it. Christianity, not the Church, is believed by Norman Drummond to be important and he emphasises the significance of spiritual as well as physical wellbeing. In his opinion, Christ is always alongside us and he refers to 1 Corinthians 13:13, where there are three things that last for ever: 'Faith, Hope and Love. But the greatest of them all is Love'. If you have these, Reverend Drummond believes, you can fulfill your potential and help others to fulfill their potential. He goes on to state that even if you do not believe in aspects of the Bible, such as the virgin birth and resurrection of Christ (which he does believe in), the morals given in the Bible are still a good way to lead your life.

Church or religious life is sometimes described as part of a community structure that can help to define the level of security and stability that children receive in their formative years.

'Positive imprint'

Stability and security

Growing up in a stable and secure environment is thought by George Robertson to give perspective and grounding. In particular, he thinks that being brought up on an island, Islay, assisted in giving and maintaining his sense of self-knowledge, perhaps more so than if he had been brought up in, say, a city. This gave his formative years a secure environment, which he describes in the introduction to his book of photographs, *Islay and Jura*, as '... a near idyllic environment which had space, freedom, no crime...'. Lord Robertson believes that stability and security provides a platform that assists children to realise their potential whilst retaining a balanced view of life. In a similar way, Norman Drummond believes that having a Scottish background helps 'keep you grounded' through a positive identity and sense of belonging. This is something that Jackie Stewart considers 'smaller countries', such as Scotland or those in Scandinavia, engender through a national pride. Sheila McLean thinks that by understanding the place you come from you can better understand yourself and, in turn, gain an improved sense of self. Calum Colvin agrees with this and he thinks, in general, Scotland provides a stable and culturally rich environment for children to grow up in. Professor Colvin was raised in a 'normal Scottish family', where his father was the first in the family to go to university and the extended family gained a living from painting and decorating. George Mathewson considers that Scotland has been a positive influence on him through a strong respect for education and hard work. Sir George's father was an electrician and his uncle a bus driver who, along with the rest of the family, were 'open and hardworking'. This provided him with a secure environment where he was encouraged in education and to 'get on' in life. A stable, secure and good home life is credited by William Stewart as forming his character and he believes that 'security, love and stability are the keys in childhood'.

Robin Harper concentrates on the physical surroundings that people live in and he observes that those who are economically poor tend to live on the outskirts of cities while the 'green and central bits' are reserved for the rich. He describes the three housing estates in which he has lived as 'bleak, windswept, not kept well, grim, no colour' and he sees such places, in themselves, stifling progress. Alan Finlayson includes in these wider influences the 'power of the media'. He thinks that, for example, television advertising can be aimed at influencing children, who are not necessarily mature enough to deal with messages promoting material goods. He believes that this puts undue pressure on children, and in turn parents, to own 'the right mobile phone or training shoes'.

Sheila McLean was brought up to be 'socially aware' and Kenneth Murray grew up at a time when he thinks there was more cohesion in society. He puts that unity down to the Second World War and immediate post-war period, where people were perhaps more willing to help each other due to their shared experience of war. Norman Drummond feels that being brought up by wartime parents informed his approach and made him proud to be Scottish and 'proud to be British as well'. Margo MacDonald thinks that her generation has a sense of community responsibility that comes from the rebuilding that followed the Second World War. This is something she saw her mother display and as a child she would, for example, never dream of standing on a bus seat as she was taught that someone else had to sit there. This 'sense of community' was also felt by Noreen Murray during her rural upbringing that centred around the church and village activities. This, along with her parents' influence, gave her a stable and secure upbringing which left her with a 'positive imprint'.

A secure and stable environment is described as a strong base from which children can gain positive influences, with that not necessarily determined by financial wealth.

'A help'

Financial wealth

Tom Farmer views the caring environment that he was brought up in as more important than having financial means and Brian Gill claims that a less financially privileged upbringing may in fact give a 'better training for life'. Lord Gill explains that a poor economic background can give an empathy with people from similar circumstances and allow for a better understanding of why some of these individuals end up in the legal system. Jonathan Long thinks that experiencing 'tough realities' can provide resilience, with Michael Atiyah suggesting that a difficult upbringing can give someone a strong determination. Sheila McLean came from a 'council house background' and, while she describes her upbringing as 'not poor, not rich', she believes that people can be held back by their relative financial poverty. Professor McLean does also think that those born into great financial wealth can lose the incentive to do well. Certainly, William Stewart recalls that Sir Hermann Bondi, an eminent mathematician and Cambridge College Master, selectively encouraged the recruitment of students from state schools, because their achievements in getting good entrance requirements were determined solely by their work ethos and intellectual talent, without the benefit of a privileged background, and that showed in the standard of degrees that they most usually attained.

Jackie Stewart notes that some people from a financially wealthy background have gone on to achieve. However, Sir Jackie does advise that it could be argued that it is easier to create more from an existing large base than to establish yourself from scratch. Having said that, Sir Jackie sees great merit in both and he does not view 'one type of person as better than the other'.

Like others, William Stewart did not feel underprivileged financially or otherwise and he reiterates that if you have 'drive, resilience and enthusiasm' you can succeed. Although he does moderate that with the view that it is 'twice as hard if you are an outsider without the benefit enjoyed, for example, by being part of the Oxbridge network'.

Regardless of economic circumstances, the influence of parents and others is seen as the crucial element in providing a positive upbringing, although Irvine Laidlaw points out that financial poverty and low ambition often make easy bedfellows. Lord Laidlaw was 'shocked' to meet fellow students, during his first year of study at Leeds University, who were financially less privileged than him. This affected him to the extent that he became a welfare officer helping others to gain improved accommodation. Robin Harper contends that, despite there being greater overall wealth, the differences between the rich and poor are more marked now than a century ago which, he thinks, restricts social mobility. Lewis Robertson advises that he was fortunate to be born into a well off, although not wealthy family, something that he can only see as 'a help'.

While financial wealth is not necessarily given as the defining factor during childhood, it is thought difficult for people to pull themselves out of certain circumstances if there is a mix of negative influences in upbringing.

'It is exceptionally difficult to pull yourself up by the bootstraps'

Exceptions

When considering individuals that became leading thinkers in their field, despite their impoverished upbringing and rudimentary formal education, Michael Atiyah dips back into history. He names Michael Faraday (1791–1867), who was the son of a blacksmith and is best known for establishing electricity as a viable source of energy; George Green (1793–1841), who was a miller's son and prompted modern thinking on mathematical physics with *An Essay on the application of Mathematical Analysis to the Theories of Electricity and Magnetism*; and Benjamin Franklin (1706–1790), the son of a candle and soap maker. As well as being a signatory of the United States Declaration of Independence (having been one of the Committee of Five appointed to draft that Declaration by the 2nd Continental Congress in 1776), Benjamin Franklin was a renowned scientist who worked on electricity theories. He also set up the mutual improvement *Junto Club* in Philadelphia in 1727 and published self-improvement proverbs in his *Poor Richard Almanack*, which was printed from 1732 until 1758. However, Sir Michael believes it is difficult to compare these people with the present day because that was a 'different era' when education was less widespread and more limited than he considers it is today. He does though believe that talent will rise and that if someone has 'real genius' then they will 'shine through'. Sheila McLean also believes that some people will 'simply shine', something she sees in those university students who 'breeze through' their postgraduate studies.

Tom Devine contends that there are still examples of people achieving from the 'deep working class', although he sees these as very isolated, and Calum Colvin suggests that there are many people who achieve from 'a traditional working class' background. Professor Colvin does though put that down to how parents support their children. Irvine Laidlaw agrees that there are exceptions, but advises that for the 'average good person' it is more difficult for those who come from less privileged circumstances. For example, Lord

Laidlaw mentions Philip Harris, Lord Harris of Peckham, as an example of someone who succeeded despite his circumstances in upbringing. Philip Harris established Carpetright in 1988 and by 1998 it had 308 stores across the United Kingdom. Further expansion saw it developing a presence in Europe and, in addition to the United Kingdom, it now has stores in Belgium, Holland, Poland and the Republic of Ireland. However, Lord Laidlaw describes Philip Harris as 'an exceptional man'. In a similar vein, Tom Farmer recalled a conversation with a Government Minister who told him that people should 'pull themselves up by their bootstraps'. Sir Tom responded that for people from hard social circumstances it is very difficult to do that, to which the Government Minister replied that Isaac Wolfson managed it. Isaac Wolfson was the force behind the growth of Great Universal Stores. When Sir Tom asked the Minister to name another person there was no response and the conversation came to an abrupt end. Sir Tom contends that 'it is exceptionally difficult to pull yourself up by the bootstraps' if there has been a mix of difficult circumstances in upbringing.

'Children are entitled to happiness'

Action being taken

John Crofton notes that government action is being taken to better educate parents and assist nursery schools in helping youngsters with vocabulary, something he deems essential if children are to benefit from primary schooling. Sir John does counsel that any benefits will only be revealed over the long-term because 'we are all victims of being part of groups', where influences are derived from the thinking of the people and of the society that we are born into. Robin Harper also emphasises the importance of such early intervention. He believes the Government is 'vaguely' doing this through education, but that such intervention has to be earlier still, 'even before birth' to assist expectant mothers. In particular, he argues that this would assist those people that come from a long-term history of dysfunctional behaviour and have limited experience of 'love, care and attention'. He thinks that dysfunctional behaviour is likely to continue throughout life if these 'basics' are not learnt in the early formative years of life. He goes on to refer to a 'powerful speech', made by a community policeman on behalf of the Scottish Children's Commission, which recommended employing more health visitors. This is something he thinks would have a beneficial impact on very young children and their mothers as, he believes, health visitors are considered helpful due to the practical advice that they give. He compares this to social workers who, he thinks, tend only to get involved when there is a problem and are often seen as authoritarian. Thus, he believes that a health visitor has more chance of 'getting people onside' during a child's first few years of life. In addition, he advocates 'targeted investments' in early education to, for example, reduce class sizes of schools in poor economic areas. Furthermore, he sees the need to move away from an attitude that 'poor people will make do with poor housing' and a view that housing is often considered adequate as long as it fulfils minimum building regulations. He argues that it would not cost a lot of additional money to make 'nicer places to live' by 'brightening them up' through better city planning and housing design. He emphasises the importance of not putting 'people in boxes', either literally or metaphorically, or underestimating their abilities. Thus, with a focused approach on the very young and early education, coupled with a re-think on housing, he believes, society can address the issues of 'poverty, health and violence'.

Alan Finlayson thinks that all 'children are entitled to happiness' and that further opportunity would be created for youngsters if society took more interest in children. He includes in this primary schools and youth organisations that allow children to participate in enjoyable activities, whilst learning the 'boundaries of acceptable behaviour'. 'Dynamic and successful in realising the potential of people of all ages and backgrounds' is how Princess Anne describes Columba 1400. The founder and Chairman of Columba 1400, Norman Drummond states that at the heart of this initiative are leadership academies for young people from socioeconomic 'tough realities'. Columba

1400 was opened in 2000 on the Isle of Skye and has four main programmes: 'The Young People's Leadership Academy', which aims to assist those from deprived circumstances into education or employment though an intensive residential course; 'The Head Teachers' Leadership Academy', which enables Heads and Deputies, from both primary and secondary schools, to rediscover why they entered into teaching and thus assist them to fully realise their leadership potential; 'The Ambassadors' Leadership Academy', which encourages the development of leadership in schools, for both pupils and teachers, and communities; and 'The Gemini Project' or 'Coracle Programme', which pairs corporate business managers with those from deprived circumstances in a two-way mentoring scheme. This is delivered in a framework that promotes awareness, focus, creativity, integrity, perseverance and service. Columba 1400 is supported by a number of sponsors, including Tom Farmer and the Laidlaw Youth Trust, which gives financial support to charities that aim to make 'a real difference to vulnerable young people in Scotland'. Such programmes are seen as applicable to everyone, not only to those from more obvious 'tough realities' as, Jonathan Long notes, we all have 'tough realities'. Dr Long goes on to explain that those from materially privileged backgrounds might, for example, lack emotional connectedness or the ability to appreciate some of the more subtle values in life, which is their 'tough reality'.

Jackie Stewart describes dyslexia and other learning difficulties as forcing people towards the 'fringes of society', and he points out that the majority of the prison population cannot read or write. Sir Jackie believes that learning difficulties often remain unrecognised and he comments that no organisation would ignore 10 per cent of its workforce, the percentage of the population he gives as being dyslexic. In his role as President of Dyslexia Scotland he encourages early recognition of dyslexia plus timely intervention and equality in both education and employment. To assist these aims, Sir Jackie raises awareness and lobbies Parliament and, in particular, he stresses the need to provide understanding within the framework of the teacher training colleges. As an example of the progress being made in supporting children with learning diffi-culties, he highlights the work of the specialist unit at Kaimhill Primary School in Aberdeen. However, Sir Jackie feels that overall progress in this area is not moving quickly enough, and he believes that this means that many people are not getting the opportunity to fulfill their potential.

Jonathan Long compares the development of an individual to the approach taken by Michelangelo when he was making a statue. Michelangelo said that he was revealing what was always there, hidden in the marble, which Dr Long refers to as 'removing clutter'. Dr Long goes on to say that the right type of relationship must be created in order to help someone rid themselves of the 'clutter' of negative influences. He believes that relationships should be based on truth, respect and vulnerability, and that by sharing vulnerability whatever 'clutter' someone is hiding behind is more likely to be removed rather than reinforced. This view of drawing out what is already there is shared by Norman Drummond who quotes the writer John Buchan, 'our task is not to put the greatness back into humanity, but to elicit it, for the great-ness is already there'.

'Immune to gloom'

Attitude

More often than not, attitude is referred to as a way of thinking or behaving, while personality tends to be seen as part of someone's nature or disposition. It is personality that is generally viewed as having a limited bearing on the ability to fulfill potential. For instance, Irvine Laidlaw advises that there is 'no one personality type which attains success'. Lord Laidlaw summarises the dichotomy in personality types by saying that you can 'be a numbers person or more charismatic' and thus certain personalities are more suited to certain roles. To illustrate this, George Mathewson advises that it is unfair to expect an excellent sales person to change immediately and fulfill an administration role due to the differences in personality and experience required. For example, someone may be decisive in their business dealings but unclear in their personal life. Lewis Robertson believes that character comes down to an individual's personality and he considers this to be a difficult and interesting area, due to the debate over what is gained from nature and what comes from nurture. A mix of nature and nurture is given by Sheila McLean, who thinks that, while personality may well be inherent, it is the environment that someone is brought up in that determines how their personality blossoms.

Certain personality traits that he retains, through 'my tongue and thinking', are thought by Jackie Stewart to be very Scottish. Sir Jackie is a 'proud Scot' and he suggests that thoroughness, determination and a natural aggressiveness are all Scottish traits. That aggressiveness is, he thinks, evidenced by the relatively high number of Scots in the police force and armed services. Lewis Robertson also sees himself as having Scottish traits and he includes in this the 'iron will' which he saw in his grandfather. Scottish traits are described by Norman Drummond as being straight, loyal, responsible and kind without fuss, while Evelyn Glennie thinks that Scots are stubborn and are able to keep things in perspective by 'not making a mountain out of a molehill'. To this she adds thrift (not to be confused with meanness), friendliness, an interest in meeting people and a strong work ethic. Tom Farmer and Calum Colvin also believe that Scots have a strong work ethic. Sir Tom adds that Scots tend to be 'fair people' and Professor Colvin sees Scots as tolerant and friendly people who can be creative in their use of language, which is why he thinks there are 'good Scottish writers'. Tom Devine sums up his view of Scottish traits in *The Scottish Nation* when writing '... it was the Presbyterian inheritance that shaped the values of thrift, independence, sobriety, the work ethic and education, which were the very foundations of the middle and "respectable" working class culture. Those values were propagated in such seminal texts as *Self-Help* by the Scot, Samuel Smiles from Haddington...'. Professor Devine advises that these are still very much relevant today.

In contrast to an inherent personality, Tam Dalyell believes that people can choose their attitude to a particular situation. Lewis Robertson also thinks that people can choose their attitude but, he adds, you must recognise that when someone is acting inappropriately it may be due to circumstances that you are unaware of. Alan Finlayson notes that these different attitudes are due to people being 'complex beings' because of the many and varied influences on each individual. Similarly, Tom Farmer sees this as part of the complexity of the mind, and he notes that people can take different attitudes to similar situations on an almost daily basis. Sir Tom observes that you can buy manuals explaining how machines work but that there are no equivalent instruction books for the most complicated of machines, the human brain. During his tenure at Kwik-Fit, the main reason for a customer complaint was the poor attitude of a member of staff, rather than the quality of work completed. In such instances, Sir Tom would ask the employee involved to get back in touch with the customer and rectify the position by demonstrating more appropriate behaviour. Normally, this would turn a disgruntled customer into a loyal customer, who would often then only want to deal with that employee. Sir Tom says that 'you employ people, not machines' and he sees learning to choose the most appropriate attitude as part of an employee's training. However, Margo MacDonald believes that attitude cannot be taught, but for attitudes to alter, someone must really want to change. Thus, she sees lifestyle coaches having a limited effect.

Calum Colvin links attitude to experience, within which he emphasises the influences received during upbringing, and it is through experience that Tam Dalyell thinks a more appropriate attitude is learnt. Professor Colvin's own attitude of 'I want to do something then I want to do it well' is driven by anxiety, sometimes coupled with external criticism and informed by role models. As an example of learning a different attitude from experience, Evelyn Glennie comments on a television interview given by Gareth Gates, who shot to prominence in 2002 as runner up to Will Young in the television show 'Pop Idol'. Dame Evelyn observed that he had found the reality of the music business somewhat different to the impression that he had been given at the onset of his career by agents and his parents. However, she notes that he has had time to 'listen to himself and find his own voice'. This has allowed him to adjust his attitude and do things his own way, rather than simply doing what other people would want, something that Dame Evelyn can relate to. The individual attitude of volunteer crew members from the Parachute Regiment was of particular concern to Chay Blyth when he was preparing to skipper *Great Britain II* in the Whitbread Round the World Race of 1973–74. This concern came from the need for crew members to get on well when living in close proximity to each other over extended periods of time. To evaluate and teach appropriate attitudes he gathered the prospective crew members together at a remote cottage in the Scottish Borders. Then, after a series of exercises, he selected those who had demonstrated the most appropriate behaviour. With that crew, *Great Britain II* went on to win the Elapsed Time Prize.

Unsurprisingly, choosing a positive attitude is viewed as beneficial, although Sheila McLean contends that a positive attitude requires confidence which, she thinks, develops from good health and good education. Chay Blyth maintains a positive approach as a matter of course, and he always looks to turn negatives into positives. Sir Chay takes this approach even in difficult circumstances and he describes himself as 'immune to gloom'. He gives the example of when *Virgin Atlantic Challenge* was sinking during its failed attempt to beat the transatlantic speed record. He telephoned his sponsor, Richard Branson, from the sinking boat to inform him of the bad news. However, he then explained a positive approach of re-investing the insurance money in an even better boat, which would allow them to try again. The following year, 1986, Sir Chay was once again co-skipper but this time of the successful Blue Riband attempt by *Virgin Atlantic Challenge II*. Sir Chay takes this positive approach in everyday life and, instead of giving up, losing heart or complaining 'that we haven't got something', he thinks that people should look for positives and ways of making do. Kenneth Murray is another who takes a positive approach. However, he did encounter a more negative environment in the Civil Service, where his colleagues' ambition was to 'keep their heads down and serve their time'. This attitude is something that Sir Kenneth cannot understand, and was highlighted to him by the realisation, at age 19, that he knew more about chemistry than his older and more experienced manager. He therefore left an established position, in spite of the 'temptation' to retire on full salary at age 60, to return to industry as a technical assistant with Glaxo, where he had an inspiring supervisor in Arthur Best and the opportunity to continue part-time education at Lancaster Technical College. Alan Finlayson thinks in terms of taking a 'proactive' attitude, rather than a 'positive' attitude, where someone does not just let things happen around them or to them. He does though advise that he has not been consistent in this as he was a 'poor student' when at university.

Robin Harper believes that it is very difficult for someone to change their attitude because it is something that can be ingrained from an early age. Norman Drummond compares a negative attitude to an illness when people try and disassociate themselves from other people, 'like a vandal wishing to escape in the same way as a flu sufferer does not want to be around people'. He relates this to the work of Camilla Batmanghelidjh who established Kids Company in 1996. Kids Company offers practical, emotional and educational help to support children, after what have often been extreme experiences.

Overall, Jackie Stewart believes that it is those who try hard and who have the right attitude that will do well. Sir Jackie also makes the point of adding that people who are quiet or deep thinkers should be recognised and not ignored. Thus, he recommends 'be yourself', because if you are false you will only get so far. He does though suggest being approachable and making an effort because it is better to be 'nicer to people'. Tom Farmer believes that, in general, people take a positive attitude because 'when you get out of bed in the morning you are looking to have a good day, you are not looking for hassle'. The attitude that Lewis Robertson recommends is to be 'open minded and intelligent' to new thinking, and Norman Drummond tries to live life to the full, stay open minded even after periods of difficulty and 'heal yourself' through having a balance in life. In his book, *The Spirit of Success*, Reverend Drummond expands the theme of how a balance in life can help to keep you grounded. He describes this as a combination of 'six cylinders' which are: 'stand back from your life'; 'discriminate between what is important and what is not'; 'do whatever sets your spirit free'; 'know yourself well'; 'manage the many agendas of your life'; and 'give without expectation of receiving'. Reverend Drummond believes that attitude is the single thing which an individual can control, and he states that 'you have a choice' in the attitude you take as it is 'the only bow that you have'.

It is thought that people can choose their attitude to any given situation. In contrast, personality is generally viewed as innate, although the influences on someone can define how their personality flourishes. As well as an inherent personality, people are thought to have an inherent type or level of intellect and talent.

'How I am set up'

Intellect and talent

To get to the very top, George Robertson thinks you need to be quick minded and Lewis Robertson believes that you require a 'certain intellect'. Tom Devine agrees and explains this in terms of the changes that Scotland has seen from the late 1970s until today, something he describes as 'a greater transformation' than between the 1850s and 1950s. He refers to the move from manufacturing to a service economy and the substantial numbers of people who have risen above their parents' standard of living. Professor Devine believes that social change has gathered momentum since the Second World War, with about 40 per cent to 50 per cent of each generation progressing into further education. He thinks this is fuelled by grants, even if these grants are less generous than when he attended university. Thus, he puts forward the view that people with higher intellect can take advantage of education opportunities and go on to secure better jobs. This, he thinks, gives the 'horrible possibility of genetic creaming', where the less able are left behind in areas of economic deprivation and become alienated as they find themselves in a situation where their abilities are unlikely to be satisfied. A similar view is given by George Mathewson. When he attended Perth Academy he thinks pupils were predominately 'working class' with up to two-thirds living in council housing. Sir George thinks that many of these people are now middle class, and that the 'brains have moved out' of poorer economic areas. Alan Finlayson believes that a 'high IQ' gives someone a 'tremendous advantage'. He explains this in the context of the Parable of the Talents, Matthew 25: 14–30, where three individuals are provided with differing amounts of talents (coins) from which they either increase or try and protect their share. Thus, he believes, it is about recognising the 'gifts' that you have and making the most of these, even if other people have a higher 'optimum level'.

Tam Dalyell suggests that intellect can be important but is 'not a huge part' of why someone fulfils potential and Tom Farmer believes that 'God gives you three things; intellect, energy and common sense'. Sir Tom goes on to say that 'I was born with a lot of the last two'. In particular, he feels that the common sense factor and the ability to keep both feet on the ground are often wrongly neglected. Jackie Stewart agrees when saying that people have a 'God-given common sense', something he describes as applying when implementing safety measures that reduced the risk of serious injury to motor racing drivers. Sir Jackie does add that common sense can be learnt from example and through being exposed to other people's thinking. Chay Blyth also thinks that common sense is underrated, but he does believe that 'intellect' is needed for certain roles, especially those he describes as requiring more complex thinking, such as mathematics. Margo MacDonald 'always wanted to be known as an intellect'. This came from an 'intellectual inferiority' caused by the 'snobbish nature of education' which labelled those, like her, who chose physical education as 'thickoids'. However, she describes herself as having 'common sense' and is now unsure if there is any difference between that and 'intellect'.

Intellect is often referred to in terms of academic learning, while talent tends to be associated with an aptitude for a particular discipline, although the two are sometimes used interchangeably. Robin Harper thinks that intellect has to be nurtured and that it will not be 'revealed' if the barriers in upbringing prove to be too strong. This is something Michael Atiyah agrees with. He thinks that people have an inherent intellect and talent, but it is the environment which defines how they will flourish. Sir Michael goes on to compare intellectual development to a plant that will wither if it is not tended properly. Sheila McLean believes that nature affords someone a set of skills and level of capacity for a whole range of options. However, she also thinks that these may not be realised due to the barriers encountered during upbringing. Professor McLean does add that intelligence and/or talent requires to be coupled with hard work. For example, Evelyn Glennie sees musicians who possess incredible talent but lack the will to work, which results in at least '50 per cent' of that talent being wasted. Dame Evelyn puts much of this down to a society where everything, especially financial reward, appears immediate and causes some individuals to forget the need to work hard in order to improve. Tom Devine believes that hard work can perhaps take someone to the top in some professions. However, in academia he thinks that hard work can only take a person so far due to intense peer review. As an example, Professor Devine advises that hard work at university can achieve a 2.1 but 'with talent that hard work becomes a 1st'. Calum Colvin concurs in this sentiment when saying that, ultimately, you need talent. He considers it 'an unfortunate fact of life' when a more gifted but lazy art student receives a better rating than a hard-working but less gifted individual.

Certain people, such as Irvine Laidlaw, may have a natural aptitude towards particular disciplines. Lord Laidlaw recounts his mother, who had a double 1st from Aberdeen University and was fluent in both French and German, not understanding why he was unable to get to grips with foreign languages. Instead, Lord Laidlaw advises that he has a good memory for numbers.

Similarly, when given the option to study mathematics or chemistry, Michael Atiyah chose mathematics as he found learning mathematical rules and then applying them through thinking easier than learning the large number of facts required for chemistry. Sir Michael adds that this is just 'how I am set up'.

Jonathan Long contends that there is a 'spectrum of intelligence' which encompasses cognitive thinking and 'social intelligence'. He describes social intelligence as heightened self-awareness that allows people to interact with each other in a meaningful and mutually satisfying way. This spectrum of abilities and styles of intellect is seen in the Scottish Parliament, which Margo MacDonald describes as 'representative'. She goes on to say that the Parliament contains people who have a mixture of intellect and capabilities, 'some good, some stars'.

Upbringing: Summary

'We are all victims of being part of groups'

Economic, cultural and spiritual barriers, which can be created by society, are thought to inhibit individual development and the ability to fulfil potential. Within that, parents are usually viewed as the key influencers of children, although teachers, other adult role models and the wider community or society are all seen to have an impact. There is a spectrum of views on religion, from those who gain great inspiration from their religious beliefs to those who take little or no inspiration from religion. However, church life and religious beliefs are thought to have some influence through being part of the community structure. While financial wealth is not described as the defining factor in upbringing, in certain instances financial poverty is considered to be an inhibiting factor and linked to low ambitions. If there is a mixture of negative influences during upbringing, it is thought that people may find themselves locked into poor economic and cultural circumstances from which it is considered difficult to get out of. This, in turn, may lead to intellect, talent and merit being ignored and remaining unfulfilled. In contrast, a mix of positive influences in upbringing may provide the secure and stable environment that is described as the best platform from which children can develop.

Action is being taken to counter the difficulties that some people experience in upbringing and to enhance existing positive approaches. This is seen to apply to all members of society, and includes the improved education of parents to help them to assist their child's development, particularly in language. In addition, there are programmes which mentor those from 'tough realities' alongside people who would not normally be bracketed in need of assistance.

Personality is usually viewed as innate, with no one personality type seen as advantageous over any other. Although, personality is thought to determine the type of work that someone enjoys or is most suited to. Unlike an inherent personality, it is believed that an individual can perhaps choose his or her attitude.

The influences received during upbringing, and the ongoing experiences that someone has, are described as affecting how intellect or talent is developed and used. However, it is considered that society can place greater value on an intellect that is more in tune with academic learning. Having said that, intellect is seen as only part of the equation and a range of attributes are believed to be important. These include hard work, energy and common sense. While intelligence is defined in different ways, to get to a high level of achievement, it is argued that hard work requires to be coupled with talent or intellect.

Furthermore, during upbringing, it is considered important to have a positive attitude to education.

Learning

'Grain of the brain'

What attitude do people have to education?
What are people's preferred methods of learning?
What gives real understanding?

In this chapter education and learning styles are discussed alongside what can give a deeper understanding of new information. Chapter IV then considers the value of help and advice, which may provide opportunity for learning to be applied or increased.

'Glorious insight'

Attitude to learning

George Robertson believes that, as a country, Scotland has a positive attitude to learning supported by a formal system of education that is, in general, 'democratic' due to pupils of all abilities and social classes going to local schools. Jackie Stewart thinks Scotland delivers high standards of education, although he emphasises the need to maintain and improve upon those standards. He sees much of this being provided by universities which, he believes, accounts for the strength of Scotland's financial sector. In particular, Sir Jackie highlights Glasgow University and he describes it as 'renowned' for its high standards. Lord Robertson believes that it is this positive approach to learning and education that helps Scots to reach high standards, and Chay Blyth notes that, in his experience, Scots tend to be well educated. However, Irvine Laidlaw argues that quality education in Scotland tends to come from the private sector, and he thinks this is evidenced by the examination results that these schools produce. He does add that there are some notable exceptions in the state sector. This is seen by Sheila McLean in parents who try to maximise their child's potential by sending him or her to a specific school, where they consider teachers and facilities, both academic and sporting, to be better. Alan Finlayson suggests that pupils attending certain schools may have an advantage over other pupils. In particular, he believes that those who attend, for example, a fee-paying school will have higher expectations placed on them by their teachers, and often their parents, compared to their counterparts in the state sector. Also, he feels that schools in poor economic areas can place lower expectations on pupils, which can mean that their ambitions and ability to fulfill potential are restricted. The importance of taking the right attitude to education at a national level is summed up by Lord Laidlaw when advising that he does not dwell on the past, as he prefers to look forward, because 'the future lies in education'.

Realising what they had missed in education, Brian Gill's parents put great effort into attaining the best education that they could afford for their son. This resulted in his love of learning, which was given to him through the 'glorious insight' of his Jesuit teachers. The need for good teachers is recognised by Tom Farmer, who sees knowledge coming from teachers and other role models that shape the environment someone is brought up in. Sir Tom goes on to say that learning continues throughout life, stressing that 'it is a myth that learning is only for young people' because it is what you learn after you think you know it all that often counts the most. He does not limit his view of learning to purely academic studies but includes other areas, such as interpersonal skills. While he contends that people are born with a certain intellectual aptitude, Sir Tom considers that knowledge can be learnt and added to if an appropriate attitude is taken and he recommends 'be inquisitive'. Tom Devine encourages an 'intellectual humility' that, he believes, assists in promoting new learning, and George Mathewson encourages an open-minded attitude to education. Sir George stresses that education promotes wealth creation and increasing standards of living. In addition, he recommends pushing yourself in education and striving for learning, as this will provide the 'discipline of logic and the ability to communicate effectively', something he considers vital in creating opportunity and fulfilling potential. However, Sir George is dismayed by what he views as a reduction in the education quotient and a corresponding drop in the respect for learning. In part, he puts that down to students sitting 'easy exams' and getting the same rewards as those who tackle more difficult subjects. Sir George is concerned that a less conscientious approach to education will lower the education standard of school leavers and cause a cultural poverty that may lead to a reduction in living standards.

People can find themselves fascinated by a subject or area, which may encourage them to learn more about it, such as John Crofton, who has 'always been fascinated by clinical medicine'. The same is true of Brian Gill, whose fascination with agricultural law and town and country planning started '40 years ago' and carries on to this day as he continues to learn about those areas. Such an attitude to learning is, Jonathan Long believes, the natural curiosity that people have to find out more and that learning can be characterised as going with the 'grain of the brain'. In other words, it is a form of learning which is based on our natural capacity for learning.

'Everyone is different'

Preferences in learning

All the contributors agree that, as Tom Farmer puts it, 'you should get an education'. In addition, there is a belief that, dependent on learning preferences, both formal academic and skills-based education play their part. As Tam Dalyell points out, 'everyone is different' and thus different types of learning will be more appropriate for different people and for different topics. Sheila McLean notes that some people are more talented in academic learning and she remembers a classmate who failed the entrance exam to go to a senior secondary school 'by one per cent'. Instead, her former classmate attended a junior secondary school where her skills were not evaluated and she was simply kept on at school until she was 15 years old and 'that was it'. Post

Second World War in Scotland there was a system of senior and junior secondary schools with pupils selected at age 12. Those who were seen as more academic attended a senior secondary and followed a five year course that aimed to prepare them for university. The other pupils attended a junior secondary where they followed a three year course designed to equip them with skills to go into the workplace. In England, Wales and Northern Ireland there was a two school system of secondary education with an exam, at age 11, deciding which type of school pupils would attend. Those that were viewed as academically minded would go to a grammar school while the others would attend secondary moderns. The secondary modern provided a skills-based education to prepare pupils for a career in industry or manufacturing. Since the early 1970s all Scottish education in the state sector has been delivered in comprehensive schools, where pupils of all abilities are taught at the same school. In general, England and Wales also provide comprehensive schooling, although some grammar schools remain, while Northern Ireland retains a stronger grammar school system.

Calum Colvin feels that he was 'written off' by what he sees as the narrow academic definitions promoted through Scottish schools in the mid and late 1970s. He considers that school was more concerned about conforming to the norms of education, rather than promoting independent or alternative thinking. This eventually led him to focus on the arts and the immediate ambition of going to art college where he went on to enjoy a skills-based education. Jackie Stewart refers to his dyslexia and difficulties in written language when saying that 'you categorically know what you can't do'. He thinks that as people mature, at around age 11, they start to see what they can do, Sir Jackie finding that he was better 'at football and in the gymnasium rather than in the class-room'. These differences in approach can also be prevalent within subject areas. For example, Michael Atiyah notes that in mathematics there are those who are into the 'nitty-gritty' and those who prefer, like him, to look at the 'big vision'. Such preferences are seen with Ron Hamilton, who favoured a mathematical bias in the subjects he studied, but declined the chance to go into academia because he prefers to remain 'hands on'. Instead, he chose to practice mechanical engineering. To accommodate different learning capabilities and styles, Robin Harper thinks that the formal education system needs to be 'relaxed' to allow people to grow at their own pace. Sir Jackie does see benefits in these different approaches to learning and he poses the question 'why would you want to be the same as everyone else?'.

These learning preferences and aptitudes can mean that some people tend to favour skills-based learning, while others may prefer an academic learning environment.

'Absolutely essential'

Academic

Margo MacDonald states that formal academic education is 'absolutely essential'. However, she describes primary schools as trying to do 'too much' by including science and other subjects. This, she thinks, is an approach to primary education that 'threw the baby out with the bathwater' and which we are 'paying for now' due to the removal of the previous 'hierarchical approach' where reading, writing and arithmetic were learnt prior to other subjects being taught. In particular, she believes that there should be more of a concentration on the 'building blocks, such as learning times tables and the alphabet'. She considers that people will gain a poor understanding of how language is constructed if there is not a proper focus on these basics. This, she thinks, may cause some youngsters, including 'graduates, clever people', to truncate language and, by using language imprecisely, find themselves unable to communicate effectively. This is something that Sheila McLean sees in some law students and, she notes, can cause difficulties because law requires precision in the use of language. Professor McLean points out that putting a comma or full stop in the wrong place can change the intended meaning of the words used. In addition, she observes that tertiary education is dispensing with more formal lecturing styles. This, she thinks, is due to students being of an age where they have the maturity to interact with different types of teaching. However, Professor McLean believes that traditional styles of teaching are required to 'learn the basics' and she therefore advocates an approach to primary schooling that ensures children are taught in a structured manner. Chay Blyth thinks that primary school education tries to fit in 'too much' and that a larger part of the school day should be about allowing children to develop by 'having fun'. Also, Sir Chay believes that the primary school day is overly long. Alan Finlayson contends that, in general, primary schools provide a 'happy' environment that is supported by parents taking an interest in their child's education. However, he thinks that parental interest, and acceptance of that by the child, can wane during secondary education. This, he believes, is because children become more independent and parents are seen as more of an intrusion which, he thinks, in some cases can contribute to an increase in disruptive behaviour, truancy and school exclusion.

Concerns about academic education tend to come from the experience of how people were taught at either school or university. For example, Ron Hamilton was not a fan of his secondary education and he describes it as 'purely a memory test and I have a hopeless memory'. He credits his sister with teaching him algebra and without that he would have failed his school Higher Mathematics examination. After school he completed Engineering Degrees and a Business Diploma at night school, which he particularly enjoyed. Irvine Laidlaw describes his schooling as 'narrow looking'. However, he does see that changing, as pupils now have more opportunity to try many different subjects, almost to the point where it is at the opposite end of the spectrum of limited options that were available to him. This change in emphasis at his old school, Merchiston Castle in Edinburgh, he puts down to an 'excellent headmaster'. The importance of the headmaster is emphasised by Jonathan Long. In particular, he sees it as the headmaster's responsibility to create the best 'atmosphere' for pupils by hiring the right type of teachers and maintaining a role as the custodian of ethos within the school community. Alan

Finlayson feels that a headmaster can inspire staff to inspire their pupils by making them feel important and, on a more general approach to education, Calum Colvin thinks banning the 'tawse' was a great step forward in the ethos of teaching. He considers that this moved teaching away from an often heavy handed approach to discipline, to one where positive support and motivation emerged. This dim view of corporal punishment perhaps comes from his father, who removed all his children from the local primary school after Professor Colvin's sister received a 'thick ear' from a teacher.

Particularly in tertiary education, Irvine Laidlaw contends that some students have to specialise too early. This meant that when he attended the University of Leeds he did not take to his degree course of Economics. He found the first year particularly hard and describes his choice of course as 'a mistake', adding that there was nothing wrong with the subject, it 'just wasn't for me'. Lord Laidlaw went on to study a Masters of Business Administration (MBA) at Columbia University, which he enjoyed more and where he 'was worked harder'. Robin Harper also contends that formal education tends to specialise too early or not give a wide enough breadth of learning. He notes that only English and Mathematics are seen as core subjects at school and pupils can opt out of sciences and foreign languages at an early stage in their education. As an example of choices being limited he points out that music and art are seen as 'add-ons'. This is something he disagrees with and he thinks that they should be core subjects. In addition, he observes that musically talented pupils are also often talented in the visual arts, but cannot study both art and music at school and must choose one or the other. In a similar way, he thinks that universities specialise too much in core subject areas, which means that topics like humanities are not included in many university courses. This, he believes, is driven by the business interests that he sees permeating all aspects of life. He includes in that the view that learning is a means to a job and not something that is done for its intrinsic value. Even though he contends that this inhibits students from gaining a fuller education, and despite thinking that the system teachers work in is becoming more restrictive, he does believe that teaching standards are improving.

These experiences and views are not thought to lessen the need for academic learning, with some, such as Tom Devine, emphasising the benefits of formal academic study both at school and in further education. Professor Devine believes that 'the future lies in the mind', due to a knowledge-based economy 'run by intellect', and he backs up this view by stating that only 16 per cent of people in Scotland are now employed in manufacturing. Michael Atiyah considers himself 'lucky' to have been well educated and able to study at 'the world's best universities', and Tam Dalyell encourages academic learning through focused reading. While Lewis Robertson comments that he does not think that a university education would have altered greatly how things turned out for him, he would have liked to have had that experience. Although Tom Farmer does think things would have been different for him if 'say I'd gone to university, I probably wouldn't have done this'. However, Sir Tom advises that personal differences will mean that different types of teaching will work for different people, where some prefer an academic environment while others may be better suited to a skills-based approach.

'Sense of achievement'

Skills-based

Brian Gill believes that there is a preoccupation with examination success and then moving on to a university degree. However, he considers that academic education is not for everyone and that 'we have lost sight of a skills-based education'. Robin Harper also believes that education has lost sight of skills-based learning, where people were taught to 'work with their hands', and he wonders where the 'crafts people' of the future will come from. To this he adds the question, what has happened to the people who wanted to be 'train drivers'? In addition, Alan Finlayson believes that many young people are being sent on academic courses in tertiary education, for which they are not suited, but would benefit from skills-based courses that they would enjoy and gain a 'sense of achievement' from. Similarly, Jackie Stewart feels that skills-based learning has been neglected and that society is wrong to place less emphasis on practical skills as 'we need more tradesmen' and require 'plumbers and mechanics'. He includes subjects such as domestic science, which he feels should be available to everyone at school. Sir Jackie gives the infrastructure build for the 2012 London Olympics as one example of where those with a trade are in demand. Kenneth Murray concurs in this overview when saying that he felt it appropriate for some youngsters to attend 'trade schools', where pupils could study practical subjects. Sir Kenneth thinks that a choice in the type of school allows people to follow a more academic or practical course of study dependent on their preferences. He is a firm believer in practical study and feels that being able to conduct experiments allowed him to gain a full understanding of the various components he was using in his chemistry studies. This is something he now sees less of, due to universities accommo-dating larger class sizes and the restrictions imposed on laboratory work by stringent health and safety regulations. As he did not consider himself the most academic school pupil, Calum Colvin feels that he only really started learning when he left school to attend Duncan of Jordanstone College of Art in Dundee. It was there that he was taught practical skills such as welding.

Chay Blyth left Hawick High School, at age 15, to take up an apprenticeship as a frame worker with a local knitwear company. He valued the skills this taught him, as it gave him on-the-job training that enabled him to obtain a qualified position. He describes the role of frame worker as much sought after and well paid in the knitwear industry. Tom Farmer always encourages formal education but points out that for some people who are less academically minded, it is better to 'get out and work'.

In addition, learning is viewed as a lifelong process that continues out-with formal education.

'It is easy to stop thinking'

Ongoing learning

Ongoing learning that takes place outside of school, college and university can be seen in people attending organised courses and in a continuous process of learning from experience and observation. This type of learning is thought to enhance an academic or skills-based education, plus perhaps inform attitudes and an individual's sense of self.

'Sloppy practices'

Observation

Jonathan Long suggests that people are apt to learn through observation, something that he thinks continues throughout life. He sees this as forming learnt habits and thinks that it is these habits that dictate individual choices in attitude and the value system that people follow. To underline this point, Dr Long quotes Iris Murdoch who said that the way people react in new situations is dependent 'partly, perhaps largely, on the quality of our habitual objects of attention'. For this reason, Norman Drummond states that adults should demonstrate exemplary behaviour because children are greatly influenced by what they observe.

With his concentration on the visual arts, unsurprisingly, Calum Colvin describes observation as a keen learning resource, and Tom Farmer also advises that he has learnt through observation. Sir Tom believes that by demonstrating a point you provide a lasting lesson. In addition, he thinks that an important part of teaching in the workplace is explaining to employees why they are doing a particular job and how that fits into the overall business. Sir Tom believes that this allows people to better understand their contribution, gives more meaning to a job and enables employees to take more pride in a job well done. Providing learning through observation is something that Ron Hamilton has also done. In the 1960s, when he was working in paper mills in Toronto and North Carolina, he struck on the then novel idea of filming the manufacturing process for the production of a four inch paper cube tissue holder. The aim of the film was to allow managers to observe procedures and make recommendations on improvements. This revealed some 'sloppy practices' that were then rectified. The film proved so instructional that it was sent to the United Kingdom to help train those working in similar areas.

As an example of applying learning from observation, Chay Blyth recounts when he was in the Army on desert operations and, along with three other Corporals, he was ushered into the Commanding Officer's tent. They were told that he was considering promoting one of them to the rank of Sergeant. Sir Chay decided that to give himself the best chance of promotion he had to think and act like a Sergeant and he started to observe and mimic the officers' behaviours. This approach succeeded and he became the youngest Platoon Sergeant in the Parachute Regiment's history. Alan Finlayson also points to his time in the Army, when he completed his National Service from 1955 to 1957 as a Trooper, mainly based in Hong Kong. He observed how the officers used their authority and that the 'good' officers operated through persuasion and example, while the 'bad' used 'bluster, threats and arrogance'. Looking back, he is certain those experiences and observations informed his approach of trying to follow the 'good' examples in his own management style. In addition, he watched how Judges and Sheriffs behaved in court. In particular, he mentions the equal courtesy and consideration that Charles Shaw, Lord Kilbrandon (whose vision the Children's Hearing System was) and Sheriff Ronnie Ireland showed to everyone. To illustrate this, he gives the example of when Ronnie Ireland suggested, perhaps insisted, that all court officials work beyond the normal 4 pm finish time in order to conclude a case. This was due to Ronnie Ireland seeing the distress that the court proceedings, involving allegations that a child had been abused by his stepfather, were having on the mother and his desire not to add to that by having her return to court at a later date. These observations have informed Alan Finlayson's own approach of trying to practise tolerance and courtesy to everyone.

'Very effective'

Experience

George Mathewson sums up experience as 'just an ongoing process of learning, not a single thing or instance', where incremental ambition and improvement happen over time, supported by increased learning which provides evolving opportunity. Jackie Stewart believes that theory and reading can be of assistance, but that there is no substitute for practice or the practical application of learning. This, he thinks, provides the experience that gives knowledge, which in turn may lead to wisdom and 'maturity in thinking'. This 'maturity' then allows people to better handle situations and avoid or address problems, as it forms part of a 'no problems, only solutions' mindset. For that reason, Sir Jackie prefers to work with people 'that have been through the mill' because, he believes, experience coupled with 'some creative thinking' best equips someone to tackle any related set of circumstances. Lewis Robertson has learnt from the experience of doing, particularly when working at the family textile business J.F. Robertson Limited (latterly Robertson Industrial Textiles) and as Managing Director and Chairman of merged company Scott & Robertson Limited. This experience developed his people management skills and, from implementing good business practice, informed his later approach to company recovery situations. The learning from experience that Glasgow University law students gain from working with those at the Citizens Advice Bureau is described by Sheila McLean as 'very effective'. Similarly, during his student apprenticeship with Hoover Ltd, the experience of working across all parts of the business provided Ron Hamilton with a practical overview of how the company fitted together and gave him invaluable insight and learning.

Brian Gill refers to the need to gain experience, and says he has met people who have academic knowledge but lack ability because they do not have the corresponding life experiences. Lord Gill believes that it is these experiences that 'illuminate you'. In addition, he advises that, even as an experienced lawyer, he is learning every day from dealing with appeals by those lawyers who have less experience than him. Calum Colvin considers that the ongoing experience he gains each time he produces a new piece of art updates his knowledge and helps him to improve his standards, and George Robertson states that he prefers to learn from the experience of doing. Jonathan Long follows a similar thread when advising that he learns from situations that he has been involved in and emphasises that there is 'often a lot of talk but people must do'. It is from experience that Noreen Murray and others believe that confidence grows, with Tom Farmer adding that to gain experience you must 'push yourself' in new situations. For example, Evelyn Glennie thinks that it is only through the experience of playing in front of an audience that she can learn to improve her performance technique. To this she adds, it is the learning accumulated from experience that allows her to pass on practical knowledge to other musicians as, she believes, there is 'nothing like experience'.

'Not many men can touch type'

A conscious effort

Some individuals make a more 'conscious effort' to improve, often through attending academic or practical skills courses. This is something that Chay Blyth is very clear on and committed to doing. Since leaving the Army, in 1968, he has gone on at least one self-improvement course every year. These include courses recognised by the Chartered Institute of Marketing and by the Institute of Project Management, with the 'best course' a Diploma from the London Business School, which he describes as 'not a full MBA but preparing for that'. Sir Chay gives particular mention to the touch typing course that he went on at the age of 55. This took him five afternoons of formal study plus 'a lot of practice' to master. He believes that those practical typing skills are very worthwhile due to the increasing use of computers and he is proud to have completed the course as 'not many men can touch type'. Irvine Laidlaw very much believes in committing time and energy to improvement, something he does on a regular basis. Despite not seeing himself as a natural scholar, Lord Laidlaw regularly enrols on courses. Some of these are academic and related to business, such as his studies at INSEAD (a graduate business school), and others widen his interests, such as taking tuition in digital photography and attending a wine tasting course run by the Greater London Council. George Mathewson also makes a conscious effort to improve his learning and he gives the example of completing a Master of Business Administration through night classes whilst in full-time employment. Robin Harper considers that such self-improvement tends to be more at the back of his mind although, on occasion, that can be a more conscious decision, for example, when he taught himself the guitar in his 20s and the trumpet in his 30s, attended an art college course in his 40s and gained a Diploma in Guidance from Edinburgh University in his 50s. He includes in this self-improvement his physical fitness but, he does add, there are certain areas that he feels he should concentrate more on but neglects, such as learning about information technology.

A deliberate approach to deepening and broadening knowledge is also taken by Calum Colvin. In general, he tries to improve through reading, which gives an outlet for his intellectual enquiry as 'it is easy to stop thinking'. This habit of reading started as a youngster when he read a wide range of subjects, 'really whatever came to hand'. He now takes a more focused approach and tends to concentrate on history and psychology to 'sharpen knowledge' of visual culture. Likewise, Michael Atiyah reads outside of his field to broaden his understanding, for example, of history and philosophy.

This 'conscious effort' to improve is not necessarily restricted to academic or practical skills knowledge as it can embrace methods of thinking and a sense of self. For instance, Michael Atiyah comments that it can be for either academic learning or developing as a person and Jonathan Long advises that he works hard to build and retain positive habits. These habits are informed by his almost daily reading of books like the meditations of Marcus Aurelius. Dr Long believes that reflecting on this type of literature can help to promote self-control, fortitude and a certain detachment from emotions that encourage clear thinking via an unbiased approach. This is certainly influenced by Dr Long's spirituality as he quotes from the New Testament that 'blessed are the pure in heart for they shall see god'.

Others, such as Tam Dalyell and Margo MacDonald, do not see themselves as making a 'conscious effort' to improve, and Ron Hamilton refers back to the innate drive that pushes him forward, rather than any 'conscious' thought process. Likewise, Norman Drummond does not see himself making a 'conscious effort' to improve, although he does believe that 'self-thought is important', and Sheila McLean sees improvement coming from trying to do her best as opposed to any 'conscious effort'. Brian Gill does not make a 'conscious effort' but instead sees himself becoming more competent through increasing interest and knowledge over time. While Robin Harper does at times make a more 'conscious decision' to improve, he normally tends just to 'pick things up'.

In addition, Sheila McLean stresses that improvement should not be 'self-regarding' but should include thinking about others, and Robin Harper cautions against a 'restrictive view' of self-improvement that focuses on moving upwards in society. In a similar sense, Brian Gill views all forms of self-improvement as laudable, but he warns against losing sight of creating a socially aware society that promotes the helping of others over any narrow view of oneself.

Furthermore, there is the suggestion that 'softer skills', which tend to be learnt from experience and observation, should be promoted or taught more proactively.

'Too much testing'

Training for life

Norman Drummond believes that schools place too much 'emphasis on passing exams' and that there should be better opportunity for all round development. He refers to prize lists which tend to be for academic achievement and not 'life skills', although he is not purporting 'daft things like prizes for everyone'. Reverend Drummond argues that two-thirds of the school curriculum should be reserved for academic learning and the remainder for 'training the mind and the heart'. He believes that this should concentrate on 'ethics, sociology and core values', rather than leaving these just to be picked up by chance throughout life. Robin Harper also believes that there is 'too much testing', as schools 'tick boxes', and that courses in philosophy or logic should be given some prominence. In addition, he thinks there is scope for more learning to be done outside of the classroom. As an example of that, he points to Norway where he advises that one day a week children are taught in the community or outdoors. This, he contends, gives youngsters a more rounded education and a better appreciation of their environment. Irvine Laidlaw advises that a wider breadth of subjects are taught at a later stage in the United States of America, particularly in degree qualifications. A broader topic range, he thinks, is advantageous and the school syllabus should be widened to include 'softer subjects'. Jonathan Long suggests that there should be less emphasis on 'academic' subjects at school. In particular, he promotes the teaching of honesty, citizenship and discipline whilst encouraging positive habits through a focus on 'virtue ethics'. The importance of forming positive habits is underlined by Reverend Drummond when he says that 'fires can burn negatively as well as positively'. Virtue ethics, which are rooted in the teachings of Aristotle, inform Dr Long's belief that teachers can help children to understand what it is to be human and thus make society more humane. He believes that fostering positive traits would negate the need to impose rules as these are only required to curtail destructive qualities. To enable this, Dr Long stresses that the 'right tree must be planted'. However, he argues that this is inhibited by schools, which are locked into a mechanistic 'socio-economic model' that brings everything down to the lowest common denominator through a teaching culture that 'is afraid of offending'.

However, Norman Drummond does counsel that people cannot be taught how to react in all circumstances. He gives the example of when at the age of 24, he held the hand of a young man who was dying. This is something that he feels he could not have been trained for. As a further example, he refers to the circumstances that Rudolph Giuliani, the Mayor of New York, faced in the aftermath of the attack on New York's World Trade Centre in September 2001. Reverend Drummond believes that nothing could have taught Rudolph Giuliani how to deal with that situation. However, he does believe that in such extreme circumstances people revert to their natural or learnt sense of humanity, which, he thinks, is determined by the habits and values they have practised and formed.

'Work hard to piece everything together'

Real understanding

In order to gain a full understanding of a subject there is a belief that hard work is required. For instance, Noreen Murray advises that you have to construct and piece together all the different sources of learning. When at university she would listen to lectures, take notes, then read textbooks and papers to obtain an understanding of the topic and permit the amplification of her notes. She sees this as the typical approach of a university student in the 1950s and 1960s. However, she thinks that some of today's students are inhibited from gaining an in-depth knowledge of their topic, because they are more often than not 'spoon fed' pages of information that they can memorise to pass their exams. This, she thinks, can cause students to take things for granted and not study the basics of a topic, which stops them from fully comprehending all aspects of their subject. Calum Colvin also thinks that students are sometimes obstructed from attaining a thorough understanding of their subject. He puts much of this down to advances in the technology that some students use, for example in photography, which can lead to the false impression that they need not learn the underlying basics. In addition, he considers that there is an increasingly complex art college curriculum, which means that lecturers have to spread their expertise more thinly. He thinks this can cause some students to miss the skills-based tuition that he enjoyed.

However, Tom Devine points out that the tools or sources of knowledge, like the 'treasure of historical research not in the public domain', are available but require to be found, taken and thought through.

In order to gain a comprehensive understanding of an area, Evelyn Glennie assesses herself as a person and as a musician. It is then, only after she has a full understanding of the subject, that she will put her learning into practice. This is perhaps shown in her approach to teaching, as it is only recently that she felt she had a thorough enough understanding of percussion to allow her to teach it effectively. Michael Atiyah considers that 'unless you think hard enough, you won't learn' and, as a lecturer, Kenneth Murray enjoyed speaking with students, but was dismayed that a large number of them did not fully understand the basics of the subjects that they were studying. For example, students would not know exactly what items they were using in biochemical experiments, having merely read that certain constituents should be mixed together. He attributes this to students not going back to scratch, but taking short cuts through using commercially prepared kits of materials. Sir Kenneth's approach is to build his knowledge from studying the fundamentals that will enable him to fully understand the subject as, in his experience, he has to 'work hard to piece everything together'.

Learning: Summary

'Grain of the brain'

The attitudes of the state, parents and teachers, along with an individual's natural inquisitiveness, are thought to shape the approach that someone takes to learning. Acquiring an education is viewed as essential, in particular a primary education that provides the skills of reading, writing and arithmetic. Following that, aptitudes and preferences are thought to dictate whether someone tends towards academic or skills-based learning. Although, in some instances, primary school education is described as trying to do too much and not concentrating enough on fundamental learning. In contrast, secondary and tertiary education are sometimes considered too narrow in their focus. Also, there is a view that skills-based education is to some extent neglected.

People are seen to start learning through observation from a very early age, which may provide learnt habits that can go on to define someone's attitude and their own sense of self. All methods of learning, whether academic, skills-based or through observation, are believed to be of value. However, experience is given as the key to gaining an improved understanding of how to apply knowledge and what attitude to adopt. While experience is believed to be gained naturally throughout life, it is thought that it can be accelerated if people push themselves to experience new or more challenging situations. In addition, some people make a conscious effort to improve by attending formal learning courses, although others see that as simply adding to skills and learning from gaining experience over time, rather than any 'conscious' effort to improve.

There is a view that people could be better served by being taught 'softer' skills in a more formal teaching environment. It is believed that by promoting habits in this way people may develop positive attributes, which will inform the basis of their approach to life. Nonetheless, hard work in thinking and in bringing together all sources of learning is viewed as a requirement if a real understanding of a subject is to be gained.

Learning and improvement are not just thought of in terms of self-improvement but also in assisting the improvement of other people and society as a whole. This spreading of knowledge can be encouraged by taking and giving help and advice.

Help and Advice

'What do you think?'

Why seek or give help and advice?
Who do people turn to for help and advice?
What type of help and advice may be available?

In this section the value of including other people and giving and taking help or advice is discussed. In addition, the type of advice that may be available and the other influences people take inspiration or encouragement from are considered. The opportunities that help and advice may furnish are then explored in Chapter v.

'You can't do it on your own'

Helping others

Brian Gill advises that he would not have reached his present position without the help of countless other people. Lord Gill asserts that people cannot succeed through their own efforts alone, but only with the help of others. This is something that Tom Farmer also believes. In particular, he considers it important to have people with whom to share successes and trials and tribulations. Like Lord Gill, Sir Tom says that there are 'too many people to mention' who have helped him, and that his approach has often been defined by the advice or suggestions he has received. Jonathan Long also highlights the importance of giving and receiving help or advice and, in addition, he emphasises the need to do that 'at the right times'. Dr Long stresses that often it is the timing of when help or advice is received or given that makes a real difference. George Mathewson appreciates the advice that he has received at important junctures in his career and he thinks it right and proper to consult with and take advice from others. Having said that, in business, he tended only to consult within the organisation he was working for.

Alan Finlayson appreciated the help and advice he received from Senior Legal Partner Richard McPake. In particular, he refers to when he was working on a large property deal in 1966 that 'went wrong', costing the client approximately £2 million, and Richard McPake supported him by explaining to the client that he was not to blame for the loss. Again, it was Richard McPake who provided support, help and advice to prioritise his work when it 'was getting on top of me'.

Furthermore, he learnt from the standards, values and equal treatment of others that Richard McPake displayed, for example, on the occasion when he, as Court Partner, was criticised for the delay in progressing a minimal value claim for an elderly established client of the firm.

Margo MacDonald believes that it is important to seek and take the advice of experts. To illustrate this, she states that she takes the advice of those with expertise in Parkinson's disease, a condition that she suffers from. Likewise, Chay Blyth considers it important to seek and accept advice from those with more experience or knowledge than him. As an example, he mentions that he sought assistance to understand company accounts. Sir Chay appreciates the help of other people, in particular the 'host of friendly helpers' that are available via radio contact when he is sailing solo. When seeking guidance, Tam Dalyell highlights the importance of receiving impartial advice, and he recommends only taking advice from those who are not dependent on you. Also, he is reluctant to give advice unless he knows the situation that he is to comment on well. Discussing work with colleagues whose insight they value is something that both Tom Devine and Calum Colvin make a point of doing. Professor Devine refers to a small and trusted group, while Professor Colvin uses this approach to foster mutual support and peer review, something that he thinks is valuable in challenging people to improve via constructive criticism. In addition, he thinks that by talking to colleagues and other 'interesting people' he can 'open up new consciousnesses'. However, in hindsight, Professor Colvin wishes he had taken more advice from others as he 'made a lot of mistakes'. He does add, rather wryly, that he is stubborn and probably would have ignored the advice anyway. This is something that he sees in a lot of students who, he thinks, are like him and may be obstinate to the point that they take the opposite tack to the one advised.

Taking and giving advice or help at the right times is considered important, but there is also a view that people should depend on their own self-reliance, something that both George Mathewson and Calum Colvin contend. In particular, Professor Colvin stresses that people should take responsibility for their own approach and not always rely on other people. Also, while Michael Atiyah agrees that it is important to take advice from other people, he believes that ultimately you have to go with your own 'gut feeling' and 'try it out'. By doing what you want, Sir Michael thinks, you will take more responsibility for your own actions and 'can't blame others' if things are not going as you might have hoped.

This can give rise to the premise of the 'self-made man', which Tam Dalyell believes may be seen in some people, although 'no obvious examples' spring to mind. Robin Harper sees the self-made man in one of his friends who left school at 15, with no qualifications, and went on to become a successful businessman. It is people who have followed through on a vision that, Sheila McLean thinks, to some extent can be described as self-made, although Professor McLean does believe that everyone requires a supporting network. Jackie Stewart contends that, in so much as everyone has their own commitment and enthusiasm, people can be 'self-made'. However, Sir Jackie does add 'but you need assistance'. For William Stewart, the self-made man is reflected in people who have attained, in the main, thanks to their own resilience, perseverance and drive. If the concept of the 'self-made man' is taken to mean that people spurn help or advice, then Jonathan Long believes it is bogus. Dr Long contends that people cannot make it through life on their own, a sentiment that Brian Gill concurs with when saying 'there is no such thing as the self-made man'. Norman Drummond adds to these views when commenting that 'while we are all able to self-help, we all need accompanying assistance', something that Tom Farmer wholeheartedly endorses when saying 'you can't do it on your own'.

When seeking advice, generally it is thought that people are pleased to provide their assistance or give their opinion.

'You want my opinion?'

Including others

George Robertson advises that the key to increasing knowledge and obtaining support for any particular aim is to engage and include other people. Lord Robertson gives the instance of a fellow student, at the then recently constituted University of Dundee, who went out of his way to ask other people their opinions on the subjects he was studying. He then developed these views into his own thinking which, Lord Robertson believes, assisted the student to gain a 1st Class Honours Degree. As a further example, when he was a relatively young member of the Scottish Development Agency, Lord Robertson turned to Lewis Robertson for counsel on a particular area. He was told that he should concentrate on the output as that is what people would judge him on. This advice has stayed with Lord Robertson and has informed his approach on a number of projects. Sir Lewis was more than happy to assist Lord Robertson and, like others, he is pleased if he can help other people to achieve their ambitions. Another person who takes an inclusive approach is William Stewart. He gives the example of when he led the White Paper on Science and Technology programme, 'Realising Our Potential', which evaluated potential technological advances and their likely impact. To do that, he set up groups which consulted with a range of experts. As he is not a member of any political party, he was not frightened to include those of different political hues. Approximately 11,000 individuals eventually participated in this, the most wide-reaching technological study in 20 years. Tom Farmer also considers it good to ask other people for their opinion. Sir Tom adds that you need not agree with the opinion for it to help clarify your own thinking and your chosen course of action. Similarly, Calum Colvin does not take on board all the advice that he is given, as sometimes he considers it 'better to ignore advice and go your own way'.

Those people that have more experience and knowledge are often very willing to make themselves available to provide help and advice. As an example of this, Jackie Stewart mentions the International Advisory Board, which he is part of. The Board was established in 2002 by Scottish Enterprise and gives guidance to Scottish companies that have international business potential, by providing access to senior business figures who are Scots or strongly associated with Scotland. However, in general, George Robertson believes that people are reluctant to take advice or include others. He is unsure why this is the case as, he believes, it is beneficial to canvass opinions. Also, he notes that people are more than happy to provide advice and 'nobody feels used', partly because it flatters them due to the inference that their opinion counts. For example, when visiting central Asian countries prior to NATO going in to Afghanistan, Lord Robertson asked one President for his specific advice on handling another regional leader. That President, who had seemed disinterested and 'almost asleep, came to life' and not only gave useful input but also 'revealed a lot about himself'. He sees this as the typical response of someone being pleased to provide information and flattered to do so, almost saying 'you want my opinion?'. This reinforced Lord Robertson's view of the need to canvass opinion to increase his own learning and to assist him in moulding ideas from the outset.

'You must be true to yourself'

Types of advice

It is considered that when giving advice in a formal way, in the main, one of three distinct approaches is taken: that of advisor, mentor or teacher.

'Sympathy is not enough'

Advisors

Jackie Stewart thinks that a good advisor will have relevant practical experience as opposed to, or in addition to, the academic knowledge that a teacher may concentrate on. When working as an advisor, Sheila McLean looks to provide a logical and well thought out conclusion by explaining the 'facts and options'. However, she notes that the ultimate responsibility for the decision lies with the person taking advice, who may choose to follow advice that is different from what she has provided. Thus, even though she does want her advice to be taken, it does not necessarily mean she is trying to convince someone. When giving advice, Professor McLean notes that some people hope to have their existing ideas verified and that, if someone has a particular conviction, no amount of reasoned argument will dissuade them from that view. Also, she considers it important that advisors do not push their own personal beliefs, especially when advising on medical and ethical issues. To illustrate this, she refers to presenting advice on the sex selection of embryos for non-medical reasons to the United Kingdom Government, which she did without including her personal view. William Stewart recommends that the message 'be given straight', regardless of how unpalatable that message is to you or your thinking, or whether or not the message will be agreeable to the recipient. As well as providing the message, Sir William believes that alternatives should be offered that will assist the recipient to evaluate the advice and come to a decision on the best approach. Sir William describes himself as 'more of an outsider', which meant that he took on the role of Chief Scientific Advisor to the Cabinet Office with 'no baggage'. This allowed him to give the Conservative Government, under Prime Minister Margaret Thatcher, straightforward, honest and impartial advice without fear or prejudice. Sir William adds that people fall from positions of power or influence when they do not listen to the true or full story but only to what they want to hear. He concludes by saying that to be a good advisor 'you must be true to yourself'.

George Mathewson has looked to advisors at certain points in his career. For example, when he was offered senior positions at both the Royal Bank of Scotland and the New Zealand Power Authority he turned to Ian MacGregor, whose opinion he valued. Sir George was advised to go with the Royal Bank of Scotland, which reinforced his own thinking that the Bank had the most opportunity for commercial growth, and he accepted its offer.

Robin Harper saw himself acting as an advisor to pupils in his role as a guidance teacher, although he thought it was important to maintain a 'distance'. He felt it would have been easy to become 'very involved' in other aspects or difficulties that children were experiencing, and he was trained to refer any such case in the first instance, because 'sympathy is not enough' if you are not equipped to give proper advice.

'Removing unnecessary clutter'

Mentors

Alan Finlayson advises that a mentor tends to assist the development of another person, often at an emotional level, by forming a longer-term and more intimate relationship than an advisor may expect to have. Also, a mentor is described, by Evelyn Glennie, as someone who assists in creating an environment where things can be discussed openly. Tom Farmer mentions that he has had many mentors in both his business and personal life and John Crofton suggests that, alongside parental influence, a 'buddy or mentor' can greatly assist development. Irvine Laidlaw wishes that he had a strong mentor, because he considers that a good mentor is the key to development. Norman Drummond points out that mentoring is not just a one-way process and, as an example of that, he refers to the 'Gemini Project' or 'Coracle Programme' run by Columba 1400. This pairs youngsters from difficult circumstances with corporate business leaders. The benefit of this two-way mentoring approach is seen in the reaction of one corporate participant who said 'if before the week, you'd told me that a 16-year-old girl from Dundee, measuring 4' 10" would have coached me into understanding my life values and sense of purpose, I would have said you were mad. But it happened'.

Mentoring does not need to be a formal process, with, for example, Chay Blyth describing the conversations that he had with Walt Ormiston, when working as a delivery boy and pie maker, as mentoring. Walt Ormiston was the local butcher and a former Paratrooper who had served during the Second World War, including Operation Market Garden in September 1944. Sir Chay was enthused by the stories that Walt Ormiston told him about the Parachute Regiment, and he was a direct influence on Sir Chay joining that regiment, aged 18, in 1958. In his turn, Sir Chay has mentored other people in this informal way. If embarking on a more formal mentoring programme, Sir Chay believes, time must be allocated over an extended period. He contends that should be at least two years, perhaps more. However, Sir Chay thinks the dynamics of mentoring, particularly between an adult and child, are changing. The main reason he gives for that is the 'umbrella society' which, he thinks, deters an adult from spending time alone with a youngster. He argues that this inhibits the effectiveness of mentoring by hindering the ability to build an understanding and bond between the two individuals. Sir Chay believes that this will eventually lead to mentoring becoming more academic.

Jonathan Long describes a mentor's work as intuitive and based on a judgment that is informed by a 'sense of trust'. This means that he does not think that mentoring lends itself to a checklist, against which people can tell if they will be a good mentor. He does though consider that a mentor should possess certain qualities, such as an ability to live with ambiguity and a willingness to form a partnership with the other person. In addition, he advises that the mentor must start at wherever the other person may be in their thinking. From that starting point, he sees the aim of a mentor as 'removing unnecessary clutter' and drawing out positive attributes. In particular, Dr Long contends that people often have to be believed in by someone else before they can believe in themselves, something he thinks a mentor is well placed to do. To do that, Dr Long emphasises, the mentor must be credible in the eyes of the other person. He thinks such credibility comes from a mentor's background, experience and by demonstrating their own personal development (more important than professional development). This, he contends, allows both parties to relate to one another by not being too far removed from each other's circumstances. He hopes that he has made a positive contribution through the mentoring he has provided, but believes that many individuals are not necessarily aware of the impact that a mentor has had on them. Dr Long reiterates that mentoring is 'trying to get something out' and he makes a clear distinction between a mentor and a teacher, who is 'trying to put something in'.

'Catalytic combination'

Teachers

While an advisor is described as providing advice to assist in immediate decision making and a mentor as trying to elicit skills or attributes, a teacher is thought to provide people information that can have a future purpose. A further distinction between teachers and mentors is that the former are seen to concentrate on academic or skills-based learning, while the latter are thought to focus on personal development.

Jonathan Long comments that the onus is on the teacher to make the relationship with his or her pupil work. This, he thinks, comes from applying learning from experience and, for example, it is only recently that Evelyn Glennie has felt confident that she has the necessary levels of experience to teach competently. Dame Evelyn believes, with inspiration and an ability to review their individual approach, teachers can add pressure gradually to pupils' expectations and thus encourage incremental improvement. To do this, she feels that teachers must respect their pupils, know their topic well and challenge pupils by asking appropriate questions to gauge and then develop their levels of understanding. Robin Harper thinks that every teacher has his or her 'own style' and he has seen good results come from teachers that make their subject as interesting as possible, from a 'total dedication' to preparing their lessons. Also, he thinks that good teachers have an empathy with children and enjoy teaching for its own sake. He enjoys reacting to young people and believes it important to be as nonjudgmental as possible, as he considers that there is no such thing as a 'bad child'. This led him to take the view that once children were in his class they became 'one of mine' and he would be defensive about them, something he acknowledges may be seen by other people as a weakness in his teaching approach. Sheila McLean believes that teachers have to really know their subject and be able to present it in an interesting manner. She also thinks that teachers must be able to present themselves well and have an ability to engage with their class or audience, something that she thinks can be done by using humour. Alan Finlayson also suggests injecting humour to make a lesson more memorable. To this he adds, in order to meet expectations, know your subject and audience. George Mathewson considers that good teachers can empathise with and hold the respect of their pupils, either by their intellect or the passion that they demonstrate for their subject. Sir George considers it crucial that teachers are enthused by their subject matter, and feels this is why he was 'on my game' during the second of three years working as an assistant lecturer at the University of St Andrews. In the first year he was gaining experience of lecturing and by the third year his interest was starting to tail off. However, during the second year he was able to combine learning from experience and enthusiasm for the subject.

One of the reasons Tom Devine accepted the Sir William Fraser Chair of History at the University of Edinburgh was that it brought him back to 'main-stream teaching', which he enjoys. However, he comments that some university lecturers enter academia due to their strong and laudable desire to conduct research, but that a good researcher does not necessarily make for a good teacher. When teaching, Professor Devine employs the approach he learnt from his father of 'total fairness' and he lets students know that they are being judged by the 'highest possible standards' in a completely 'impartial manner that ignores personalities'. Norman Drummond thinks a teacher, like a mentor, should instil confidence in pupils by providing them with support, while Jackie Stewart believes that teaching boils down to one thing, 'communication', although Sir Jackie does stress that teachers must be given the correct levels of support and training. Margo MacDonald sees a good teacher as someone who listens, observes, enthuses and explains, while Evelyn Glennie says that teachers ought to provide 'support and guidance'. Calum Colvin agrees when saying that a good teacher will identify areas of support, act to assist in those areas and help clarify ideas. Professor Devine hopes to give pupils clarity and inspiration by providing them with a clear structure of approach, something he describes as a 'catalytic combination'.

'The chance of a lifetime'

Pupils

A pupil who demonstrates certain characteristics is thought best placed to take advantage of the advice on offer, regardless if that advice is given by an advisor, mentor or teacher. In this sense a 'pupil' may be a school pupil, university student, trainee or, more widely, a person seeking advice. Calum Colvin believes that pupils have a choice about what to learn and from where or whom to learn it, and must therefore weigh up what advice to take and when to act on it. Evelyn Glennie echoes Professor Colvin's remarks when stating that there are always choices in learning and sums up her view of a good pupil as someone who is 'eager to learn from others'. Dame Evelyn teaches privately plus gives master classes and she likes pupils who already have some direction, which she can shape and encourage. For Tom Devine, a good pupil can appreciate when they are being judged fairly and that personality is not a factor in the guidance and feedback being given. However, he adds that some people do not appreciate that and take criticism personally. Noreen Murray believes that unless pupils are committed to their subject they will not improve upon existing standards or fulfill their potential. She detects a lack of commitment in some university students and wonders if that is due to an increase in the student population, where, in addition to the motivated students who have always accepted places, students that are less committed to their studies are now entering tertiary education. Kenneth Murray picks up on this point when saying that he notices a lack of application in some students, which he cannot appreciate, as university is 'the chance of a lifetime'.

In addition to the help and advice that people may take from advisors, mentors or teachers, it is emphasised that people may also learn from and be influenced by their peers.

'You'd call that bullying now'

Like-minded people

In his youth Chay Blyth used to hang about in gangs, but one day when at the swimming pool someone flung him in. 'You'd call that bullying now' he says. He was hauled out of the pool by Tom Robson, the local swimming champion, who was a contender but was not selected for the British Olympic Swimming Team. Sir Chay could not swim and he accepted Tom Robson's offer of swimming lessons. Sir Chay noticed that the other team members had higher expectations, 'thought differently and communicated differently', which rubbed off on him. This, he thinks, helped him raise his standards of personal conduct and he now appreciates polite behaviour. For example, he cannot understand people tolerating inappropriate language. Sir Chay goes on to say that if you confront someone on poor behaviour and they tell you to 'go to hell', then all well and good as you have lost a bad influence. This is seen in Kenneth Murray's desire to 'escape' the environment he encountered when working as a civil servant and his ambition to improve being mirrored by his friends, all of whom were determined to increase their learning by attending day and evening classes. Sir Kenneth used his evening class qualifications to gain a place at Birmingham University where he went on to attain a 1st Class Honours Degree and PhD in chemistry. This led him, eventually, into pioneering work on DNA and the development of a vaccine against viral hepatitis B, one of the earliest and most practical applications of molecular biology.

While Calum Colvin emphasises a need to communicate and collaborate with others, like Evelyn Glennie, he can feel the need to preserve a degree of independence and not be overly influenced by peers. When studying at the Royal Academy of Music, Dame Evelyn observed that students would follow each other's lead, for instance, if 'one went to the pub the others would follow'. This does not mean that people pick their peers or those they wish to collaborate with in an impassive fashion as, for example, Michael Atiyah does not seek out individuals to work with. Rather, he describes how collaborations come from 'spontaneous meetings', such as from being introduced to other people's friends or when discussing items with colleagues (including former students who have become colleagues) and those with different expertise to him. Indeed, John Crofton did not have any close friends who were medically inclined and only met others who shared his interest in medicine when he commenced university.

As well as the influence of peers, people can be influenced by inspirational figures.

'Amazing people with amazing stories'

Inspirations

To this day Calum Colvin is inspired by a host of photographers, artists and musicians. While he prefers not to name one above the others, he aspires to the high standards that they set. In particular, he notes that the notion of Scottish artists working and living in Scotland 'did not exist' when he embarked on his degree course at Duncan of Jordanstone College of Art. Now he sees many artists doing just that and Professor Colvin hopes they will inspire other Scottish artists to follow suit. Tom Farmer is also reluctant to name those who have inspired him. However, he views it as important that he has never been disappointed by these people, particularly when he met them, and that they lived up to his expectations. Chay Blyth refers to butcher Walt

Ormiston and swimmer Tom Robson as inspirational and influential in his teenage years, while fellow musicians are referred to by Evelyn Glennie as giving her ongoing inspiration. She includes the British cellist Jacqueline Du Pre, whose career was tragically cut short by multiple sclerosis, and the Canadian pianist Glen Gould. Dame Evelyn goes on to describe them as 'amazing people with amazing stories'. She is also inspired by those students that push musical boundaries through challenging themselves and the norms of the music world. In addition, she takes inspiration from 'self-help' books, from which she will read extracts from time to time to give herself 'a top up'.

Margo MacDonald talks of the inspiration that she took from the career and achievements of swimmer Eloner Gordon. Eloner Gordon was trained by her father at her local 25 m pool in Hamilton and won a bronze medal in the 200 m breaststroke at the 1952 Helsinki Olympics, beaten by two Hungarians who used the new and faster butterfly technique. In addition, she was inspired by the saleswomen at shoe shop Saxone on Sauchiehall Street in Glasgow. She describes them as having 'limited education' but being 'sharp, clever and confident'. A further inspiration came from her school gym teacher, who 'smoked like a lum', always wore a well-cut suit, only occasionally wore white gym shoes and who encouraged her to study physical education at college. This included the observation that she would find the exams a 'scoosh' and would therefore be able to go dancing, 'the best piece of advice I was ever given'. Likewise, Robin Harper gained inspiration from his school teachers, particularly his history teachers, as well as his Professor of Moral Philosophy at Aberdeen University.

William Stewart names former Prime Minister Margaret Thatcher as an inspiring down-to-earth pragmatic figure. One of George Robertson's 'heroes' is former Czech President Vaclav Havel, who was a leading figure in the 'Velvet Revolution' that emancipated Czechoslovakia from Soviet rule. Vaclav Havel went on to become the first President of Czechoslovakia and then the Czech Republic, and oversaw its move to a free-market economy. Lord

Robertson believes this will give Vaclav Havel an enduring legacy. When considering a legacy or inspiration to future generations, John Crofton thinks of personality as leaving a pattern in time that is remembered by family and friends or, for the most notable of people, recorded in history. Sir John names William Osler as an example from Western medicine of someone who has a continuing legacy. William Osler pioneered medical residencies and bedside teaching that focused medicine on patient practicalities, rather than a more theoretical approach. The ability of historical figures to continue to resonate is demonstrated by Robin Harper naming former Prime Minister Winston Churchill as an inspiration, as a 'great speaker' rather than as a politician, and Norman Drummond mentioning Mary Seacole (Mary Jane Grant). Mary Seacole travelled to Britain from her native Jamaica to volunteer as a nurse during the Crimean War (1853–56) and had experience of military nursing, plus respect for the armed services through her father being a Scottish soldier. However, on arrival in London her application was rejected by the authorities. Undaunted, she travelled to the war zone where she set up nursing facilities under the glare of battle and her work in assisting wounded soldiers was recognised both by the men she helped and by the British public, with her fame rivalling that of Florence Nightingale. Mary Seacole continues to be an inspiration to Reverend Drummond.

As well as a person being influenced or inspired by others, an experience or event may have an effect. For instance, Robin Harper has taken inspiration from the work of the Centre for Human Ecology, which promotes ecological understanding and social justice. Similarly, while no one individual inspired Lewis Robertson, he was 'impressed' by those he worked with during his Second World War service at Government Code and Cipher School (GC&CS), Bletchley Park (since renamed Government Communication Headquarters, GCHQ). Sir Lewis began his war service as a photographer with the Royal Air Force in 1942, but was transferred to Bletchley Park due to his knowledge of Italian. At Bletchley Park he learnt German and worked on breaking enemy ciphers. Like Sir Lewis, Ron Hamilton does not name any particular individual as giving inspiration, although he does relate his approach to that of James Dyson, who is perhaps best known for the invention of the bag-less vacuum cleaner, as he sees parallels in the persistence shown in inventing and bringing their products to the market place. Similarly, no one person is given by Sheila McLean as inspiring her. She does though admire the 'kind of person', like businessmen Tom Hunter and Bill Gates, who 'do good' through what they have achieved. However, events have been influential on Professor McLean and she mentions the assassination of United States President John Kennedy in 1963 and, in particular, the Cuban Missile Crisis of 1962, when the United States of America blockaded Cuba in order to compel the Soviet Union to dismantle a nuclear missile base. This made her, a 10-year-old at primary school, suddenly aware of the realities of the world and she describes being 'shocked' when, along with her classmates, she was told of the precautions she should take in the event of a nuclear attack. These included painting windows white, to reflect the explosive light, and taking refuge under a table with a mattress propped on top of it. Her concerns were further underlined when she considered the geographic proximity to her school, in Glasgow, of the Faslane Naval Base, which continues to house nuclear submarines. These experiences made her more politically aware and were discussed at home during her childhood. As part of the influences on him, George Mathewson refers back to the 1960s and early 1970s when he was employed by Bell Aerospace in the United States of America. It was there that he worked with top intellectuals, 'both Jewish and Nazi', who had arrived in America following the end of the Second World War. He was very impressed by such intellect and, while he did not consider himself of the same specialist standard, this exposure helped him realise his strengths as an administrator and communicator. Sir George also likes to think that he has been a positive influence on others and he has received letters to that effect. In particular, he took great satisfaction when a telephone receptionist at the Royal Bank of Scotland contacted him to say that his business approach had 'given her back her pride'. Kenneth Murray was greatly influenced by Frederick Sanger, whom he contacted, looking to work with him for one year on return from Stanford University, but with whom he ended up completing three very influential years. In the 1970s Frederick Sanger was at the forefront of many of the developments in genomic biology, which remain relevant today as they include the fundamental method of reading DNA. Frederick Sanger was awarded his second Nobel Prize in Chemistry for his work on the creation of a method for sequencing DNA, having received his first Nobel Prize in 1958 for his determination of the amino acid sequence of insulin. This pioneering work on DNA led to the complete sequencing of the human genome and many applications, such as the DNA fingerprinting used by forensic laboratories, and had vast implications for the understanding of the genetic basis of many diseases. Noreen Murray lists a number of scientists as being particularly influential on her thinking, including George Beadle (1958 Nobel Prize winner in Medicine for work on the biogenetics of fungus), and many outstanding scientists she encountered, or heard lecture, during her time in Stanford, California and Cambridge University (including Sydney Brenner, Naomi Franklin, Dale Kaiser, Frank Stahl and Charles Yanofsky). She also mentions David Perkins, who, during the five years she spent working in his laboratory, created an intellectually stimulating environment that encouraged her to follow her own ideas and interests.

Along with the influence that may be gained from role models, peers or inspirational figures, the stability that is viewed as important in childhood is also considered influential in later years.

'Generated some positive scientific collaborations'

Continuing stability

The security and stability William Stewart enjoyed in childhood have continued throughout his life, as he remained close to his parents in his adult years, with further stability coming via secure marriage. Similarly, Tom Devine recognised his family for their support when he was working on *The Scottish Nation*, writing that 'the book could not have been completed without them', not least because of the death of his son, John, the year before he started the book. In his autobiography, *Winning Is Not Enough*, Jackie Stewart writes '... I feel extraordinary lucky to have been blessed with such a robust, loving family unit'. Ron Hamilton stresses that his wife of over 40 years, Moya, has always 'provided moral support and practical help'. Alan Finlayson gives special mention to the support he receives from his wife, Dorothy, and her encouragement of his wishes to embark on career changes without regard for income expectations. Lewis Robertson credits his wife, Elspeth, for practical improvements that were made when he was Chairman of the Eastern Regional Hospitals Board, Scotland, during the design and construction of Ninewells Hospital in Dundee. Elspeth Robertson was a nurse and recommended, in addition to the proposed showers, installing baths in the nursing quarters as she was aware of the benefit and appreciation of a relaxing soak after completing a long shift. She also picked up on the omission of a dedicated religious facility in the hospital and put forward the idea of using a central but under-utilised space to create a chapel. Both of these suggestions were implemented and appreciated.

Tom Farmer says that one of the 'tricks' of his success was 'to marry the girl next door', and John Crofton refers to his wife as his 'inspiration'. Eileen Crofton is a doctor and was a leading campaigner for the anti-smoking lobby ASH (Action on Smoking and Health). Sir John was concerned with tobacco and involved in the foundation of ASH, both in Scotland and the rest of the United Kingdom, and, more recently, he has been involved in similar action regarding alcohol. These campaigns are driven by an ambition to improve quality of life and are shared with a passion by John and Eileen Crofton. Kenneth Murray and Noreen Parker were married in 1958 and have formed a strong scientific partnership, which Noreen Murray rather modestly says 'generated some positive scientific collaborations'.

Help and Advice: Summary

'What do you think?'

Help and advice is described as best sought from those who are respected, have knowledge in the area of interest and who can be impartial in providing advice. Also, the timing of it can have a significant impact. If asked, it is believed that people are generally happy to give their views, although it is also thought important to give, as well as take, help and advice. In addition, there is emphasis placed on a degree of self-reliance and people taking responsibility for their own decisions and choices.

Help and advice may be provided by an advisor, mentor or teacher. An advisor is thought to give straightforward advice in a dispassionate manner, a mentor is seen to build strong relationships to assist personal development and a teacher is viewed as providing or inputting further information. A 'pupil' is believed to have a choice about what advice or learning to take, as it is recognised that someone cannot learn everything or take every single piece of advice that is available.

It is emphasised that people can be influenced greatly by those they associate with in adult life, by particular experiences and sometimes by inspirational figures. Furthermore, as in childhood, a stable and secure environment is considered to be influential during adult life.

From taking and giving help and advice, it is believed that ideas and new learning can be gained from which opportunity may be created.

CHAPTER V

Opportunity

'The talent or skills to cash in'

Where does opportunity come from?
Does luck play a part?
Are there risks involved?

This section considers opportunity and how it is created and then acted upon, along with the risks and potential for mistakes that may bring. To allow people to act on opportunity, confidence is thought to be required, which is the topic of Chapter VI.

'Success does not happen by accident'

Creating opportunity

Opportunity may be created by an individual for either themselves or for other people and is generally thought to be developed from ideas or the merit of having the right skills and knowledge. In addition, opportunity can be provided by luck, such as from a chance meeting.

'Batting a ping pong ball'

Ideas

The ability to come up with ideas is perhaps a habit gained from the exposure to other people's innovative thinking. This may be seen in John Crofton, who describes his father as 'extremely original', and George Robertson, who gives the school debating society as an early influence that helped sharpen his thinking. Similarly, Lewis Robertson experienced imaginative thinking, coupled with innovation and the setting of high standards, when working at Bletchley Park during the Second World War.

New ideas are seen as a stimulus for improvement with, for example,

Sheila McLean suggesting that 'pushing ideas gives opportunity'. George Mathewson comments that in business 'it works' to introduce new ideas, for example by replacing a company Chief Executive. That is one reason why he thinks the average tenure of a Chief Executive is 'a couple of years'. In addition, Sir George considers that by taking on challenges in fields he is not familiar with, he can provide fresh thinking to an organisation which cuts through the bureaucracy that can inhibit innovation. Michael Atiyah also sees great benefit in a fresh approach. For example, he regularly leaves a problem that is 'niggling away' at him and then comes back to it after a space of time, which allows him to tackle it from a new perspective. Lewis Robertson and his colleagues were innovating, setting new standards and increasing expectations when developing Ninewells Hospital in Dundee. Now though, Sir Lewis thinks such projects may be compromised, because ideas on set standards are established, which restricts new approaches. He thinks this may be further limited by the increasing number of people who tend to be involved in that type of project, because there comes a point when too many stakeholders hinder progress by increasing bureaucracy and slowing down decision making.

A desire to take an innovative approach was given by Kenneth Murray as one of his motivations for establishing the Darwin Trust of Edinburgh. Having seen the death of carers who had contracted hepatitis B from their patients, Sir Kenneth, together with colleagues in the new biotechnology company Biogen, began a research project in that area. This led to the introduction of reliable diagnostic reagents and an effective vaccine against hepatitis B. As the vaccine was patented it earned huge royalties from which Sir Kenneth donated his share to establish the Trust. In addition to wanting to continue the University of Edinburgh's strong presence in natural sciences, Sir Kenneth wanted the Trust to set high standards through taking the 'innovative approach' of supporting promising overseas students and researchers, who may otherwise have found it difficult to further their scientific studies and research. Such originality in approach can also be seen in the Edinburgh food cooperatives that John Crofton was instrumental in establishing. These cooperatives encourage healthier eating through an increase in diet of fish, fruit and vegetables.

In the engineering commercial world, Ron Hamilton believes that a good idea is one that can be patent protected. However, he considers it very difficult to get ideas 'out of the lab'. As well as inventing daily disposable contact lenses, he invented optics for road signs, which at the time were deemed too expensive to be implemented, and he designed an improved handle for curling stones. As an example of innovative thinking, Alan Finlayson gives the very practical idea that his Reporter colleague, Helen Petrie, used to reassure young people that the information held on them would not be re-used. She invited them into the office to shred their own file. This allowed the young person to feel that they were in control, and it demonstrated to them that they had a potential new beginning following what had often been difficult circumstances. Creativity and innovative thinking is something Jackie Stewart often sees in dyslexic people. That, he thinks, is due to them not accessing learning in the same manner as the majority of people and, thus, having to 'think out the box'. Sir Jackie describes this in terms of most people travelling on the M1 motorway, while those who are dyslexic have to find alternative routes, something he sees as often beneficial because it 'gives more room for manoeuvre'.

When creating and developing ideas some people prefer an inclusive approach. George Robertson proactively canvasses other people's opinions and Irvine Laidlaw makes a point of discussing ideas with other people. For example, Lord Laidlaw compares a discussion with his former Head of Worldwide Marketing at the Institute of International Research to 'batting a pingpong ball', where the conversation sparks ideas. Lewis Robertson also believes that ideas come from interaction, particularly through 'intelligent conversation', something that he considers the Royal Society of Edinburgh provides an excellent forum for. In contrast, Calum Colvin takes a solitary approach to idea generation and trusts his instincts to allow thoughts to evolve. He does not panic if it is taking time for them to become clear, as it will 'just come to you'. Usually, this is done with a 'vague plan' in mind, which Professor Colvin keeps deliberately loose so as to allow scope for change. Having said that, he does discuss work with colleagues and recommends taking advice, reading lots and trying to see things from different perspectives whilst retaining some autonomy by thinking for yourself. Professor Colvin adds to that list 'get drunk and have regular sex'.

Technology is given as a strong stimulus to ideas because, as Ron Hamilton puts it, 'you can't put technology back in the box'. He notes that, especially in the United States of America, companies like to be seen as leading technological innovators and he places great emphasis on protecting intellectual property rights. However, he advises that technology is not necessarily a panacea to riches. For example, he was ready to invest in Internet opportunities 'pre bubble', as he never saw the 'bubble bursting', but was able to come in after the event and now operates the world's first Internet based 'direct from manufacture to consumer' contact lens supply company. George Mathewson includes sportspeople and musicians amongst those which he sees increasing their potential income from technology, such as from television revenues and the exposure given by other forms of mass media. Tom Devine emphasises the need to develop ideas and to participate intellectually as he views the future, certainly in Scotland, lying in areas where brain power is valued over brawn. In particular, he sees computer, artistic and financial disciplines coming to the fore, supported by universities which promote ideas generation and development in those areas.

In the same way that ideas may be stimulated by a mixture of positive influences, conversely negative influences can curb idea generation. For example, someone who worked with Evelyn Glennie stopped giving her opinion and ideas, because these were always rubbished by another member of staff. It was only when that person's detractor left that she regained the confidence to start inputting ideas again.

Chay Blyth considers that it is the potential of ideas which must be recognised. He adds that the idea need not be original and he gives Richard Branson as an example of someone who takes and improves on existing ideas through his Virgin brand. Irvine Laidlaw is another who does not subscribe to 'the not invented here syndrome' and he is 'happy to steal an idea' from somewhere else, which Tom Farmer refers to as 'happy to be second first'. Sir Tom describes this as taking the opportunity to observe and learn from the pacesetter, and then improve upon its practices with a view to becoming the established leader in that field. As an example of the re-use of ideas, Alan Finlayson advises that critical elements of the Children's Hearing System were incorporated into the Juvenile Justice systems, which now operate in both Cleveland, Ohio and Boston, Massachusetts.

In order to train the mind and provide creative thought, Tom Devine tries to retain an 'intellectual humility', George Mathewson keeps an 'open mind' to new ideas, and Evelyn Glennie has a system of recording the ideas suggested by those she works with. Dame Evelyn equates this to planting a seed that may germinate at some future date and she describes it as 'therapeutic' to review these ideas alongside her own approach, in order to establish which ideas are worth pursuing.

Michael Atiyah explains how he starts to distil thoughts 'by tossing ideas about with others', to define the problem or question to be tackled. This is followed by an often solitary period, when he thinks hard about the topic in order to solve the problem. However, he does always break this period up with social interaction, as he believes that too much solitude can cause people to become overly introverted. Once the problem has been solved 'you know it', and Sir Michael then moves on to 'the least enjoyable bit' of showing proofs and writing it all down.

'Demonstratable expertise'

Merit

Robin Harper looks to develop ideas in order to broaden his experience and stimulate incremental improvement by increasing knowledge, rather than gaining any financial reward. Such an approach is thought to provide opportunity based largely on merit. That is the merit which may be realised from skills and achievement, not the potential merit that can remain unfulfilled due to the circumstances of upbringing. Thus, opportunity is considered more likely to be provided to those who have the right learning and qualities to take on any given task or, as Michael Atiyah says, 'the talent or skills to cash in'. Similarly, Calum Colvin believes that opportunity comes from the substance of someone's work and not the overt self promotion he has seen in the art world. He has witnessed some artists spending more time on drawing attention to themselves, through puerile 'bizarre stunts', than on their work. This, he thinks, tends to make those artists fashion orientated and their work dispensable.

As an example of progressing through merit, or the substance of work, William Stewart recounts how he led the clean up of anthrax from Gruinard Island, which had been used for biological experiments during the Second World War (Gruinard Island sits just off the coast of Wester Ross in the northwest of Scotland). In particular, he insisted that, following decontamination treatment, sheep should be put on the island to verify that it indeed was safe for human habitation. Decontamination was successfully achieved. Following this, he was offered the position of Chief Executive of the Agriculture and Food Research Council because, as Sir William puts it, 'I had demonstrable expertise in the use of microbes, plants and animals, a fellowship of the Royal Society (the stamp of approval by the scientific establishment) and experience of dealing with Whitehall'. Through gaining more experience and demonstrating an ability to apply knowledge, often in an advisory capacity, further opportunities were offered to Sir William, including Chief Scientific Advisor to the Cabinet Office, Chairman of the Microbiological Research Centre at Porton Down, and of the Health Protection Agency. Sir William believes that it was his broad experience, knowledge and capacity for work which got him noticed. It was demonstrable achievement rather than influence. He also makes the point that sound judgement is crucially important. Sir William recalls the anecdote that 'the problem with clever people is that they often find cleverer ways of being stupid', he watched out to ensure that did not apply to him.

Alan Finlayson also thinks that people gain jobs or positions on merit. As part of that, he believes, it is important to have a good reputation and, at times, be a 'good talker'. Evelyn Glennie creates opportunity for herself by increasing her learning through being proactive in gaining experience. This was particularly evident when she was studying at the Royal Academy of Music, when she would bring percussion music to an orchestra's attention, to show how she might add value to its performance. Some of these orchestras agreed to her participation, which provided her with valuable playing experience and created further opportunity due to her increased learning. Dame Evelyn highlights the Kent Youth Wind Band as being particularly receptive to her proposals and it even allowed her to try new arrangements. This is something that she has not forgotten and now, with her experience, she is happy to reciprocate and help its members to progress.

Sheila McLean thinks that opportunities come from confidence, talent and concentrating on the job you are doing. Plus, she believes that opportunities may be presented to those who have a particular expertise and more experience. For example, she thinks that opportunities have been provided to her because there are 'not many in my field' and she has worked in it for 'longer than others'. She does though believe that opportunity can be constrained by the type of job that someone does and its associated career path. This, she thinks, can inhibit 'entrepreneurial spirit' or thinking on alternative careers. In particular, Professor McLean considers that may be the case for those working in some service sector jobs, such as in call centres, compared to the manufacturing roles that used to be more available and, perhaps, more fulfilling. For Tom Farmer everyone can create and make the most of opportunities, whether for themselves or for the companies they work for. In that sense, he says that 'everyone can be an entrepreneur'. Potential new avenues of opportunity and interest are thought, by Chay Blyth, to come from an open minded approach that develops learning and increases experience. To do this, he encourages people 'to go along' and meet new people and learn new things. Sir Chay provides the example of when he felt one of his employees missed the chance to find out more about his experiences and future plans, and thus potential opportunities, when she chose not to attend a talk he was giving.

Patience can also play a part. For example, John Crofton advises that he had to wait on vacancies becoming available during his medical career (he practised at a time when people tended to gain positions in hospitals where they already worked, rather than by changing institution). A case in point was when he had to wait on an elderly tuberculosis consultant to retire, before he could take control of that person's remit and fully integrate it into his plans to tackle tuberculosis in Edinburgh. However, Sir John did not waste that time but spent it ensuring that he was ready to act when the eventual opportunity arose. Being well placed and ready to take advantage of opportunity is something that Evelyn Glennie recommends. To do that she suggests keeping in touch with what is going on, developing the required skills and having an element of independence that allows you to act quickly by not relying overly on other people.

A concentration on the short-term is not thought to restrict future opportunity. This is seen with George Mathewson, who does not subscribe to long-term planning. A view he maintained even when he was Director of Strategic Planning and Development at the Royal Bank of Scotland. Sir George believes that the further you look into the future, the more unpredictable assumptions become and the more volatile forecasts will be. He thinks that such uncertain forecasts are of limited value in decision making. However, his concentration on the near term does not mean that future opportunity is ignored. For example, Sir George fostered the relationship between the Royal Bank of Scotland Group and Spanish banking group, Grupo Santander, which proved critical in the Scottish bank's acquisition of National Westminster Bank in 2000. It was the culmination of 15 years spent building mutual trust, learning and respect between the two banks, which ensured Grupo Santander provided the decisive £2 billion in financial support that allowed the largest merger in United Kingdom financial services history to go ahead. He advises that the relationship was not nurtured with that aim in mind, but rather to allow each bank to take best advantage of any future opportunities.

Irvine Laidlaw thinks that people who work hard and have the right skills should merit advancement, regardless of their background, creed or colour. As part of his own approach, Lord Laidlaw prioritises by focusing on where the biggest opportunity may be and, by giving precedent to the right things at the right times, George Robertson contends that 'success does not happen by accident'.

'Time and chance'

Luck

When considering opportunity, Tam Dalyell refers to former Prime Minister Jim Callaghan's autobiography *Time and Chance* where, prior to the main body of the text, Ecclesiastes 9 vs. 11 is quoted, 'I returned, and saw under the sun, that the race is not to the swift, nor the battle to the strong, neither yet bread to the wise, nor yet riches to men of understanding, nor yet favour to men of skill; but time and chance happened to them all'.

Kenneth Murray considers that luck is 'immensely important', and Irvine Laidlaw feels that good fortune was with the Institute for International Research when it conducted events in the Middle East, as it was 'lucky' to be operating in a stable political climate. Luck also plays a part for Margo MacDonald and she gives the example of being 'fortunate' when it was decided that the person who came first alphabetically in her college class would be assigned the role of interim student representative, until an election was held. As her maiden name is Aitken, she was given the job and, having had the opportunity to do well, she won the election. The feeling that people have luck at certain times is shown in Lord Laidlaw describing some people as 'luckier than others' and Chay Blyth quoting Napoleon Bonaparte, who used to ask about a general 'but is he lucky?'.

Brian Gill thinks that to be successful in life people must have hope, help other people and require the assistance of others. He adds that opportunity is not necessarily engineered but, for example, can come from a chance meeting. Kenneth Murray also thinks that 'meeting someone over a coffee or in the pub can prove very useful' as, for example, when John Crofton met Guy Scadding 'just by chance' when he was posted to the Middle East during his army service. It was Guy Scadding who offered Sir John the position of unpaid clinical assistant at the Brompton Hospital in London. Having proven himself in that role, Guy Scadding then suggested that Sir John take the position of part-time member of the Medical Research Council Tuberculosis Unit. This gave Sir John responsibility for administering tuberculosis trials at the Brompton Hospital and started his involvement in an area that he was to become synonymous with. Sir John also thinks that chance may have played a part in his personal life. When he received leave from the Army he wanted to visit his sister living in Dublin, but no visas were available for the Republic of Ireland, except for children or parents. 'By good luck or kindness' those that organised the leave despatched him to Northern Ireland from where he was able to visit the Irish Republic. He met Eileen Mercer during that leave and they married at the end of hostilities in 1945. A rather different, unhappy, wartime event shaped Lewis Robertson's early career. Prior to the Second World War his older brother, James, worked for the family textile business and Sir Lewis had accepted a place to attend Cambridge University. Lieutenant James Robertson RNVR was lost at sea along with 840 others when HMS *Barham* was torpedoed and sunk in November 1941. Due to the death of his brother, Sir Lewis forsook university and joined the family firm at the end of the War.

Michael Atiyah and Calum Colvin both refer to the luck of being in the right place, or meeting the right people, at the right time. In hindsight, things 'seemed to unfold' for Sir Michael when he was a student and graduate, while Professor Colvin considers himself 'fortunate' that he was part of a group, in London during the early 1980s, that experimented with and used photography differently. Alan Finlayson refers to 'happenstance' when talking about being in the right place at the right time. In particular, the timing of when the position of Reporter to The Children's Panel became available when his 'CV was OK for the job'. The same, he thinks, was true when he was offered the position of Sheriff and, having thoroughly enjoyed both these roles, he reflects 'how lucky can you be?'. Being in the right place at the right time, or perhaps put better the wrong place at the wrong time, played a major part in where Kenneth Murray and Noreen Murray developed their research. They were driving in Lancashire when a participant in a car rally drove through a junction without giving way and collided with their car. Thankfully, no one was seriously injured. The accident caused them to request a short delay in taking up appointments at a new university in England, but that university was totally inflexible and refused their request. This meant that, fortunately, Sir Kenneth was able to remain in the inspiring environment of Frederick Sanger's laboratory for a further two years, before moving to the new department of Molecular Biology at Edinburgh University.

As well as events, the chance of circumstances that people are born into or where they are brought up can also play its part. There is the example of the young George Robertson protesting against the United States Naval Base, with its Polaris nuclear submarines, at the Holy Loch. This was no doubt a key factor in him entering politics. Dunoon Grammar School, which he attended, lies just to the south of the Holy Loch. In a similar fashion, Tom Farmer refers to Edinburgh as a 'great city' and says that he was 'lucky to be brought up' there. In addition, Sir Tom thinks that his Scottish nationality is viewed positively wherever he has travelled in the world, something he describes as 'a tremendous advantage'. Irvine Laidlaw considers that his Scottish roots are important to him and could on occasion be advantageous, particularly in banking in Hong Kong where 'everybody seemed to be Scottish'. Ron Hamilton advises that being Scottish and an engineer used to 'open doors', although he no longer believes this to be the case.

Chay Blyth refers to synchronicity and the thinking of Swiss psychiatrist Carl Jung when purporting a view that there are logical interdependencies to events that do not have a seeming cause and effect. This provides a connecting thread that can be described as 'luck'. Sir Chay uses two examples to explain this. The first was when, along with John Ridgway, he was a guest of Aintree race course owner Mirabel Topham at the 1967 Grand National. Sir Chay and John Ridgway had rowed the Atlantic Ocean in 1966. Prior to the race they met the Duchess of Westminster who had been happy to sell a 'dog of a horse' called Fionavon which, like Arkle, was named after hills in Sutherland. Sir Chay's house was called Fionavon and with that coincidence of circumstances he placed a bet on this 100–1 outsider to win, 'for a bit of a laugh'. During the race a large number of horses refused to jump and piled up at fence 23, but Fionavon steered a clear course, jumped successfully and went on to win the race. Fence 23 was renamed Fionavon and Sir Chay notes that, while the Duchess of Westminster was not overly pleased, he was delighted. The second example came in 1987 when he was asked to do some consultancy work for a company that wanted to evaluate the practicalities and associated costs of sponsoring a boat in the Whitbread Round the World Race. He contacted the race organisers to obtain a copy of the rules, but was incredulous when they insisted on charging £200 per copy, even although he wanted the copy for a potential sponsor. At that moment he decided he would organise his own round the world race. Soon afterwards, Ron Melvin of British Steel contacted him for advice on sponsoring a boat. That 'advice' quickly took the form of a wider sponsorship deal to support a race between identical boats, each with an experienced skipper, that would be crewed by individuals with limited or no sailing knowledge. The 'British Steel Challenge' was held over 1992–93 and leveraged on the 21st anniversary of Sir Chay's previous association with British Steel, when he sailed single-handed non-stop round the world onboard *British Steel* in 1970–71. Sir Chay went on to organise subsequent 'BT Global Challenges' over 1996–97 and 2000–1. In both of these examples Sir Chay sees synchronicity, where the whole picture is interconnected and not just down to 'luck'.

Thus, luck is seen to play a part in shaping a course of action or in providing opportunity. However, it is highlighted that people still have to see and then act on the potential that allows them to take advantage of that luck.

'Make the most of whatever luck comes your way'

Seeing potential

Noreen Murray advises that 'the trick with opportunities or luck is recognising the significance'. This is something that Calum Colvin agrees with and he says that you should 'make the most of whatever luck comes your way', while Eileen Crofton suggests that John Crofton can see the opportunity and, importantly, 'seize the potential'. Jonathan Long also thinks that opportunity should be 'seized', particularly if you are following your passion. Perhaps Norman Drummond goes even further when saying that his 'vocation' is moving forward the opportunities that are presented to him. In addition, George Mathewson considers that it is important to capitalise on opportunity and that he makes the best of the 'luck' that comes his way, while Michael Atiyah thinks the key with opportunity is having the ability to take advantage of it. Sir Michael believes that ability comes from having the right skills.

Ron Hamilton advises that it is important to sense and recognise opportunities. As an example of that, he describes how he gained a number of employees via Hamilton job centre, when other employers in the area were closing down. During a job interview a good candidate informed him that a former colleague was also looking for work and that they got on and worked well together. Both were soon employed and a similar approach of gaining 'a ready made team' was repeated several times. Chay Blyth names Ann Gloag and Brian Souter as examples of people who can see and make the most of opportunity. Ann Gloag and Brian Souter saw the opportunity that transport deregulation in the United Kingdom offered and, having established Stagecoach with two buses in 1980, they built a company that operates rail, bus and tram networks. This includes a fleet of approximately 7,000 buses and coaches in the United Kingdom and a further 2,800 or so coaches in the United States of America. Sir Chay adds that it is his own ability to see opportunities that eventually led him to sail round the world 'the wrong way'. After Francis Chichester had circumnavigated the globe eastwards in *Gypsy Moth*, stopping once on route, Sir Chay noted that there were at least 11 individuals vying to complete the same journey non-stop. Robin Knox-Johnston was the first to achieve this feat between June 1968 and April 1969 in his yacht *Suhaili*. So, rather than compete with them, Sir Chay saw the opportunity to complete the journey nonstop westwards, which is 'infinitely more difficult' due to sailing against the prevailing winds and currents.

Seeing potential and seizing opportunity is something that Tom Farmer has done throughout his career. For example, when embarking on his first tyre distribution business, Sir Tom was approached by a newspaper who wanted to do an article on discounting against manufacturer pricing guidelines. This was topical at the time due to the loosening of price competition regulation. Realising the publicity this may give, Sir Tom agreed to an interview and the Monday following the article in *The Sunday Post* there was a queue of cars waiting to buy tyres and 'it never stopped'. Sir Tom sold that business and moved to California where he noted the move towards specialising in component parts. Seeing the opportunity that presented, he implemented a similar approach on his return to Scotland through the Kwik-Fit brand, which specialised in replacement tyres and exhausts.

In order to take an opportunity, it is emphasised that people require to have the right ideas or skills. In addition, there can be associated risks involved when implementing an idea or acting on an opportunity.

'I am not a gambler'

Risk-taking

Lewis Robertson sees some people as natural risk takers, who can better recognise the right moment to take action, and George Robertson considers that there is a thin dividing line between success and failure. That, he thinks, is determined by the decisions taken and the risks inherent in those decisions. Lord Robertson gives the example of the Labour Government holding a referendum on Scottish devolution in 1997. The decision was driven by the view that it was right to let the electorate decide, even although that brought the risk of just a slim majority in favour or even a 'no' vote. In hindsight, Lord Robertson believes it was the correct approach regardless of the risks that were involved. Drawing on his experience from the Industrial & Commercial Finance Corporation (now 3i), George Mathewson considers that there are two types of entrepreneurs; those that have no alternative due to other opportunities not being available to them, perhaps through a lack of education, and those that are financially well off and can afford to take risks. Sir George goes on to say that his whole career could be seen as risk taking, as he joined companies in industry sectors where he had 'no experience'. He gives the examples of joining the Scottish Development Agency, 'a then discredited public sector company', and when he joined the Royal Bank of Scotland, which 'was failing'. However, in both of these examples, he not only saw risks but also great opportunity and following almost three years of learning and reviewing the Royal Bank of Scotland's business, he implemented wide ranging developments that started its progression into the top echelon of world banking groups.

Jonathan Long thinks that risk taking is required when working with young people. In particular, he says that you must invest trust in youngsters with the risk that trust could be betrayed. Even if that trust is broken, Dr Long believes, the acceptance and understanding that giving trust provides may plant a seed of positive thought that will be harvested at some future date.

Tam Dalyell sees himself as a risk taker as, for example, when he stood for Parliament 'I did not know whether I would be any good at it'. Norman Drummond also describes himself as a risk taker and there comes a time when he feels 'why not do it'. Reverend Drummond includes the examples of becoming a Head Teacher at age 32, without any training for that job, and then leaving that position, which entailed a 60 per cent cut in salary, while supporting a family of five children. Reverend Drummond considers that you should have courage, be open-hearted and think of the potential service to other people when taking risks. Bravery is something Evelyn Glennie thinks people taking risks must have. She describes that as the ability to try something new, even if it has the potential to fall flat. The need to take risks is, she thinks, part of wanting to be the best that you can be. When she was younger her 'youthful fearlessness' meant that nothing was frightening and that she was willing to take risks and responsibility for her actions. During this time, especially on moving to London, she 'was like a sponge'. However, as she grows older she has tended to become more risk averse, due to thinking things through more rigorously. Chay Blyth sees himself as a risk taker and comments that he has taken the ultimate risk, with 'my life'. This was seen when John Ridgway and Sir Chay were rowing across the Atlantic Ocean and their lives were perhaps saved by Captain Mitchell of Shell tanker *Hausellum*, who stopped to provide them with provisions as their food supply dwindled. Sadly, that risk to life was demonstrated when a rival bid to row the Atlantic Ocean ended in tragedy with the upturned boat, *Puffin*, recovered and rowers David Johnstone and John Hoare lost at sea.

When people describe themselves as 'risk takers' it does not mean that they are careless in the risks they take. For example, Ron Hamilton advises that he would not have left his job with CooperVision if he had known that the expected £4 million in venture capital funding to support his disposable con-tact lens business would not materialise. In addition, when taking risks he always tries to stack the odds in his favour and states that if there is a one in 10 chance that you will succeed 'then you must try it ten times'. He adds, if you try it only once then it is unlikely to work. Michael Atiyah takes a similar stance when advising that you may have to pursue a number of ideas before one pays off, 'like throwing a dice many times to get a six', and he observes that 'if you don't try, you don't succeed'. Irvine Laidlaw refers to 'containing failure', even although he is 'a huge risk taker'. He ensures that the balance of odds in any one transaction are 'about 80 per cent' in his favour, because he 'wouldn't bet the company'. If that ratio starts to move against him, then 'you are in trouble'. This theme of calculated risk is taken up by Tom Farmer, who reduces risk by thinking through a plan of approach. For example, he sees the biggest risk when expanding a business by acquisition as ensuring that you follow through after the purchase to make the new entity work, not the actual purchase itself. This was the case when Sir Tom doubled the number of Kwik-Fit outlets to 200 by purchasing another business and then securing another 180 outlets via a further acquisition. In each instance, he had a plan to integrate these units into his existing operation to ensure that all the out-lets ran as efficiently as possible. Similarly, through analysis, Chay Blyth tries to understand risks and whether he wants to take them. If he does proceed, he looks to minimise those risks by detailed scenario planning. However, Sir Chay believes that after you take a risk you should be prepared to take the consequences if things go wrong. This happened when the trimaran he was sailing capsized southwest of Cape Horn and he spent 19 hours in the water before being rescued. He had thoroughly planned and rehearsed for this pos-sibility, and had attached emergency equipment to the bottom of the boat, which he was able to access if the boat overturned. This does not mean that Sir Chay advocates removing risk from everything as, for him, risk taking gives adrenalin. Although, that does not correspond to him seeking increasing thrills by taking greater and greater risks. Regardless of whether the risk is physical, emotional or financial, for Jackie Stewart, it is the same commodity. Sir Jackie tries to 'remove hazards and avoid failures' by taking a thorough approach where he pays attention to detail, is precise in the application of learning, and is focused on and committed to the task in hand. Sir Jackie considers it 'common sense' to remove unnecessary risk, and he refers to when he was at the forefront of the practical application of safety measures in Formula One racing. Despite the sometimes very hostile response that Sir Jackie received as the figurehead of the drivers' campaign, including the uncertainty of some drivers and death threats from the public, he continued to pursue the aim of improving safety. The approach taken included a drivers' boycott of certain racing tracks that were deemed too dangerous. This saw overall safety improving, with more and better safety barriers installed and the introduction of proper medical facilities. Included in that was the removal of hazards from around racing tracks, such as trees and walls, which had contributed to the death of 57 of his fellow drivers over the 11 year period that he raced professionally. This has led to such a concentration on safety, that since the death of Roland Ratzenberger and Ayrton Senna at the San Marino Grand Prix of 1994, there have been no fatalities in Formula One racing. Sir Jackie further illustrates his attitude to risk by advising that he only spends what he can afford and has never operated an overdraft because 'that is not my style'. He contrasts this with people he knows who 'use credit to do everything'. Sir Jackie describes his approach as 'not wanting to step outside what I do not know', to which he adds 'I am not a gambler'.

In general, Irvine Laidlaw believes that people are not large risk takers with, for example, John Crofton reeling at the idea that someone may 'lose, say, four out of five times'. Sheila McLean does not consider herself to be a risk taker and describes herself as 'a bit staid'. Professor McLean is a trained lawyer and considers that it would be more of a risk if she was in legal practice compared to her main role in education. She does though refer to risk when she became the first International Bar Association Professor of Law and Ethics in Medicine at Glasgow University in 1990 and the risk of having to create a course on Medical Law, as she might have been 'talking rubbish'. Professor McLean includes changes in ethics, medicine and the law, such as when a legal definition of Persistent Vegetative State was accepted which meant that her teaching had to alter. Furthermore, she thinks that there are risks when dealing with the media, something she does regularly, because you have to make sure that you 'get the facts right'. Robin Harper describes himself as a 'cautious risk taker'. As an example, he mentions the instance when, along with seven others, he went out in a force seven gale on the Moray Firth to lend assistance to a stricken dinghy. However, prior to setting off, they assessed the situation and understood the approach they were going to adopt. Also, he thinks that in politics, risks are taken all the time and, for example, he refers to a debate on fisheries policy in the Scottish Parliament. He felt that a more precautionary approach to fish stocks should be taken and ended up writing the motion submitted by the then Labour and Liberal Democrat Government. This brought the risk that his own Green Party would not receive any credit or publicity and its members would be dissatisfied by his approach. However, he took the view that there was a greater risk of the motion being rejected if it was labelled 'Green', rather than the approval it received thanks to government backing. Similarly, William Stewart does take risks but employs a prudent approach and does not 'let my heart rule my head'. This was the case with the Stewart Report, the output of an Independent Expert Group on Mobile Phones led by Sir William, which is defined by its precautionary approach in recommendations to both government and industry.

Margo MacDonald does not see herself as a risk taker, although she notes that other people have described her as such. However, she does believe that risk taking creates opportunity but considers that money is often required to enable a risk to be taken. In addition, she believes that children 'want to fit in' and not worry about a lack of money 'or the embarrassment or shame of, say, electricity being cut off'. This, she thinks, may make children 'super careful' and unlikely to take risks in later life. Robin Harper thinks that schools can limit a child's approach to risk. He gives the example of visiting primary six and seven classes (11 and 12 year olds) to see the 'great work' they had done on a project about the Amazon and the eco structure it supports. Afterwards, he asked their teacher if they had taken the opportunity to enjoy the wooded area close to the school, but was told 'no', because that would mean risk assessments and other difficulties in arranging an outdoor activity. Thus, he advises that the opportunity for the children to 'enjoy the open air' was lost.

Some people do not think in terms of risk, for example, Calum Colvin preferring to trust his own instincts and not overly worry about risks, such as what an audience will think about his work.

Even although people describe taking a precautionary approach to risk taking, success cannot be guaranteed as risk taking brings with it the possibility of mistakes or failure. Indeed, Irvine Laidlaw believes that if one of his business offices had no failures then its staff were either not doing enough work or were not pushing themselves hard enough to gain new opportunities.

'The greatest teacher'

Learning from mistakes and failure

Brian Gill counsels that 'everyone makes mistakes', although he stresses the importance of not making the same mistake twice. Tam Dalyell agrees and notes that it is important to learn from failures, and Jackie Stewart says that people do not want to be associated with a 'serial mistake maker'. Sir Jackie thinks that many mistakes come from 'spontaneity' and he tries to avoid or minimise mistakes by planning ahead. Through such forward planning, he considers that the 'inevitable' mistakes are 'not severely damaging and don't destroy you'. In addition, Sir Jackie believes that 'the corrective medicine is more expensive than the preventative medicine'. As he gets older, Sir Jackie thinks it has become easier for him to say 'I made a mistake' and he has come to dislike the time wasted when people try to justify their mistakes. Irvine Laidlaw also considers that mistakes are 'almost inevitable' and that he has learnt from his own mistakes. However, this does not mean that he finds mistakes acceptable and Lord Laidlaw emphasises that if a mistake is made, learn from it and do not repeat it. Sheila McLean and Tom Farmer take a similar stance. Professor McLean says that she will 'tolerate failure', but that she feels an 'obligation' to resolve problems and learn from failures, although she notes that particularly in her personal life these may prove to be 'one-offs'. Sir Tom advises that he will 'tolerate things going wrong', as long as people learn from them and make efforts to correct them. He sums this up as 'tolerate, not accept'.

Michael Atiyah believes that you learn more from failures than from successes and he views mistakes as part and parcel of the creative process. However, if he sees something failing repeatedly then usually a 'wrong turning' has been made at the outset, which requires a review of the fundamental approach. When things have gone wrong, Evelyn Glennie believes that people must be resilient and pick themselves up again with, for example, George Robertson advising that he does not get knocked down easily and, when he does, he has an ability to get back up and keep going. An early instance of this was when he was running for Deputy President of the Scottish Union of Students and was confident of winning, but lost. Lord Robertson soon picked himself up from that setback and took from it the learning of relying more on his own resilience and not necessarily trusting those people who said they would support him.

Chay Blyth always encourages people to try new things but, in doing so, recognises that there will be setbacks because the 'world is full of failure'. The key for Sir Chay is to learn from failure and 'persevere, as when the successes happen they are great'. Margo MacDonald also considers that failures will occur when taking risks, but that these are 'unlikely to kill you', while

Norman Drummond discerns a more positive approach to failure in the United States of America than that taken in the United Kingdom. He advises that, in America, failure is referred to as the platform for your next success. Jonathan Long argues that 'human arrogance' causes people to steer others, particularly children, away from failure. He believes that in some instances it is better to let 'nature take its course' and allow people to experience failure because that is 'the greatest teacher'.

Others though would not say that they have learnt much from failure per se. This includes William Stewart, Noreen Murray and George Mathewson, all of whom prefer to concentrate on successes. In addition, Tom Farmer does not see himself 'learning from failure' but rather just learning from the daily ups and downs, as he tries to make sure that everything is working as well as possible. Like Sir Tom, Evelyn Glennie sees this as a process of learning over time and if something does not work in her music it is not a 'failure' but instead 'it gives you something to practice on, something to correct'.

Opportunity: Summary

'The talent or skills to cash in'

It is thought that opportunity is more often than not provided on merit to whoever has the most appropriate skills, learning or levels of experience. Ideas are also seen to create opportunity and may be stimulated by the habit of innovative thinking, or perhaps instigated and developed from events or collaborations with other people. It is considered that such new thinking can provide the opportunity to progress a certain area by offering a fresh approach and an alternative perspective. These ideas do not necessarily have to be 'original', as improving upon existing ideas or applying them to a new field is also viewed as important. Dependent on preferences, some people emphasise a collaborative approach to idea development, while others hold a more solitary line. However, there is likely to be a mix of approaches dependent on what stage of development an idea is at. Luck can also play a part and a chance set of circumstances may shape events or provide future opportunity. Although, it is thought that someone still requires to have the right ideas, skills or attributes in order to take advantage of luck.

It is emphasised that an opportunity has to be recognised and then acted upon. This is thought to bring with it a decision on how comfortable someone is with the risks implicit in that action. People take a different approach to risk dependent on their knowledge of how significant the risks are, the area to which the risks apply and the levels of comfort that they have in a positive outcome. An ill prepared or careless approach is not followed when taking risks, as risks are described as being managed to individual acceptable levels by thorough preparation and scenario planning. Even still, mistakes, failures or setbacks may occur when taking action. Resilience is seen as required to overcome any setbacks, and the importance of learning from mistakes is highlighted, which may be viewed as applying learning and improving on a day-to-day basis as experience is gained. In addition, to act on an opportunity, it is thought that confidence is required.

Confidence

'One of the keys to progression'

What are the right levels of confidence?
Why may confidence be lacking?
Where is confidence gained from?

The importance of having confidence in the right measures and how that confidence can be built are discussed in this section. Confidence is given as something that helps to support perseverance, which is the subject of Chapter VII.

'In the right doses'

Importance

The importance of self-confidence is stressed by Margo MacDonald and Lewis Robertson, who contends that it is vital to have a belief in yourself. George Robertson thinks that confidence coupled with a belief in what you are doing is central to achievement, and Alan Finlayson advises that it is confidence which allows people to persevere. George Mathewson states that gaining confidence is 'one of the keys to progression' and Calum Colvin explains his views on confidence by saying 'that if you live in fear of being kicked then you will never do anything' and 'if you are scared of falling down the stairs every morning then you may never get out of bed'. Michael Atiyah links confidence to opportunity and risk taking as, he thinks, without confidence people are less likely to stretch themselves and more likely only to do 'a little' and 'play safe'.

Having confidence is seen as important but, as Tam Dalyell says, 'in the right doses' where there is neither over-confidence, nor a shortage of confidence.

'A timid schoolgirl'

Lacking confidence

A number of influences or emotions are thought to cause a lack of confidence. These include an inbuilt shyness or poor self-perception, particularly when young. For example, George Robertson started to increase his confidence during childhood when a squint that he had in one eye was rectified, and George Mathewson only gained in confidence from about age 15, as he had been 'small and ill as a child'. Chay Blyth sees many youngsters lacking confidence due to 'low self-respect'. He thinks this can be due to poor communication skills caused by children not learning vocabulary from an early age. In particular, when children or young adults are outside their own peer group they can often have 'nothing to say'. Sheila McLean also links confidence to childhood. She thinks that confidence is developed during someone's formative years from health and education opportunities, and she describes herself as having been 'a timid schoolgirl'. Calum Colvin felt uncomfortable speaking about his work at the onset of his career due to a natural shyness and John Crofton was shy in his youth to the point that he would leave the family home in an effort to avoid meeting visitors. In addition, confidence may be undermined by overly negative criticism. This is something George Robertson sees in Scotland where he feels that people have a tendency to 'knock others down'.

Anxiety can also undermine confidence. For example, Brian Gill says that the same worry about not meeting his own standards, which pushes him forward, also ensures that he is never wholly self-confident. Likewise, Tom Devine advises that the 'profound sense of anxiety', which drives his improvement, also provides him with insecurities through a lack of confidence. At times, Alan Finlayson has attempted to mask his lack of confidence by trying to be 'popular and funny'. This is something he now regrets because he occasionally resorted to putting other people down. He gives the example of losing a game of bridge for money, when there were a number of onlookers, and he blamed the loss on his partner. In front of everyone, he explained to his partner where he had gone wrong and his partner replied by saying 'you should write a book', to which he responded 'and you should read it'. This 'got a cheap laugh' from the onlookers. However, he thinks that remark was hurtful to his partner, a personal friend, who felt diminished by the riposte, which would have been better left unsaid. A confident façade is something that Jackie Stewart observes some people have an ability to project, even when they are feeling anything but confident, and Margo MacDonald views a show of confidence as one way people hide their insecurities in order to 'defend themselves'.

'Give it a go'
Gaining confidence

It is thought that confidence can be built from experience, with that perhaps enhanced by the maturity gained from being self-reliant from a relatively young age. Furthermore, it is considered that being prepared and receiving encouragement will boost confidence.

'Try new things'
From encouragement

The same encouragement that can foster ambition and the ability to fulfill potential in upbringing is also believed to furnish confidence. Much of this is seen to come from adult role models, especially parents, who can give young people belief in their own abilities. This may provide an almost inherent confidence, which is perhaps seen in Chay Blyth, who gained much of his self-belief from his mother, and Lewis Robertson, who has an inbuilt confidence, which means that he does not have much self-doubt and is generally satisfied with his approach. Kenneth Murray sees people varying greatly in their confidence levels. He thinks that is influenced by upbringing, particularly school, and he suggests that those from a fee paying school background have more confidence than others. However, Sir Kenneth adds that he believed that was the case 20 years ago, but is less certain if it still holds true today.

Margo MacDonald believes that the encouragement gained from

participating in sport can help build confidence, something she experienced from playing team sports. Alan Finlayson gained confidence from sport and he was 'football daft' but also played tennis, cricket, golf and hockey. This continued throughout his school days and his time in the Army, until he was 'crocked' during a university football match from which his knee has never really recovered. As a keen member of his local swimming club, Chay Blyth also gained confidence from sport in his youth, and George Mathewson's lack of confidence in childhood was partly dispelled when he started to participate in rugby. Jackie Stewart also gained confidence from sport, in his case from playing for the school football team. This confidence was further enhanced by the praise he received as a youngster for his work at a local farm during harvesting. Such encouragement is thought by Norman Drummond to be very important in giving someone confidence. In particular, he reiterates the significance to children of having a consistent adult role model who provides them with good guidance and instils confidence in them through showing faith in their capabilities.

Encouragement is linked to help and advice with, for example, the help of others very much appreciated by Brian Gill. As a young lawyer Lord Gill was assisted by those who could have, in his view, instructed better counsel than him. However, for reasons that he does not know, they showed faith in him. Similarly, Chay Blyth does not know what his employers saw in him or why they showed confidence in his abilities when he was selected for the 'well paid factory job' of apprentice frame worker from a field of 30 candidates. In her early career, Evelyn Glennie cites the faith that James Blades showed in her, plus the encouragement that he provided in helping to give meaning to her work and confidence in her approach. This ability to instil confidence is something that, she thinks, James Blades was aware of and was willing to use to assist others. In addition, when still a novice performer, Dame Evelyn was informed by a French conductor that she would not be able to play the French piece she was about to perform because she 'was not French'. This upset her and undermined her confidence, but the orchestra members rallied round, saying that she should 'take no notice as we are on your side'. The encouragement of the orchestra helped her to regain her composure and this came through in her music as she performed well. Ron Hamilton realised that Boots the Chemist was serious about distributing his invention of daily disposable contact lenses when it said it would send representatives to visit him to discuss its potential. This demonstrated belief in the product, as he would normally have expected to visit them, which gave him the confidence to carry on.

Michael Atiyah thinks that confidence is often gained by interacting with other people. Through such interaction, Sir Michael advises that ideas are challenged and tested, which makes them more robust and increases confidence in them. Irvine Laidlaw believes in giving people the confidence to 'try new things'. For instance, at the Institute of International Research, if it was felt that a particular conference was likely to succeed but was not in the normal bounds of someone's work, perhaps due to a new geographic location, then he would underwrite any potential loss and thus take the risk away from that individual. This security would give the person involved the encouragement and confidence to proceed. Alan Finlayson also thinks that encouragement can give the confidence to 'give it a go'. An example of this is provided by Calum Colvin, who was approached to create the theatre design for *The Breathing House* at the Royal Lyceum Theatre, Edinburgh in 2003. Professor Colvin was reluctant to participate as he had never undertaken a similar project and is not a regular theatregoer. Nonetheless, those from the theatre company encouraged him and showed such belief in him that he felt confident enough to 'give it a go'. The production went well and Professor Colvin received the Critics' Award of Best Design for Theatre in Scotland. The encouragement of achievement or recognition can breed further confidence with, for example, John Crofton seeing his father's self-confidence grow in line with his successes and Professor Colvin overcoming his shyness in discussing work thanks to the encouragement from the praise that he received in the early part of his career.

'Good training for self-confidence and leadership'

From experience

Noreen Murray believes that confidence can be derived from experience and practice as, for example, when Kenneth Murray presented their joint research to universities. She only presented at Glasgow University while Sir Kenneth presented at many universities across the United Kingdom, this gave him more confidence than her in speaking about their work. However, she does suggest that experience can, to an extent, be substituted by teaching and she would like to have been taught public speaking techniques because she thinks that would have boosted her confidence in presenting and lecturing. Sheila McLean advises that she used to be terrified of speaking in public and 'hated it'. However, through practice and the repeated experience of public speaking she grew in confidence to the point that she no longer has an issue with this. Like Noreen Murray and Professor McLean, Tom Farmer thinks that confidence comes from experience. For him, this means that you must 'push yourself' in new situations, even if that feels uncomfortable at first. Sir Tom recounts, when he was 20 years old and working as a tyre salesman, how he would feel unsure when visiting a company with a large fleet of cars at their 'fancy offices', almost to the point of 'making excuses not to go'. He puts that down to a new environment that he was not used to, as these were not the type of customers he normally serviced. However, once he was there he would discover that he was alright and he would enjoy the meetings, finding that the people 'might even like me'. As part of having confidence from the outset and gaining a positive start to a meeting Sir Tom would 'take a moment' to ensure that he remained calm and focused. Gaining confidence from experience is seen in a further example given by Sir Tom. He recalls that when he first attended a senior management meeting he thought those present were cleverer than him and that 'I must have really made it'. However, after attending a few such meetings, he realised that the other participants were not cleverer than him, it was just that they had more confidence through the experience of attending more of those types of meetings.

Robin Harper also believes that confidence comes from practice. This, he thinks, starts in people's formative years from 'learning to express yourself' by getting the opportunity to speak up in class and join in debates at school. It was his experience of serving as a Medical Officer in the Army that really grew John Crofton's confidence and ensured that his natural shyness was completely overcome, something he credits to the responsibilities that came with a role that interested him. Sir John joined the Army Reserve in May 1939, was called up in August of that year and was based just south of Dunkirk, but managed to 'get out' before the area was overrun by the German Army in 1940. Postings followed to Mesopotamia and Greece, where he describes sheltering wounded troops under lorries and having very limited medical supplies with which to treat them whilst under enemy attack. During this time he caught typhoid as all sterilising equipment was lost when the truck transporting it was destroyed and he was left deaf in one ear from a 1,000 pound bomb exploding '15 ft away' from him. That explosion did not cause more serious harm because, along with his comrades, he was sheltering in a slit trench. Sir John goes on to say that the experience of 'retreat from the Germans' was 'good training for self-confidence and leadership'.

Confidence may also come from preparation and using knowledge. For example, Alan Finlayson ensures that he is properly prepared prior to a meeting in order to get 'keyed up' on the subject. He compares this to a sports person and the preparation that he or she goes through to get into the right frame of mind for a match. Whether knowledge has come from experience or more formal learning, William Stewart advises that 'using an evidence based approach is crucial. You must be able to justify your conclusions'.

'Pick tatties'

From independence

Both Chay Blyth and Evelyn Glennie cite the independence and responsibilities that they had from a relatively young age as helping to build their confidence. Sir Chay refers to starting work at age 15 and the responsibilities that brought, while Dame Evelyn was taught from an early age to be independent in her thinking and finances. The approach was very much, 'you won't get something for nothing' and that you should 'give and share'. For example, Dame Evelyn could not just ask her parents for money to buy Christmas presents so, along with her brothers, she would 'pick tatties' on the farm to earn enough cash to buy the gifts. The independence that she went on to experience when she left home to study at the Royal Academy of Music further developed her confidence and gave her the strength to try new things in the knowledge that she can get back up again even if she 'falls flat'. In a similar way, William Stewart experienced independence when he was relatively young. From age 15 he spent time away from his home on Islay to attend school in Dunoon on the Scottish mainland. The independence and resilience that taught him was, he thinks, an advantage when he attended Glasgow University. This was because he was well versed in looking after himself, unlike some of his fellow students who found that difficult and dropped out of university.

Resilience is something that George Robertson values and has learnt to apply in certain political circumstances. He considers that such resilience was required when he was steering through the policy for a referendum on devolved government in Scotland, as 'the sniping in Scotland at that time was incredible, often venomous'. It got to the point that on one day he refused to read the newspapers, the only time he has ever done so (former First Minister Jack McConnell took the same approach that day). However, Lord Robertson believes that people now see the referendum as the correct approach.

While building and having confidence are seen as positive, there is thought to be a fine line between having confidence and being over-confident.

'Off-putting'

Over-confidence

Jonathan Long thinks that it is good for people to believe in themselves, but in the right quantities. Dr Long considers that 'unquestioned confidence will come to nothing' except maybe arrogance which, he thinks, sits next to confidence. George Robertson also points out that there is a thin dividing line between self-confidence and arrogance, something he views as 'off-putting', and Norman Drummond believes that it is right to exhibit confidence but not over-confidence. William Stewart cautions against misplaced confidence or over-confidence bordering on arrogance which, in addition to calling 'off-putting', he thinks can blind people to their own weaknesses. This is the experience of Brian Gill and he describes meeting lawyers with too much self-confidence who could not see and thus address their own shortcomings. It is that inability to asses your own capabilities, coupled with a lack of empathy with other people, that Robin Harper believes causes over-confidence. Alan Finlayson thinks that the best way to stop over-confidence is to tell someone that they are acting in that manner, and Calum Colvin has observed over-confidence in some students and recent graduates, which he refers to as 'the arrogance of youth'.

Tam Dalyell has witnessed over-confidence in politicians and he names former Prime Ministers Margaret Thatcher and Tony Blair as examples of people that he thinks displayed a general over-confidence. Michael Atiyah sees over-confidence in fellow Mathematicians who fall into the trap of always speculating. This means that they do not get into the detail or proof of theories, as their over-confidence causes them to believe that their higher level suppositions are correct.

Sheila McLean thinks that over-confidence can come from someone believing themselves to be established in a position to a point that they regard themselves as 'Teflon'. She has seen this in speakers who 'swan in' and deliver 'dreadful talks'. Margo MacDonald thinks that the over-confidence she has witnessed comes from individual 'stupidity', while Tam Dalyell believes that over-confidence stems from people thinking themselves 'close to perfection', something he describes as 'dangerous'. Through his great grandmother five times removed he is related to the 33rd President of the United States of America, Harry S. Truman. With that connection he was pleased to attend an event in May 2004 to mark the 120th anniversary of Harry Truman's birth in Independence, Missouri. At that occasion he was reminded of when, in 1945, news arrived from Palm Springs of the death of Franklin Roosevelt, and the speaker of the House of Representatives, Sam Rayburn, told Harry Truman that from then on he would call him 'Mr President'. Sam Rayburn added that many people will tell a President that he is 'perfect' but that 'I know and you know that you are far from perfect'. He believes that this thinking contributed to Harry Truman being a 'great President'.

Due to the tendency to 'knock others down', over-confidence is not a trait that George Robertson sees excessively in Scottish people. However, Jackie Stewart argues that over-confidence is 'more dangerous', because he thinks that if you lack confidence you are more likely to pay attention to the detail that can minimise mistakes and possible failures. To curb any potential 'arrogance', Jonathan Long believes in practising a humility that is informed by his spirituality, from which a strong but invisible and quiet confidence may emerge that is neither superficial nor blasé. In addition, Michael Atiyah believes that misplaced confidence can be avoided if confidence is built on a solid foundation of sound values that grow in line with achievement.

CHAPTER VI

Confidence: Summary

'One of the keys to progression'

A strong, maybe even understated, confidence that is built on knowledge and achievement is seen as desirable. In particular, the right measures of confidence are thought to provide people with a belief in what they are doing and the approach they are taking. However, it is considered that a lack confidence can be due to anxiety, poor self-perception or a natural shyness. Such a lack of confidence may inhibit progress but self-doubt can be managed and overcome or, in the case of anxiety, may even be a driver of improvement.

Confidence is thought to be built from an early age through the influence of parents and other adult role models. Continuing encouragement from other people is viewed as important throughout life because it may help to instil or maintain the confidence to take action. Participation in sport is also given as something that can boost confidence.

In adult life, confidence is thought mainly to be gained from experience, with that likely to be enhanced by practice or regular involvement in an area. The experience of early independence and the responsibilities that come with that are also highlighted. In addition, confidence can be derived from proper preparation. However, there is sometimes a thin dividing line between confidence and over-confidence, with over-confidence viewed as off-putting and something that can stop people from addressing their own shortcomings.

Having confidence in what you are doing is described as a spur that can encourage perseverance.

Perseverance

'Just to keep going is often the supreme act of courage'

What is perseverance?
What attributes support perseverance?
What behaviours can perseverance promote?

In this section the meaning of perseverance is discussed and how that manifests itself both in terms of action and the type of behaviour displayed. Perseverance is given as a requirement to follow through on plans and decisions that are encompassed in a structured approach, which is the topic of Chapter VIII.

'Great successes'

Keep going

Most of the contributors emphasise a need to persevere with, for example, Jackie Stewart advising 'never stop trying, never give up' and Tom Farmer recommending that 'you must keep at it, you must persevere'. Margo MacDonald speaks pragmatically when saying that in persevering with Parkinson's disease 'you just have to get on with it' and, for the 'average person', Brian Gill suggests that perseverance means 'never giving up on the standards that you set'. Lord Gill and George Mathewson both name James Dyson as an outstanding example of someone who has shown perseverance in inventing and marketing the bag-less vacuum cleaner. Norman Drummond gives a slightly different slant, when saying that he perseveres in order not to let other people down. He describes his approach in a cricket analogy, 'I never declare in an innings', and adds that 'often when you think you cannot go on, in fact, you can'. Sheila McLean sees perseverance in people who can get back up after setbacks, not let go of original aims and insist that they are right, often by being 'bloody minded'.

Jackie Stewart is very straightforward in recommending that 'if you want to do something, do it'. Although he believes that people should avoid 'delusions of grandeur' and concentrate on doing well in whatever it is they do. Sir Jackie sees this as the approach of people such as entrepreneur Tom Hunter who, he thinks, did not focus on potential financial wealth but concentrated on the job in hand. Irvine Laidlaw emphasises the need to focus and persevere in the most promising areas as he considers it 'human nature to chase failure'. He comments that some people put great effort into turning a failure into a break even situation 'and they think they're heroes, well I think they're stupid'. Lord Laidlaw argues that if the same effort and resource was put into a success these people would create a 'super success'. Sheila McLean notes that perseverance could entail repeating the same mistakes and therefore may not necessarily be a good thing. To illustrate this point, Lord Laidlaw advises that if the manuscript for this book has been presented to 10 publishers and they have all said 'no', then 'stop, drop it'. The thought of when to stop or change direction is taken up by Margo MacDonald when saying that the trick is knowing when to take a chance or when to revert to 'plan B'. For example, Evelyn Glennie remarks that if she is 'doing a lot just to stand still' then she has probably peaked and it is time to move on to something new.

Noreen Murray prefers to concentrate on successes, but notes that the input to generate successful experiments may take several years. Jackie Stewart points out that 'no one has seamless success' and he believes that there is a 'window of time' in which to persevere. This, he thinks, means that you should guard against writing off something too soon. Michael Atiyah thinks the question of 'what stage to cut loses?' is difficult, as if 'you pull back too quickly you may miss out'. He sees an inherent skill, which is enhanced by experience, informing when to continue or when to stop. Ultimately, he thinks, that you have to go with your 'gut feeling'. Sir Michael does contend that if something comes very easily, it is often not remembered or of as much value as the things that require perseverance and hard work, it is these that provide the 'great successes'.

Sheila McLean thinks that perseverance is more obvious in business than in education, where she considers it to be more passive and about doing 'the best you can'. Tom Farmer notes that in business, as in personal life, things will not necessarily end up as someone may hope. In particular, he points out that it is impossible for everyone to reach the top. However, Sir Tom believes that reaching the top is not the point of life but rather doing well and that 'just to keep going is often the supreme act of courage'.

'Dreamers seldom make it'

Action

Evelyn Glennie summarises how she thinks perseverance manifests itself when saying that 'perseverance is seen through action', a sentiment that Jackie Stewart shares and he advises that 'dreamers seldom make it'. Sir Jackie stresses that it is the practical application of a vision that will, for example, bring new products or services to the market place. Tom Farmer shares this view and he notes that a company acquisition often fails due to a lack of action in following through on the purchase, for example, by not integrating the new entity into existing operations. Although this does not mean that simply by acting people are persevering or that immediate action for the sake of it is proposed. In addition, perseverance is not necessarily obvious with, for example, Michael Atiyah saying that you have to 'persevere in thinking'. Dame Evelyn suggests that a further facet of perseverance is patience, something that Robin Harper also believes and he recommends, 'be patient with yourself and more patient with others'. Patience was displayed by John Crofton, when waiting on a colleague to retire prior to him taking full control of tuberculosis treatment in Edinburgh, and by Noreen Murray when the head of the Medical Research Council unit, in which she was working, left and the unit was closed. This delayed elements of her research for one year.

Thus, perseverance by action is seen to include thinking and patience. However, perseverance is perhaps more conspicuous when someone is following through on decisions or in the latter stages of a project. As an example of that, George Robertson refers to the implementation of the Good Friday Agreement which was brokered in April 1998 and fixed the basis of devolved government in Northern Ireland. It included human rights and equality commissions, early release of terrorist prisoners, decommissioning of paramilitary weapons and reform of both the criminal justice system and policing. Lord Robertson explains how that agreement would not have become a reality without the perseverance of Tony Blair in following through and driving the process, which ensured the agreement was implemented and a Northern Ireland Assembly delivered.

Robin Harper refers to the perseverance shown by Winston Churchill in returning to lead the Conservative Government of 1951, having lost the role of Prime Minster in the July 1945 General Election. He also names Mahatma Gandhi, for the perseverance he demonstrated during his 'whole lifetime', and Jane Tomlinson for her 'outstanding' perseverance after she was diagnosed with terminal breast cancer in 2000. Jane Tomlinson was given an estimated six months to live but spent the next seven years participating in many physical challenges, including marathons and 'iron man' events plus three long distance bicycle rides; from John O'Groats to Land's End, from Rome to her home in Yorkshire and a 4,200 mile (approximately 6,800 km) journey across the United States of America. She did this despite having regular chemotherapy and developing a chronic heart condition. In addition to raising close to £2 million for cancer charities, Jane Tomlinson wanted to demonstrate that people who have received a terminal prognosis can still lead an active life. 'To a lesser extent', he also gives the perseverance of those, in the Green Party, who during the best part of the 1980s and 1990s put themselves forward for election and gained only 'three or four per cent of the vote' until a seat was eventually won in the Scottish Parliamentary elections of 1999. As an example of perseverance, Alan Finlayson suggests, a Liberal Democrat who stands for the House of Commons and will perhaps never get into power but continues to work at it, as they 'think they are, and may even be, right'. He adds that he admires people who have exacting standards and are passionate about what they do. Tam Dalyell cites the scientist Max Perutz as someone who demonstrated outstanding perseverance. Max Perutz achievements were recognised by the joint award of the 1962 Nobel Prize in Chemistry with John Kendrew, for their work on the structure of globular proteins that carry oxygen round the body, such as haemoglobin and myoglobin.

Ron Hamilton says 'persist, persist, persist' because 'perseverance is the key', something he did when inventing and then marketing the first low cost sterile daily disposable contact lenses. Having had the idea of developing this product in-house rejected by their employer, both he and Bill Seden resigned in 1988 to pursue the ideas and practicalities of applying a more stable process to contact lens production. Due to production methods that were unstable and which created a large amount of 'wastage', daily disposable contact lenses were prohibitively expensive. However, the £4 million of Venture Capital funding promised to support their work was withdrawn. It was only following legal arguments, which showed the would-be investors apparent breach of contract and gave them limited financial redress, that they were able to establish a makeshift laboratory in his back garden and secure initial intellectual property rights. Fortunately, those rights were in place when they agreed to discuss the technical details with a large company. Having spent several months with that organisation's technical teams, they went to a meeting where they expected to sign a licensing and consultancy agreement that would bring their idea to the market. That view was soon dispelled when they were told 'you two can go now'. It was explained to them that the company had worked out that neither he nor Bill Seden had the finances to fund international patent protection, that their initial patents would soon go into the public domain and that they had no time to gain an alternative partner. With no patents to worry about and having seen the technical details, the company reasoned that it could start production and avoid paying royalties to the inventors. However, he turned to the British Technology Group (BTG), which helped to secure the intellectual property rights that thwarted any company from gaining their ideas for nothing. Although this agreement did entitle BTG to half of any future royalties. Further difficulties were then encountered when the initial thought of month long eye wear was rejected, following experiments that showed problems if lenses were worn overnight. So the aim became to produce daily disposable lenses. A stable process, that reduced unit costs enough to make such lenses a commercial reality, was eventually within reach. In order to establish a full manufacturing capability they then tried to interest an established company from the eye care industry in their ideas. Many representatives from those companies came to review their findings but all of them declined to believe in the product. One representative even said that, with its extensive research and development facility, he could not report back that a couple of people working in a garden shed had anything to offer. In hindsight, they see the reason for this lack of interest as 'we were a threat to them' due to existing investments in complementary eye products, such as cleaning fluid for contact lenses. They 'had a blind spot' about talking to distributors, rather than manufacturers, and the breakthrough came when they showed the product to Boots Opticians. It recognised the potential, endorsed the product and was soon selling the daily disposable contact lenses. With funding now secured, they licensed the technology back from BTG and rapidly developed a strong market position with opticians. In 1995 Bausch & Lomb approached them to purchase distribution rights but with demand running ahead of capacity they did not see a need for this. Instead, they offered to sell the business and Bausch & Lomb purchased it along with the intellectual property rights (which accounted for the majority of the amount received). The purchase agreement included a five year non-competition clause. Over that time he conducted development work and at the end of the prescription period Ron and Moya Hamilton launched daysoft® limited, which makes and sells high specification disposable contact lenses across the world.

It was through perseverance that Lewis Robertson considers F. H. Lloyd plc, then the United Kingdom's largest steel foundry business, was resuscitated. When Sir Lewis joined the company, as specialist rescue Chairman in 1982, it was in severe difficulties. These were exacerbated by over capacity across the industry, to point that the Lazard scheme was introduced to pay firms to curtail output. Sir Lewis realised that F. H. Lloyd was 'spread too thinly' for the amount of work it could win and he vividly remembers visiting the main foundry and finding it like a 'cathedral on a Monday'. There were two tank turrets sitting in the sand and 'that was it'. Sir Lewis reckoned that F. H. Lloyd could take the money available from the Lazard scheme, close the main foundry and then continue appropriate and sustainable levels of capacity at other sites. This approach was seen as 'heresy' by the Directors who thought themselves impregnable and took the view that competitors would simply close. Sir Lewis was satisfied that his approach would work and with the authority of the bank he moved ahead with his recovery plan. This involved a complete reworking of structures and the appointment of new management. His approach, which was viewed as radical, almost certainly saved F. H. Lloyd from going out of business. In parallel with that, Sir Lewis was Chairman of Triplex plc from 1983 to 1987, where he had implemented new management structures and rectified its financial difficulties. This had allowed Triplex to retain its interests in grey iron, non ferrous castings, light engineering and building components. Having persevered to ensure that both of these companies remained in business and were of a sound financial and commercial footing, Sir Lewis oversaw their merger into Triplex Lloyd plc, which he then vigorously expanded in his capacity as Chairman.

Perseverance has also been displayed by Irvine Laidlaw throughout his career. Lord Laidlaw describes his early years in business as 'really tough', especially as he wished to remain self-employed and 'was determined not to get a job'. That persistence saw the genesis of the Institute of International Research in 1973 as an international newsletter publisher operating out of the city of New York. In 1978 two conferences were undertaken in the United

Kingdom and, from success of these, focus turned to the conference market. Expansion in this field was swift and by 1980 offices had been established across South East Asia, with further expansion until the Institute of International Research became a truly global conference organisation. In 1984 it diversified into exhibitions and went on to become the largest business of its type in the world. After being the driving force behind this hugely successful company, Lord Laidlaw sold it in 2005 to T&F Informa.

The persistence in following a particular career or employment choice was shown by John Crofton. In particular, he found it difficult to get a job in medicine when he left the Army at the end of the Second World War. For example, the first position he applied for had over 100 applicants and he was not short listed. Recently married and with some savings from his army pay he persisted until he secured an unpaid position at the Brompton Hospital in London under the guidance of Guy Scadding. It was this job which eventually led to his involvement in tuberculosis research and trials. Sir John's perseverance continued throughout his career as, for example, when his team announced the strong results of the protocol they had developed against tuberculosis. 'Nobody believed them', even to the point that they were accused of 'fiddling the figures, and he was told that the results would not be accepted until people saw the improvement in their own patients. So, he set up an international trial with the help of an 'excellent coordinator', Reg Bignall, who had also initially been sceptical. Vast numbers of people were involved in the trial and it was soon evident that any deterioration in patients was due to the protocol not being properly adhered to. Outside of that, Sir John can only recall the death of one moribund patient. Sir John's perseverance in implementing, showing and sharing these treatment protocols has saved many lives across the world.

'You don't get a full bottle'

Attributes of perseverance

Perseverance is not seen as something that happens in isolation but is believed to be derived from a number of attributes. It is thought that foremost amongst these are a capacity for hard work, commitment, determination and energy.

'An internal combustion engine'

Energy

Energy is given by George Robertson as the most important of all qualities because 'if you have energy, this will drive forward the other qualities of perseverance, self-confidence and being quick witted'. In his youth, Jackie Stewart saw himself as having the energy and enthusiasm to do well in a sporting environment or one where practical skills were required and Tom Farmer emphasises the importance of maintaining energy levels. While he thinks that energy can be boosted for a short amount of time, like an athlete who eats carbohydrate prior to a race, Sir Tom tries to sustain a constant high tempo as opposed to having peaks and troughs. In contrast, Evelyn Glennie sees her own energy as 'something of a yo yo' that changes with her achievements and desire to fulfill aims. Also, Dame Evelyn thinks young people have a 'youthful energy' and she describes the energy that a youth orchestra generates as very different to that when playing with more experienced musicians. Chay Blyth likes spending time with younger people because they help keep him enthused through their energy. Sir Chay does not want to stagnate like some people of his age who 'look and act like old men'. However, Calum Colvin thinks that as he gets older, and 'your back starts to creak', he has to focus his energy better by concentrating on fewer projects.

Ron Hamilton considers that you have to 'gee up' some people to keep them going but he sees other people who have their own drive. The boundless energy that John Crofton seems to possess is perhaps best described by his wife, Eileen Crofton, who calls him 'an internal combustion engine'.

Such high energy levels can support perseverance through allowing people to do a lot by either concentrating on one field or developing diverse interests. The capacity to specialise and gain a real depth of understanding in one particular area or to gain knowledge over a spectrum of topics is seen with Norman Drummond. He describes himself as a 'renaissance man', meaning that he is comfortable doing many things, which he thinks is sometimes 'intimidating' for people who have only ever done one thing. The willingness or ability to do a lot can develop a habit of keeping busy. This may be the case with Irvine Laidlaw, who is 'always busy' because it 'never stops', and Tom Farmer, who comments that there is 'always something on the go, every day' and that he is 'always doing things'. This included, in his youth, buying and selling bicycles and cleaning cookers where he advertised a 'Kwik' cleaning service in his local newspaper. John Crofton remains busy in his retirement as he continues the battle against tuberculosis, pulmonary lung disease and the wider issues of ill health linked to poverty and social deprivation. This includes working with the World Health Organisation to publish a 'straight forward book' to assist those fighting tuberculosis in third world countries; fulfilling a request from the European Union to re-iterate the protocol steps, because tuberculosis remains an issue across 'recent accession states and through Russia right up to the Chinese border'; and promoting messages to address difficulties caused by smoking and alcohol. To try and support these initiatives he has also turned his hand to fund raising, which he finds fascinating, and has sent 'thousands of letters, each with a hand written personal message'. This habit of keeping busy is something that Evelyn Glennie got into, particularly during the demanding schedule that she undertook in London when in her 20s, and that Chay Blyth gained in the Army. To illustrate this, Sir Chay gives a light-hearted example from when he was operating in a mountainous region near Aden. There was concern during a period of little action that the men may become idle or, as he jokingly puts it, 'the troops might think'. So, to keep people busy a game of volleyball was decided upon and the order was to make a volleyball pitch, 'a volleyball pitch!', in terrain where there was not a flat space to be had. Sure enough, the pitch was made and Sir Chay uses this small example to show how he thinks the Army was very good at keeping people active, involved and positive.

Keeping busy and having the ability to get a lot done is remarked on by Kenneth Murray when saying that 'if you want something done give it to busy person'. This gives the sense that someone who is in the habit of being busy will have the capacity for further work. However, Tom Devine warns that 'you can't do everything'. For example, when he was asked to apply for the role of Principal at a Scottish university he declined because he was already Vice Principal of Strathclyde University. Professor Devine felt that he could not take on the additional scholarly and management responsibilities the new position would entail as his primary interest remained research and writing. This requirement to prioritise and focus is considered as an imperative by George Robertson. He illustrates that by giving the case of a lawyer who has lots of clients, but who must focus on each individual client in turn despite the many other distractions that may be going on. Tom Farmer believes that even those with talent have to focus and Irvine Laidlaw thinks that, unless you are lucky or talented enough, 'for the average good person' focus is required. Evelyn Glennie advises that the focus she gives to a project or objective means that she is not affected adversely by outside factors, while George Mathewson recommends trying to do well by giving focus to what is in front of you. John Crofton adds to this when saying that potential is most likely to be fulfilled if you 'find something that you are good at and concentrate on it', which is echoed by Jackie Stewart who says 'be as good as you can be at what you can do'.

In addition to the energy that supports an ability to do a lot, both commitment and determination are considered to be key components of perseverance.

'A massive signal'

Commitment and determination

Brian Gill advises that in law progress is determined by what you know plus your commitment to the profession. Lord Gill believes that if someone does not explore knowledge or lacks commitment they will fail. In particular, he states that lawyers make a promise to their clients and to the profession to commit totally to mastering their subject and applying the highest professional standards. He adds that regrettably many lawyers do not do this. As well as being committed to what you are doing, George Mathewson thinks it important that you demonstrate commitment by 'doing what you say you will do'. He thinks that sends 'a massive signal' of honesty which will develop trust and encourage participation. People may be committed to a defined goal, a way of life or to learning, something that Kenneth Murray has witnessed in his capacity as Chairman of the Darwin Trust of Edinburgh. The Trust provides support and financial backing to non-UK students, especially those from Eastern Europe, to enable them to further their scientific research and studies, mainly at Edinburgh University. Sir Kenneth notes that these overseas students tend to 'work exceptionally hard' and never complain about working in a foreign language, adjusting to a new country or the size of their grant. He observes that some even save money from their grant to send home. Such commitment to learning and improvement plus a selfless attitude is viewed by Sir Kenneth as most commendable.

Commitment is often seen to concentrate on devotion or dedication, while determination is perhaps more focused on strength of mind and will power. However, the two may be inseparable with, for example, George Robertson referring to himself as a 'determined person' who is keen to contribute through his commitment and belief in what he is doing. Calum Colvin was determined to make his way in life through the visual arts from the age of 17. That was reinforced when he 'discovered' photography at age 18. He says that unfortunately a lot of art students lack determination but 'it is those who have that you will hear about'. Likewise, Michael Atiyah considers that the force of character that determination can give is important for progression. Chay Blyth thinks that his determination first manifested itself when he started swimming and he used to train three times a day. The first session would be in the morning, when he would run the three miles from his house to the pool, then at lunch time followed by an evening session. This determination to improve led to him being selected to swim for the South of Scotland. Sir Chay refers to that same determination when he established The British Steel Challenge and when 'finding the resolve to keep going was an intensely exhausting mental struggle' during his solo round the world navigation. If difficulties are encountered, Sir Chay tackles them head on and notes that 'determination and single-mindedness are the qualities that matter most'.

Energy, commitment and determination can equip people to keep going and are thought to provide the impetus for, what is viewed as a critical element, hard work.

'Follow your bliss'

Hard work

Hard work is something that all the contributors believe in with, for example, both Norman Drummond and Irvine Laidlaw referring to the maxim '95 per cent perspiration and five per cent inspiration'. Lewis Robertson says that 'you must work hard' and Chay Blyth advises that he always preferred to work. For example, Sir Chay went straight from school into an apprenticeship without taking time off and then joined the Army on a Saturday, having left his previous job on the Thursday of that same week. Sheila McLean has 'always worked hard' but is not precious about her work and can completely 'switch off' and not 'lift a finger'. To underline this she adds that even if she moved on from the Department in Law and Ethics in Medicine at Glasgow University, which she has built from scratch, she would 'not miss it'. Hard work is subscribed to by Jackie Stewart, and Tom Farmer advises that he never watched football as he 'always worked on a Saturday'. Calum Colvin makes himself work, even on those occasions that he does not want to. Professor Colvin thinks there is something in his character that requires him to work and he wonders if that comes from a Scottish work ethic. Evelyn Glennie dislikes laziness as she tries to do her best and is 'always willing to work', and Brian Gill thinks hard work comes from the habit of discipline. Noreen Murray believes that many people achieve through hard work and she commonly worked between 70 and 80 hours per week in the laboratory. Similarly, Alan Finlayson thought nothing of working 'normal office hours' plus at least three nights a week and Saturday mornings. John Crofton used to start work at 8 am, '6 am if busy', and continue on until about 7 pm when he would take a break until starting again for two hours or so at about 8.45 pm. Eileen Crofton casts some doubt on these hours suggesting they were generally longer and she questions the length of break at 7 pm. Sir John did make a point of taking Saturday and Sunday afternoons off to spend time with his family.

Hard work is not only described as applying to professional life and building a career but is also thought to encompass those intangible things that make up character, which Norman Drummond refers to as the 'gifts of intuition, memory and compassion'. Reverend Drummond points out that 'you don't get a full bottle' and that an individual must work hard to develop as a person. This is something George Robertson does, as he 'works hard' to try and do his best in every aspect of his life, and Michael Atiyah advises that, as it is those thoughts you have had to work hardest on that are the most memorable, you learn to 'struggle hard'.

In addition, hard work is not necessarily seen as something that is disagreeable. For instance, Calum Colvin 'enjoys working' and Brian Gill comments that work is not arduous if you love what you are doing. In such instances, where something 'is dear to you', Norman Drummond argues that you will never feel that you are 'flogging a dead horse'. For example, Evelyn Glennie advises that her brother puts great effort into running a farm despite it rarely making money. Indeed, some people have questioned whether it is worth the effort and have suggested that he sells up. Instead, he perseveres because there is 'some chemistry' inside him whereby he sees himself achieving through showing commitment, determination and stubbornness. This is something that Dame Evelyn greatly admires. Michael Atiyah picks up on this enjoyment in work and recommends that you 'do what you are interested in, not what other people think you should do'. He expands on this by saying that other people 'may be wrong' and that if you do something that drives you internally then you will be better motivated and more likely to give it your all, rather than going in half-heartedly. He is not recommending that people disregard advice but rather that you are not obliged to follow the 'expected rules'. Sir Michael adds that if you do not succeed, you cannot blame others and at the very least you will have enjoyed trying. Jonathan Long gives a similar view but discusses it in the context of Joseph Campbell's research into the 'monomyth'. This proposes that myths and legends permeate across different cultures and countries but have a similar format of a reluctant hero, going on an individual quest and returning after achieving an objective. This, Dr Long believes, points towards the common human yearning to follow a passion. He ties that to the concept of 'authentic happiness' promulgated by Martin Seligman. In that, pleasure is described as a transient emotion that will lead to meaning and understanding in life if it is accompanied by 'flow' or a following of passion. Thus, Dr Long purports working in whatever you are passionate about or, as he puts it, 'follow your bliss'.

'High standards'

Perfection

Perseverance can include striving towards high standards which, in some instances, is given in the context of a perfectionist approach. This is the case with Ron Hamilton, who describes himself as a 'perfectionist' who is constantly looking to 'raise the bar', and Norman Drummond, who sees himself as a perfectionist in so much as he can always improve upon his previous efforts. Evelyn Glennie makes a conscious effort to improve and works hard in practice sessions to reach 'perfection, which of course isn't achievable'. For Dame Evelyn, putting that practice into a live performance is important because she views live performance as the real gauge of how good somebody is. In the recording studio, Dame Evelyn argues, musicians can 'fake it' through using technology that can rectify imperfections. While technology does assist live performance, she advises that it does not have the same ability as studio equipment to remedy flaws. Dame Evelyn compares this to sport where she views competition as having the ultimate say on who is the best, which means that sports people 'can't fake it'.

People may also rework something in order to improve it, perhaps doing this many times. For example, Kenneth Murray is 'fussy' in going back and correcting writing, and William Stewart is never totally satisfied with what he writes and repeatedly goes back and 'tinkers' with the text. This concern with detail is seen in others, such as Irvine Laidlaw, who is 'into the details of things', and Ron Hamilton paying 'a lot of attention to detail'. Jackie Stewart is also very much into detail and he refers to the 'thoroughness' that supports his high standards. This preference for detail is described by Norman Drummond as coming from the left side, the logical side, of the brain.

A fascination with a topic can take someone further than a perfectionist approach. For instance, Calum Colvin 'changes and adjusts' a piece until he feels that he cannot do any more to improve it. Professor Colvin refers to himself as a 'perfectionist' who is 'finicky and obsessive'. Similarly, John Crofton agrees cheerily with Eileen Crofton's description of him as 'obsessive' when referring to his fascination with clinical medicine. However, a high level of perfection can cause difficulties. Tom Devine acknowledges that 'you cannot do it all the time' but explains that, as a perfectionist, if he does not reach his expectations he gets depressed which can give way to 'black dog'.

However, not everyone takes a perfectionist approach with neither Chay

Blyth nor George Mathewson seeing themselves as perfectionists. Sir Chay does though describe himself at times as 'close to it', with sport the area where he is most likely to take a perfectionist approach, while Sir George says the he 'can be fairly sloppy in various things'. Rather than thinking in terms of perfection, Sheila McLean has high standards and, as in other aspects of perseverance, considers it is about being the best that you can be. Noreen Murray 'tries to take a perfectionist view', but would never say that anything she has done is 'perfection', and Brian Gill does not see himself as a perfectionist due to the compromises which he believes are required in life. That does not mean that someone who does not view himself or herself as a 'perfectionist' has lower standards. For example, Noreen Murray refers to her own 'high standards' and Lord Gill describes himself as a 'demanding Judge with exacting standards'. If Lord Gill feels that a lawyer has failed to meet those standards, particularly in his or her commitment to a client or the profession, then he will bring it to their attention in the hope that their standards improve. On the other hand, when Lord Gill deals with counsel who exceeds these standards, such as when a huge amount of effort has been put into the preparation of a 'poor case', it is an 'awesome privilege'.

CHAPTER VII

Perseverance: Summary

'Just to keep going is the supreme act of courage'

Perseverance is seen as an ability to continue and keep on trying, even when things are not going as you would like. Particularly in business, it is emphasised that perseverance should concentrate on those areas that have the most chance of success. In addition, it is thought that the most memorable results may come from those things that require greater perseverance. However, it can be difficult to decide when to stop or when to continue and persevere, with that described as a judgment based on instinct and previous experience.

Energy, commitment, determination and hard work are given as the main attributes of perseverance. Energy may be formed from a habit of keeping busy and can allow people to do many things or gain a real depth of understanding in one area, and in some instances do both. The dedication to continue and the determination which supplies the mental strength to keep going are also seen as facets of perseverance. The attributes of energy, commitment and determination are described as fuelling hard work in both thinking and actions. Although, it is emphasised that if people are doing something they enjoy then it will not feel like 'hard work'. Also, it is considered less important whether there is an obvious 'success' or 'failure' if someone is following their passion because he or she is likely to gain enjoyment from doing whatever that is.

Some individuals describe themselves as perfectionists, or certainly giving attention to detail, which can see them repeatedly revisiting something to improve it. Other people take a different approach and do not see themselves as perfectionists, although that does not mean to say that they have low expectations, as they too strive to improve and raise standards.

Perseverance may be seen when a process is followed that eventually delivers a desired outcome. Such a process often comes from a plan that forms part of an overall structured approach.

Structured Approach

'The most methodical man in Scotland'

How is a structured approach developed?
What part do targets play?
What are the benefits of organisation?

People have different views on the amount of structure that they apply to their professional and personal lives in terms of planning, process delivery, use of targets and organisation of time. In addition to these areas, the potential need to develop some level of business understanding is considered in this chapter. Part of a structured approach is communication, which is discussed in Chapter IX, People Skills.

'Plan B and C to fall back on'

Planning

In the main, a structured approach is referred to in a business or professional context, rather than in personal life. Included in this approach are preparation, analysis and planning. This is emphasised by Jackie Stewart, who prepares by giving full attention to detail in order to lay 'business foundations'. To prepare properly, George Mathewson believes that disciplined thinking and the application of logic is required, something he thinks engineers and scientists have. Brian Gill encourages law students to apply disciplined thinking to both analysis and discussion, which he hopes assists in expressing views succinctly, and William Stewart applies very detailed analysis when developing a precautionary approach to health issues. Sheila McLean uses 'factual analysis' in preparing details so as 'not to take sides', something Chay Blyth did when analysing yachts to identify the most appropriate specifications prior to commissioning a yacht to compete in the 1973–74 Whitbread Round the World

Race. In business, Ron Hamilton and Tom Farmer analyse the present position, competition and the markets being entered so as to define the most appropriate plan of action and understand future business potential.

Such analysis is described as being driven by a desire to resolve issues and work out solutions to problems. For example, Tom Devine believes that writing about history is not about giving a narrative but working out and understanding issues from the past, while Calum Colvin is trying to make sense of issues through art. Professor Colvin quotes the maxim that a photographer makes 'order from chaos' and adds that 'in a way a photographer frames the world, as the image tells a story as it tries to make sense of a bigger world'. John Crofton finds it useful to turn complex problems into metaphors or diagrams in order to better understand them, this being especially true when he looks at mathematical rules.

However, a structured approach does not mean an inflexible approach or one where reason is always applied. For instance, Michael Atiyah stresses that 'mathematics is not all logic'. Sir Michael describes the creative process at the start of developing thoughts as more 'like an artist' and he illustrates this with the example of building a 'cathedral or a bridge'. He describes how, to construct either, mathematics is used but, at the start of the building process, you think about what you want the structure or building to look like. Then, only after that creative element, you think 'let's see if we can make it work'. This leads to a blend of the creative and detailed logical aspects of mathematics working in harmony in order to solve problems, something Sir Michael very much enjoys and gains satisfaction from.

Initial preparation and analytical work can help to define the rest of a structured plan. This is where a systematic approach is often employed to ensure that all elements are properly explored and completed to meet a desired outcome. For example, Lewis Robertson takes an orderly approach where files are listed very carefully to ensure accuracy and he refers to himself as 'the most methodical man in Scotland'. In recent years, Sir Lewis has computerised these records and he gives one of his interests as 'list making'. A planned approach resonates with George Robertson, who stresses the importance of planning ahead because 'one step so far so good' is unlikely to succeed. As an example, Lord Robertson refers to the plans that he drew up to deliver the devolved settlement in Scotland, without which he thinks it far less likely that the Scottish Parliament would have been established. Lord Robertson adds that this was the only policy that did not go through the full United Kingdom Labour Party scrutiny process because it was considered purely a Scottish question. It was the realisation of these plans that he takes 'most pride from in politics'. Alan Finlayson has been told by others that one of his fortes is public speaking and that he must find it 'easy'. However, this is not the case and he puts in 'endless work' to prepare speeches beforehand. Usually, this includes having cards to prompt him and the whole speech in his inside pocket to refer to should he falter when delivering the speech. He also prepares fully prior to, for example, meeting children that are subject to a custody dispute. In advance of those meetings he tries to gain as much background information as possible and thinks through methods that will put the child at ease and encourage him or her to discuss their circumstances. Sheila McLean also plans ahead and advises that she has appointments in her diary for over a year in advance of meetings. She has always tended to be well organised and, for instance at the age of six or seven, she used to write down which of her clothes matched each other.

Margo MacDonald does not over emphasise planning but she does weigh up the options carefully prior to deciding which to take. This includes having a 'plan B and C to fall back on' and tackling problems head on. Chay Blyth also includes alternative scenarios in his plans and he recommends a holistic approach where 'careful planning, attention to detail, hard work and the right tools for the job' are of the 'utmost importance'. This total planning approach is one that Jackie Stewart employs and was given as key by John Crofton when tackling the rise in cases of tuberculosis that were seen in Scotland in the immediate post Second World War period. Sir John realised the need to take control of all relevant areas and insisted that he would only accept the position in Edinburgh if he was placed in charge of respiratory diseases and not just tuberculosis, although he did have to wait on a colleague to retire before he gained full patient control. Sir John had identified that a lack of integrated patient control, exacerbated by the prescription of 'bad combinations of drugs' were the critical elements that needed to be addressed and this complete control allowed him to plan all aspects of research and patient care.

Once the analysis has been considered to decide the approach to be taken and a plan has been detailed, it is recommended that the process that delivers that plan is followed through robustly.

'Doing things better'

Process delivery

The need to deliver a plan by way of a strongly controlled process, facilitated by appropriate communication, is highlighted by Ron Hamilton. Likewise, to drive forward a process, George Robertson sees the need for someone to exercise control by using the leadership qualities that he saw Tony Blair display when driving forward the process to implement the Good Friday Agreement in Northern Ireland. The ability to drive forward a process is one of the reasons that Irvine Laidlaw focuses the Laidlaw Youth Trust and other support work in Scotland. As he is 'more of a big player' in Scotland, Lord Laidlaw feels that he is able to shape the agenda and get other people involved. This, he thinks, would be far more difficult to do if he was trying to drive forward a wider remit, such as providing aid to Africa. Jackie Stewart is very process orientated and he tries to 'keep it simple' and apply common sense to the process of ongoing work. He illustrates this by saying that it only takes 'a few seconds' to pick some weeds in the garden, so 'why wait' until something becomes a big job.

Driving forward a process and looking for improvements are considered equally relevant to an established process as to a new process. This is seen in existing methods being challenged with, for example, Calum Colvin believing that improvement often comes from having existing procedures or rules in place because 'without rules you have nothing to kick against'. Ron Hamilton is always looking to reduce business costs by implementing process efficiencies, as opposed to seeking cheaper labour rates, which means that he sees no need to follow other manufacturers and move production abroad. To drive efficiencies he has harnessed the opportunity which technology provides and implemented a process, via the Internet, that offers customers a self-service purchase environment. This includes payment by credit or debit card and avoids costly distribution networks. It links into his manufacturing capability, where an automated and tightly controlled process has reduced the retail cost of a pair of disposable contact lenses from approximately £150 in 1988 to about 50p today. In this process he relies on trusted business partners and gives the example of using the Royal Mail for bulk shipping because he has always found it honest and has a good relationship with it. This does not stop him striving for further improvements and he has re-designed packaging in order to obtain cheaper postage costs.

Similarly, Evelyn Glennie challenges herself not just to improve musically but also to improve the business processes on which she relies. For example, it is usual for a music promoter to pay an agent, who then pays the musician. Dame Evelyn has altered this so that she is paid in the first instance by the promoter after which she remits funds to the agent. This ensures that she is paid promptly and also, as she has implemented an efficient payment process, that the agents receive their share at least as quickly as before. Agents were at first resistant to making this change but Dame Evelyn believes in 'pushing boundaries' and not doing things a certain way just because they were done like that previously. Her desire to become a solo percussionist was certainly against the normal 'rules' of the day, where percussion was viewed in a supporting role. For Dame Evelyn the challenge of pushing the boundaries of possibility continue to evolve with, for example, the development of percussion instruments. She gives the case of the marimba moving from the previous normal 5 octaves to 5.5 and 6 octave versions. This enlargement in the range of sound brings increased potential for the musician and is set to continue as, Dame Evelyn advises in percussion, there is 'no Steinway', no absolute standardisation of instruments, which means that the possibilities are not exhausted. These improvements, through challenging both herself and the normal methods, are something that she thinks were instilled in her during her time at Ellon Academy. She advises that the school seemed to match pupils to teachers to try and bring out each individual's skills and push boundaries, not just do things as they had been done before. Also, Dame Evelyn rails against some of the traditional approaches and gives the example of being taught, like all classical musicians, not to smile but to bow in a certain manner after a performance. She enjoys performing and wants the audience to enjoy her music so she has dispensed with that staid approach. Instead, she prefers to be warm and welcoming, which assists her interaction with the audience and, hopefully, their enjoyment of the performance.

While George Robertson emphasises the need to drive a process forward, he is pragmatic about how that process is implemented. He stresses that it is outputs which people will be judged on and not the process that has been administered, although a focused and well run process should secure a positive output. Lord Robertson recommends retaining flexibility in the approach to ensure that the correct outputs are delivered, rather than becoming 'mesmerised by process'. This concentration on outputs was first emphasised to Lord Robertson by Lewis Robertson who always 'asked for deliverables'. Ron Hamilton records key customer information in order to retain focus on outputs and to better meet customer requirements. These include contact people, pricing, productivity, and profit and loss information. Jackie Stewart looks at outputs in terms of the targeted audience because it is 'no good trying to sell to someone who can't afford it'. He takes account of that in his planning and process development and he tries to make items marketable and affordable by 'doing things better'.

Analysis, planning and driving forward a process are almost exclusively referred to in a business or professional capacity. This includes other elements of business.

'The best career move I made'

Business elements

Evelyn Glennie has become 'more savvy about business' and she feels that she must understand it as her career depends on it. Dame Evelyn says that she had to learn quickly because 'up to 80 per cent of time' can be spent on business due to the need to negotiate appearances, find venues and arrange travel, with all that coming before rehearsal time. She does not discriminate between building a career and the business aspects that form part of that, and she states that 'the best career move I made' was setting up an office and support team in 1989. This reduced her reliance on agents and allowed her to become more informed in her business dealings. She adds that, due to the costs and fees which influence decisions, 'in music, the reality is different from the ideal'. Thus, Dame Evelyn contends, music is no different from any other profession because it is not as 'glamorous' as people might think. Calum Colvin also recognises the need to ensure that he keeps on top of business matters to support his career and, while he would rather be concentrating on his art, 'I don't mind doing them'.

Within business, different approaches and emphasis are highlighted. For instance, through strong process review and improvement, Ron Hamilton has a business model which is very automated with a large investment in technology. This allows him to deal with customers directly which, he believes, assists his understanding of customer requirements. The business model incorporates self-service purchase and efficient distribution, where there are no debtors and limited amounts of paper produced. In addition, a concentration on efficient processes helps to limit company overheads, as illustrated by only three people working in the company accounts department, and brings with it financial control and understanding. The model is robust, 'liked by customers' and has completely altered how contact lenses are bought and sold. In moving that market towards self-service via the Internet a 'good customer' that has 70 optician outlets was nervous about its sales being substituted by web based sales. To alleviate that concern he conducted a re-branding exercise for that company, which in effect franchised what was already a proven business model.

Tom Farmer sees the elements of business like a chain, where each link has to be in place for the overall business to work efficiently. The part which Sir Tom concentrates on is 'firstly your own people', because he thinks that by having good employees suppliers will be keen to get involved. His definition of suppliers includes not only immediate suppliers, such as a tyre manufacturer supplying a garage, but all those who contribute to the organisation's infrastructure, such as the company's bankers and accountants. With employees and suppliers working effectively in a sound company infrastructure, Sir Tom believes, customers will receive a good service that will encourage more custom as people will tell others and return for repeat business. That growing customer business then translates into profit and shareholder value. George Mathewson gives the shareholders as the number one responsibility and starting point in business considerations. However, he adds that the Royal Bank of Scotland scored high, if not first, for staff satisfaction and customer service. Sir George is uncertain how the correlations work but he emphasises that all areas have to be borne in mind, including 'the softer issues', and he is intolerant of 'business politics' and the inefficiencies that bureaucracy can bring.

For Jackie Stewart, the corporate world 'could learn a lot from sport'. In particular, he thinks that sport provides humility due to its ability to 'knock you back'. Sir Jackie gives the example of Paula Radcliffe winning the 2007 New York Marathon, which makes her the 'best again' and means that the previous winner is no longer at the top. Sir Jackie believes the changing fortunes of winning and losing in sport has a humbling effect which, if seen in business, would reduce the 'corporate strut' of over-confidence and the dangers inherent in that.

Ron Hamilton suggests that business will defend its own vested interest. Ultimately a business requires to make money to survive and Norman Drummond gives the example of David Murray having to change school following his father being declared bankrupt and the resolve that gave David Murray never to let that happen to any of his businesses. By his early 20s David Murray had established a structural steel distributor, Murray International Metals, and his business interests have successfully gone on to include mining, commercial property and call centres, as well as ownership of Rangers Football Club. When Irvine Laidlaw first took on the Institute of International Research the company was laden with debt. This meant that he was continually looking for cheap premises, to the point that he was removed by a bailiff from a basement flat because it was not allowed to be used for commercial purposes. He encountered this problem and the same bailiff on more than one occasion! However, as the business expanded, debts were repaid and an official office was established. From this experience, Lord Laidlaw considers that in business 'cash is everything'.

However, Sheila McLean is concerned that business may now be leading the agenda in all aspects of life, with business models used 'for everything'. She sees this in healthcare, social services and academia, where something has to be easily measurable for it to be of value. Professor McLean contends that this means only certain things are measured and she gives the example of an academic, who may be a fantastic teacher, not being judged on the more intangible results of teaching and quality of students, 'that does not come into it'. Instead, that person is measured on how many academic papers he or she publishes each year. Professor McLean advises that academic institutions require a 'five star' rating for 'this, this and this' under these measures in order to access funding. She goes on to describe a University Principal as running a 'multi-million pound business'. Professor McLean is concerned about how appropriate such a model is to the likes of a university as she thinks that business 'lacks ethics' due to profits being paramount. At an international level, she believes this is why no great political pressure seems to be placed on countries or regimes that have large inequalities within them, as long as they are trading partners and buying, for example, 'arms from BAE'.

Unlike some elements of a structured approach, targets were discussed in both a professional and personal capacity.

'Doing what you've got to do'

Targets

George Robertson is someone who 'always has been' target driven and he gives the example of the targets he set when implementing the Strategic Defence Review of 1998. These were more rapidly deployable armed forces; an improvement in the joined up approach between the Army, Royal Navy and Royal Air Force; plus a reduction in nuclear capability but with the retention of Trident as the United Kingdom's ultimate deterrent. Lord Robertson described this to the House of Commons as 'modernising forces to deal with tomorrow's threats, rather than yesterday's enemies'. Robin Harper is more likely to use targets in his professional life than in his personal life, although he does set targets to improve his physical fitness. In politics, he thinks that you have to be target driven and prior to entering politics, when teaching, he used targets competitively. This included checking the marks that the pupils in his modern studies classes received to see if they compared well to other teachers' classes. Alan Finlayson can also be competitive when comparing results, but in general he is not overly target orientated although he does have a broad personal target of being of 'assistance'. Sheila McLean sets time related targets, both for herself and those she works with, such as postgraduate students. This can include defining an agreed timetable for work to be submitted, with quality targets coming from the critique of that work and by applying knowledge gained from experience. Kenneth Murray finds targets useful when setting out new areas of research and Noreen Murray believes that people are stimulated to achieve set targets, as is the case with Chay

Blyth who is motivated to beat targets. This is not only seen in Sir Chay's sailing records but also when he became the youngest platoon sergeant in the Parachute Regiment and the apprentice frame worker who was given his own frame after the shortest period of time. Sir Chay completed his apprenticeship in a record time of five weeks and three days, four days quicker than the previous best time.

Targets are used by Irvine Laidlaw and Evelyn Glennie in both their professional and personal lives. Dame Evelyn advises that she has 'always' been target driven and Lord Laidlaw puts in place measures that he thinks are often much more stringent than those that other people would apply. Brian Gill is another who sets exacting targets and, when setting targets, Dame Evelyn tries to 'keep it simple' and she takes the view that targets 'keep you going' and avoid 'you just drifting along'. Likewise, Sheila McLean sets 'realistic targets' because without them 'you drift'.

Other people describe themselves as less target driven but, as Jonathan Long puts it, 'hold targets lightly'. Norman Drummond takes this view when describing himself as 'goal orientated but not in the American way' where, for example, someone may want 'to be in Kansas in three years and New York in five'. A similar approach is described by Calum Colvin. He is not target driven in his personal life but does have a 'vague plan' for series of works where he uses deadlines to help focus his mind on the subject matter. Like Dr Long, Reverend Drummond and Professor Colvin, Tom Farmer takes a pragmatic view of targets. While he thinks that people must plan and think things through, he does not consider that necessarily needs to be to the nth degree. Sir Tom goes on to say that when Thomas Edison came up with a safe and economically viable light bulb, he knew, in general terms, what he was trying to achieve, rather than the exact method that would work. Sir Tom shows this pragmatism when referring to whether or not a target is met by saying that 'life has lots of chapters'.

Some individuals do not see themselves as particularly goal or target driven, for example, Margo MacDonald is 'not usually' target orientated. Michael Atiyah does not have defined targets but he does keep a list of things to do and notes of topics or projects that he is working on or may wish to progress in the future. Normally, he has 'half a dozen' or so such projects on the go at any one time. As 'you can't give up', this allows him to leave a topic, if he is 'stuck', and then come back to it from a fresh perspective after focusing on the others. In addition, this provides him with the variety that he enjoys. Sir Michael can recognise when he has completed a project or finished with a problem because 'you can nail it down' in a logical structure that shows it in the context of a continuum of ideas. Targets are not at the forefront of Lewis Robertson's thinking and he considers that he is just 'doing what you've got to do'. If business goals were to be set, Sir Lewis would concentrate on finances and the need to improve profits year on year to provide an acceptable return for investors. This is due to Sir Lewis' view that business is 'all about growth'. George Mathewson thinks that targets often lack meaning due to the future being uncertain, while Ron Hamilton believes that the over use of targets allows under performers to manipulate figures to give the impression of good performance. While he considers that such individuals will be found out over the long-term, for this reason he is not target orientated.

Whether or not people are target orientated, a structured approach is described as promoting good use and organisation of time.

'Limited time on earth'

Time

Lewis Robertson describes himself as very well organised and a meticulous time keeper. He recounts that a young civil servant asked him how he always had time to do the 'big things' and he replied by saying, 'organising my day carefully' and doing the trivial but often necessary tasks first in order to release time for those other items. It is this very organised and methodical approach which Sir Lewis credits with allowing him to participate in a large number of committees and groups. Sheila McLean is also well organised and she thinks it is that organisation which allows her to participate in her three main roles; as a University Professor, a media advisor and in committee work. Like Sir Lewis and Professor McLean, Irvine Laidlaw is well organised and feels that busy people will organise their time out of necessity, which allows them to do a lot. To illustrate this, Lord Laidlaw gives the example of returning a completed diet card to his personal trainer on the agreed date and being informed, by the trainer, that a number of less busy people had missed their deadline. As part of remaining organised, Lord Laidlaw ensures that he keeps on top of correspondence by providing prompt replies. Chay Blyth also advises that he uses time well, to the extent that he will plan ahead for the coming day. Both George Mathewson and George Robertson agree on the importance of using time well. However, neither of them consider themselves expert in time management but Lord Robertson thinks he must be 'better than most', although he jokes that 'my wife wouldn't consider me an expert time manager'.

William Stewart takes the view that it is 'what you do with the time that you have which is important', a thought that Brian Gill echoes when advising that it is time saved not wasted that is important. Lord Gill contends that organisation of time brings structure to life which can avoid, in particular, young people from becoming idle and wasting talent. When Lord Gill is travelling by train or aeroplane he will use that time to work and at points in meetings, where his full attention is not required, he will jot down notes on other topics. John Crofton also tries to make best use of spare time. When he was demobbed from the Army and looking for work he used that time to finish his medical thesis and, like Lord Gill, Sir John uses travel time to catch up on work. Tom Farmer reiterates that to use time well people have to be organised and that he is 'diary obsessed'. If he did not note everything properly in his diary, Sir Tom thinks, he could easily forget things that require his attention or miss future appointments. Michael Atiyah also relies on using a diary to remind him of meetings and he considers that to progress you must be organised, as if you are not you will 'not be able to do as much'.

Linked to her target driven approach, Evelyn Glennie used to maximise her work time but now feels that it is important to learn how to create 'my own time'. This includes making social time 'more interesting' by allowing her the freedom to do what she wants to do. In a similar vein, Tom Farmer believes it important to take time to enjoy your achievements, something that in hindsight he wishes he had done more of. He describes this as taking 'more time to smell the flowers'. In particular, he refers to occasions when he felt he had to attend meetings or 'always be there' when in fact that was not the case. Having said that, Sir Tom does not regret these decisions as he felt he was taking the correct approach at the time. Margo MacDonald is 'sometimes good' with time but in general she gets 'diverted by scooping up' other things. Calum Colvin tends to have elements of his work at the back of his mind, which means that, while he is not necessarily concentrating directly on a piece of work, over time he brings these thoughts to the studio to 'make things happen'.

Alan Finlayson is 'not bad with time' and he makes sure that he is not late for appointments and that he is prepared beforehand. Robin Harper thinks that he uses time well in his political life although he tends to take on 'too much' which means that minor things, that he should take care of in his personal life, can be neglected and build up into bigger issues. To use time well, Norman Drummond recommends, 'prioritise, look after yourself and sleep well'. He feels that it is important to understand how your body clock works but recognise that at times demanding tasks will have to be completed when required, not when someone may wish to tackle them. Brian Gill summarises his view on time and organisation when saying that we have a 'limited time on earth' and should therefore spend it usefully.

Structured Approach: Summary

'The most methodical man in Scotland'

Formulating a structured approach usually starts with analysis in order to better understand issues and to define a plan, where a methodical approach is seen to be taken to ensure that each part of the plan is properly covered. To deliver a plan via a process, strong control and direction are considered vital. Although it is recommended that a structured approach is flexible enough to ensure that concentration is given to the eventual output, even if this is achieved by a different route than the one initially envisaged. In addition, the application of new methods is seen to apply to existing processes as well as new processes or plans.

Planning and process delivery are almost exclusively referred to in terms of business or professional life. This includes a need for some individuals, who are not primarily seen as business people, to take care of business matters in order to support their careers. A holistic approach is usually taken in business, although different areas may be stressed dependent on the business, its sector and an individual's personal style. However, it is thought that business measures and structures may not be appropriate to all areas of society or all types of work.

There are a wide spectrum of views on the use and benefits of target setting. Some people have carefully defined targets in both their professional and personal lives, while others take a looser approach that places much less or no emphasis on targets. Especially in professional life, a good degree of organisation is viewed as beneficial in releasing time to do more things, including making time for yourself. This is seen in a concentration given to time saved, and what someone does, rather than time wasted and things not done.

While a structured approach is generally thought of in a professional context, people skills are highlighted across all aspects of life.

CHAPTER IX

People Skills

'As good as any qualification on a piece of paper'

How are people skills learnt?
What are the best methods of communication?
How is trust gained?

In this Chapter people skills are discussed alongside how they may be obtained and put into practice. This includes forming a team. People skills are viewed as an essential part of leadership, which is the topic of Chapter x.

'Be good to people'

Importance

Tom Farmer asserts that the most important aspect of either personal or business life is relating to and communicating with other people. An ability to create and strengthen relationships is viewed as vital by Jonathan Long, who notes that there is a need to work with and be close to others in all facets of life. In his professional experience, Dr Long emphasises the role of a school headmaster as 'custodian of atmosphere and ethos' which, he thinks, is provided by people skills. John Crofton considers people skills to be of immense importance and recommends getting to know other people as just because someone comes from a different background it 'does not automatically make them nasty'. In a similar way, Robin Harper thinks that people skills give an ability to empathise and he describes people skills as being 'as good as any qualification on a piece of paper'.

Most obviously, people skills allow individuals to build relationships with, for example, John Crofton making a point of getting to know patients. This, he believes, helps markedly in diagnosis and cure because tuberculosis is a 'social disease', where social problems are paramount in 'one-third of cases'.

Lewis Robertson saw the benefit of the close working relationship he established with those he describes as the 'pioneers of recovery banking' at Barclay's Bank, and both Tom Devine and Calum Colvin refer to a few friends and colleagues with whom they discuss their work. Professor Colvin takes this approach as some artists can be very competitive with the 'temptation to get nippy'. It is by having shared experiences that Evelyn Glennie thinks people are really able to connect and relate to each other. She argues that by sharing or having similar experiences people can empathise through knowing what someone else is feeling, rather than trying to guess emotions or just showing sympathy. In a similar fashion, she thinks that a shared spirituality or, maybe better, shared ways of thinking can further enhance that connection and offer more meaning to life. Importantly, adds Dame Evelyn, this allows people to take appropriate action relevant to the circumstances. An instance of this comes from Chay Blyth who, from his experiences of sailing, was able to empathise with and give practical advice to participants in the British Steel Challenge round the world sailing race.

An ability to get on with and relate to people is something that George Robertson thinks, in the main, Scots have and he describes Scottish people as gregarious with a tendency to make friends easily. George Mathewson considers himself 'lucky' that he generally 'gets on with people' and, in order to form and grow a relationship, Tom Farmer believes you should always 'be good to people' because 'what goes around comes around' or, as Brian Gill puts it, 'you meet the same people on the way up, as on the way down'.

Like other areas, people skills are thought to be moulded in upbringing and further developed from experience, although some individual's are viewed as having more natural people skills.

'Smooth out some of the rough edges'

Natural and learnt

Ron Hamilton does not see himself as a 'natural networker', and Irvine Laidlaw sees some people as being more naturally charismatic or charming and he describes himself as not having 'natural interpersonal skills'. Brian Gill advises that he has met outstanding people who lack skills as communicators because 'you've either got it or you haven't'. This is something that Evelyn Glennie sees and she believes that some people are just 'natural and genuine' in their people skills.

John Crofton thinks he has an inbuilt interest in people, even although he was shy in his youth. These people skills were bolstered by the experience of living in close proximity to other pupils and the teachers when he attended Tonbridge School in Kent. They were then further developed, in line with his confidence, from his army experiences. Alan Finlayson is naturally interested in people, something he thinks that can make him seem 'nosey'. However, he does add that the more you know people, the more you will understand them and the less judgmental you will be about them. It is from reflecting on and applying learning from experience that Irvine Laidlaw thinks he has improved his people skills, while George Robertson advises that he learns from the interactions that he has with other people. In addition, he comments that even if these experiences have proven unsatisfactory, he is not bitter and does not hold grudges. Likewise, Sheila McLean is not put off if she thinks someone has, say, taken advantage of her because she believes that you 'must engage'. However, she does think that the ability to learn new people skills diminishes over time due to repeated habits becoming more ingrained. Experience is also given by George Mathewson as the main way in which people skills are developed. Although he does believe that teaching can 'smooth out some of the rough edges' or tackle the extremes of dysfunctional behaviour. Similarly, Margo MacDonald does not believe that people skills can really be taught. Having said that, like Sir George, she thinks that teaching may persuade some people to think about and perhaps moderate unsuitable behaviour. Tom Farmer suggests that attitude and people skills should be considered together. In particular, he believes that it is your attitude to other people and yourself that will define how you come across in personal interactions. As in attitude, Sir Tom thinks that people skills can be learnt from training but more so from day-to-day experiences, something both Kenneth Murray and Lewis Robertson concur in. Sir Kenneth advises that he has not attended any type of personal skills course but learnt his people skills through experience, and Sir Lewis does not view himself as a natural people manager but has developed those skills from experience.

Tom Devine agrees that interpersonal skills are usually learnt from experience but he also thinks they can be taught. Norman Drummond and Evelyn Glennie believe these skills can be taught, as does Robin Harper, who thinks that people skills such as counselling can be taught. Chay Blyth also considers that people skills can be taught, something he did when teaching a crew of paratroopers etiquette prior to the Whitbread Round the World Race of 1973. He refers to this as a 'couth course'. From his previous sailing experience, Sir Chay was aware of the formal receptions, meals and presentations that they would attend and he was keen to ensure that the crew members were prepared through knowing the accepted manners for such events. He describes this as something he lacked in his younger days. The course proved beneficial and he sees merit in developing the 'couth course' into other areas of personal development. Sir Chay thinks it is often about how you portray yourself, including 'simple courtesies', like thanking someone in a letter and learning how to give and take compliments. 'Even just smiling and showing decency will make you stand out' and Sir Chay stresses the importance of learning these skills because he thinks that 'you have about 15 seconds' before people will make up their mind about you. Tom Farmer also emphasises the need to make a good impression, something he describes as an ability to 'sell yourself'.

Good people skills are thought to allow individuals to relate to each other in a more meaningful way, with this perhaps increased through understanding and managing each other's expecatations.

'Make sure you deliver on promises'

Managing expectations

William Stewart contends that the ability to connect with people and manage other people's expectations depends on how well you can relate to their interests or concerns. To illustrate this, he highlights the different breadth and depth of conversation that he would expect to have with a writer compared to a scientist. In addition, he stresses that a conversation is a dialogue with two sides where there must be something in it for each participant, to which he adds 'I am not into monologues'. Jackie Stewart agrees with this and states that if you 'take everything and leave nothing' that is 'greed'. Sir Jackie thinks that by 'leaving something for their benefit' goodwill will be developed which, he believes, promotes respect and credibility. As part of this, Sir Jackie emphasises the importance of making time to talk to people because that gives you the chance to 'deal with a misconception' or 'debatable opinion'. Like Sir Jackie, Robin Harper prioritises time to meet people. This provides him with the 'opportunity to understand others' and to present his own ideas. Similarly, Ron Hamilton loves to speak to and receive feedback from his customers. This gives him the chance to 'turn customers' who may be sceptical or less sure about his product and service.

The benefit of understanding others in order to manage expectations is provided in an example given by Evelyn Glennie, who was asked by a group of American business people to make a presentation to them. She explored their reasons for approaching her and, from understanding those motives, was able to give a presentation that both appealed to them and was beyond their expectations. In making that additional effort, Dame Evelyn hopes that the participants took more from the event than they anticipated and that she created further business opportunity for herself, as they may be more inclined to use her again or recommend her to other people. Tom Farmer wholeheartedly endorses an approach of managing expectations. In particular, he tries his best not to let his staff down (as he sees them as the first priority in business) although, he says, on occasion 'it happened'. To tackle any staff concerns at Kwik-Fit, Sir Tom implemented a scheme where an appointed 'Action Man' guaranteed that any staff issue would be addressed within 24 hours. In the same way that this scheme helped to manage staff expectations, employees were trained to manage customer expectations. For instance, after work was completed on a car and the customer was just about drive off he or she would be called back, 'Mr or Mrs Brown, a minute please'. The member of staff would then clean the car windscreen and headlights. Sir Tom believed that in order to strengthen and grow the Kwik-Fit customer base it was important to 'give that wee bit more than the customer expected'.

An ability to manage expectations is put to the test in what Ron Hamilton calls the 'innovation dilemma'. This refers to keeping existing customers happy when new methods are implemented as, for example, when he introduced sales to customers via the Internet. This brought with it the potential conflict of selling direct to customers who may be clients of the opticians that he was already supplying. He understood the difficulties these opticians faced due to the levels of fixed costs inherent in their business and he implemented a solution where, if a personal customer identifies the optician he or she uses (a facility for that is embedded in the sales process), he provides the optician with a financial rebate. The apparent fairness of this approach has allowed him to manage concerns and to continue to supply both opticians and contact lens users direct. He also provides that 'something extra' by taking a personal interest in service, which includes writing to customers that raise a question or concern. In addition, as contact lenses are not suitable for everyone, he provides new customers with four trial lenses as part of their order. If a customer is not satisfied a full refund is made, although any problems tend to be down to an incorrect prescription. However, overall he thinks the most important way to manage expectations is to 'make sure you deliver on promises'.

This ability to manage expectations can be prevalent in all walks of life. For example, Robin Harper describes his role when working on the Children's

Panel as a 'mediator', where he tried to balance the needs and expectations of all sides. Tom Farmer gives the example of when he saw Pope John Paul II, who was near the end of his life and wheel chair bound. John Paul II had mumbled some inaudible words to the assembled crowd but, as he was about to leave, he turned and waved to which the crowd responded positively as this final gesture gave that something extra, beyond their expectations.

Calum Colvin does not worry about things outside his control when trying to manage expectations, and Jackie Stewart says that there will 'always be somebody who is not pleased'. This is something that Tom Farmer agrees with when saying 'that you learn no matter how hard you try, you will not always please everyone'.

Also, the method of communication used is given as central to how people manage expectations and relate to each other.

'Think before you speak'

Communicating

George Mathewson describes communication as fundamental to personal life and 'key to running a business'. Ron Hamilton agrees that 'communication is so important in running a business', while Tom Farmer adds that 'building personal connections is integral to business success'. As such, communication is viewed as an essential element of a structured approach with, for example, George Robertson underlining that 'you need to be in the driving seat' in order to get your message across. In addition, Irvine Laidlaw stresses the need to use the most appropriate means of communication dependent on circumstances, be that face to face, letter, fax, telephone or email. However, Robin Harper notes that the increasing number of communication channels brought by the world wide web, such as 'YouTube and Facebook', will eventually stretch his already limited time further. For example, he comments that 'I've not even looked at my own website!'. Chay Blyth is concerned that these advances in technology can make people lazy in their communication. This, he thinks, sees people using text and other instant messaging systems because they worry about the speed with which they interact. Sir Chay believes that these communication tools are impersonal and that their over use may mean that people avoid getting to know each other.

John Crofton 'always prepared the ground well' and adapts the message and mode of communication to circumstances. For example, the Church of Scotland was so concerned by the 'scandal and public pressure' caused by the increase of tuberculosis in Scotland that it invited Sir John and others to take to the pulpits to allow them to explain these health issues. Also, Sir John mentions that, when he was Dean, there was a time when there was a great jealousy between those at the Edinburgh Royal Infirmary and the city's Western General Hospital. This caused a breakdown in the relationship between the two groups. He felt that there were good people working at both hospitals but that the Western General suffered from low funding. Thus, he determined that its capabilities would be increased by the prestige that would come from making one of its members of staff a Professor. However, the friction between the two groups continued until he decided to take all those involved away for a weekend. This allowed them to meet each other and talk through and resolve differences. Sir John describes the personal contact and opening up of communication between the various parties as a 'tremendous help' in resolving, what appeared to be, 'an impossible position'. Sir John also believes that to get people involved and to influence them it is best to go and meet the person which, 'after a quiet word', usually gets things done. In business, Ron Hamilton recommends verbal communication, to give personal contact, followed by a written communication to ensure clarity. The ability to explain something succinctly is also of great value and he states that 'if you can't explain your business idea in 30 seconds then you probably don't understand it yourself'. Communication, like managing expectations, is seen in actions. This is something that George Mathewson considers vital and he reiterates that you communicate your own commitment by doing what you say you will do.

Giving and receiving feedback is considered to be an important part of the communication process. This is seen as an exchange of ideas or a debate, something Chay Blyth thinks is beneficial in allowing people to put their point across with 'verve, in a non-violent manner'. Calum Colvin sees debate and feedback as a vital part of encouraging development and, in particular, he thinks it is important to tell people what has gone well. He describes this approach as 'better than bullying'. However, Jackie Stewart does caution that, in the same way 'you check the water before having a shower or bath', you should check or think before 'blurting something out'. This is a sentiment that Tam Dalyell agrees with when recommending that you should 'think before you speak'.

In addition, communication and wider people skills are described as an essential part of creating a good team.

'A foreign body, a virus'

The team

Jackie Stewart always looks to surround himself with the best people he can find, while Alan Finlayson likes to be around interesting people who can stimulate him. Similarly, Chay Blyth wants to be with positive and 'dynamic people' and he believes that, in the same way 'success breeds success', 'good guys attract good guys'. Sir Chay adds that even one negative person can have a very detrimental impact on the people around them.

'The team' can include all those that may provide help and advice. For example, both Chay Blyth and William Stewart note that people require to take expert advice, in addition to using their own judgment and the judgment of those closest to them. Due to the need for quick answers, Sir William considers that this is particularly true in government and he counsels that, like in other areas of life, 'do not think that you know everything but be sure you know the real experts in the relevant field'. As part of Lewis Robertson's approach he also gets the support of good people, such as when he insisted that 'a bright civil servant' should be seconded as his personal assistant when he was Chief Executive of the Scottish Development Agency.

Ron Hamilton believes that suppliers and others outside of his direct business control are part of a wider team. He thinks that this holistic view is beneficial because it can promote the stability that he values. For example, he continues to use the same toolmaker, financial advisor, bank and legal advisor as when he started out in business. He adds that the relationship is always with the individual and, therefore, when his legal advisor moved firm, he followed.

Developing people within a team is something that Tom Farmer encourages and he took it as a compliment if an employee was able to move on to other things having gained a strong base of learning in his organisation. In addition, he always welcomes back good people, something that Ron Hamilton also subscribes to, and Sir Tom takes pleasure in the trust that people put in his organisation, for example, when an employee asked for a job for his son. Sir Tom advises that those requests, to take on other workers and instances of returning employees, were reasonably frequent occurrences. Sir Tom takes an inclusive but firm view when introducing new employees or team members, stating that 'if you want to be part of the team, you are welcome to join, everyone is welcome to join'. However if, for example, a member of staff was not interested or had a could not care less attitude then 'you can leave now, go'.

Alan Finlayson notes that you will not always like the people you are working with and, indeed, they might not like you. Having said that, he emphasises the need to get on with people in a professional capacity. Margo MacDonald also comments that there will be times when people do not get on with each other but, if she finds herself working with someone who she is not connecting well with, she always tries to maintain a 'professional' approach.

In business, George Mathewson believes that people should be allowed to play to their strengths and that it is important to have the right person in the right job, something he ties to personality types and the attitude someone displays. When developing an effective team or good and reliable people to spend time with, Evelyn Glennie starts with the premise that 'everyone has something to offer'. In the business world a new team member is described by Ron Hamilton as akin to taking on 'a foreign body, a virus', which the corporate entity has to deal with and assimilate gradually into its culture and way of doing things. Getting the right person in the right job, whilst retaining freshness in approach, is something Irvine Laidlaw strives for. In particular, Lord Laidlaw actively looks to gain better or more suitable people when growing a business. This is due to the difference he sees in the skills required to grow or participate in a small company compared to those required for a large organisation. When buying companies, he often considered that they had reached a 'glass ceiling' due to keeping people for too long and he was regularly told, rather proudly, that 'Jim has been with us 15 years'. However, he feels that long retention of employees in growing companies is not necessarily advantageous. Lord Laidlaw acknowledges that it is not pleasant for an employee to be fired or made redundant but he considers that they would be worse off if they stayed in an unsuitable role because they would not enjoy the job. He adds that this would be exacerbated by the continual pressure from him if they were not performing satisfactorily. Having said that, over the 30 year period that he was at the helm of the Institute for International Research he 'met many wonderful people'.

George Mathewson recommends that you 'choose your friends carefully' and he considers that one of his strengths is 'choosing and listening to good people'. George Robertson describes the Scottish political scene as the 'toughest that I have encountered' and he advises that, at times, it was not always clear cut who was supporting him. Lord Robertson goes on to draw a comparison with the conflict in Kosovo where, he comments, you knew exactly who was on whose side. Sheila McLean 'despairs' at her inability to 'suss people out', as she always assumes that people are 'nice' and finds it unpleasant if she is proved wrong. She refers to The Idiot by Fyodor Dostoevsky when explaining that perhaps seeing the good in people, even if at times you are taken advantage off, is a better way to live than taking a selfish view of life. Also, she does not see herself as a manager because she does not like confrontation and finds it difficult to challenge inappropriate behaviour in others. For that reason she has avoided roles such as head of department. Similarly, Alan Finlayson does not think himself good at challenging inappropriate behaviour, which means that he is sometimes prepared to put up with failings.

As well as helping to build a strong team, it is suggested that through people skills trust can be established.

'Be trustworthy yourself'

Trust

George Mathewson considers that trust may be gained from managing expectations and doing what you say you will do, which he stresses requires honesty and commitment. To build trust, Sheila McLean advises that you have to 'be trustworthy yourself' which, she thinks, is demonstrated by not cheating, deceiving or letting other people down. Tom Farmer emphasises the need to trust others in the first instance, something Evelyn Glennie describes as 'positive openness'. Lewis Robertson believes that trust is often linked to length of service and that people respect and trust those with experience, which can then provide loyalty. Sir Lewis describes the trust that he established when working on public sector projects and with those at Barclay's Bank during corporate recoveries as fundamental to the success of these undertakings. In many ways, Sir Lewis believes he had more freedom to push forward ideas in the private sector because there tended to be fewer stakeholders than in the public sector. He advises that by dealing with a smaller number of stakeholders closer working relationships are established. This, he believes, leads to a reduction in bureaucracy and an increase in the speed of decision making. He thinks that position has worsened from when he was overseeing the construction of Ninewells Hospital in Dundee throughout the 1960s when he had one Government Minister to deal with, 'now there would be 22'. By having that trust, Chay Blyth believes people are more likely to speak their mind and not just say what they think is right, while Ron Hamilton contends that by nurturing loyalty, trust is built, which establishes honesty and avoids the temptation to 'bury mistakes'. This loyalty and appreciation of his own employees was demonstrated when he made a cash donation to staff when he sold his daily disposable contact lens business, 'Award', to Bausch & Lomb. To maximise the value of the payment, he argued strongly against the Inland Revenue's stance of wanting to tax each individual on that money until he won the right to make the payment tax free, including the element that would have been lost in tax. He believes in building loyalty, based on honesty, and he has a strong team of trusted people that he can turn to. For example, he places all his design work with one person who he trusts to provide the requirements at very short notice because she has a feel for the overall style of work. This curtails bureaucracy in briefing or proofing designs and is something he believes that a large design company could not do as effectively.

This need for trust and buy-in to ideas is something John Crofton has seen when tackling health problems caused by damp council housing. To help address that issue he formed a team of professionals, including a research and development officer and 'a good GP'. Although difficulties were experienced in ensuring that all the various parties worked together. However, by strong communication and ensuring everyone was engaged, trust between the different groups was established and then retained by having local people lead the initiative. That was done, in part, by local people filming the difficulties they were experiencing, with that film then used to secure the required funding. When bringing people together and establishing trust, George Mathewson thinks that the crucial element is to ensure that you are absolutely straight with people and tackle problems early on before they have had a chance to fester and become larger difficulties.

People Skills: Summary

'As good as any qualification on a piece of paper'

While some people may have a natural aptitude for people skills, it is thought that these skills are enhanced by experience and, perhaps up to a point, may be taught. Through people skills, it is believed that expectations can be better met from establishing a common understanding via a dialogue. Furthermore, a shared or joint experience may provide additional awareness that enables people to give more meaningful assistance than they would otherwise have been able to do. In addition, doing what you say you will do is given as an obvious way to manage expectations.

Personal contact, where people meet, is often seen as the best method of communication. However, different types of communication may be more appropriate depending on circumstances, and people are seen to communicate a strong message through their actions. Feedback, challenge and debate are also viewed as important facets of communication.

The influence of fellow 'team' members is described in a similar way to the influence of role models in upbringing and of later peer groups, where people can have either a positive or negative influence on each other. In addition, building long-term relationships are thought to assist stability in business. Although there may be a requirement for a certain amount of staff turnover to keep thinking fresh and ensure that, as the business grows and changes, the most appropriate person is in the most suitable role.

People skills, displayed with honesty and commitment whilst showing trust in other people, are described as encouraging people to trust each other. When establishing that trust or managing expectations it can be beneficial to give that bit more than was expected. This is thought to assist in establishing openness, which may go on to give respect and loyalty.

Communication and people skills are viewed as an important part of leadership.

Leadership

'At the top of the mountains, not in the valleys'

What should an effective leader do?
What are the key aspects of leadership?
Can leadership skills be learnt?

This section discusses the attributes of leadership and how these are obtained and displayed. Leadership draws on all the aspects discussed in this book including review, which is the final area discussed in this Chapter.

'Strength of character'

Leadership elements

George Mathewson, George Robertson, Lewis Robertson, John Crofton and William Stewart all advise that a leader must be able to see and assimilate the big picture and then transfer that into practical action. Sir William describes himself as a 'big picture person' and he advises that a leader has to be 'at the top of the mountains, not in the valleys'. Sir John adds to this by saying that he 'had a capacity to see what needs to be done', and Evelyn Glennie names Nelson Mandela as an example of a leader who she describes as having 'humility, perseverance and stature'.

Jonathan Long views a leader as someone who can exercise an influence over other people for a common good. He believes that requires determination and resilience plus an ability to coach. Sheila McLean thinks that the sign of a good leader is someone who people want to emulate. This, she believes, comes from the leader having proved himself or herself, or from having charisma and popularity. John Crofton sees 'organisation, direction and orders' as the main qualities of leadership and Norman Drummond believes that a strong leader should demonstrate 'exemplary behaviours' for others to observe and follow. Jackie Stewart also thinks leadership by example is important, to which he adds common sense, while Chay Blyth suggests that the key component of leadership is 'enthusiasm' for what you are doing and who you are doing it with. Alan Finlayson believes that good leaders need to know 'what they are talking about' which, he thinks, comes from not being too remote from the day-to-day issues that their department faces. This was one of the reasons why he opted not to move into a full-time management role but retain an element of operational work within the Children's Hearing System. By doing so, he was able to relate to staff and avoid the questions of 'what does he know?' or 'when did he last see an angry family?'. He does add that direct work with families and Hearing Panel Members was the part of the work he most enjoyed. The attributes that Irvine Laidlaw thinks leaders should have are; an ability to take risks, being dissatisfied so that they are always looking for improvements, and an ability to encourage others, especially in adversity. George Robertson sees the important qualities of leadership as listening, making the decisions, an ability to explain the decisions made and then seeing decisions through to a successful conclusion. Michael Atiyah thinks that a leader should give guidance and set standards for others to improve upon, although not in the manner of a military leader but rather by providing intellectual leadership. It is 'strength of character' that Margo MacDonald thinks gives effective leadership. However, she is unsure of the attributes that give that character as all the political leaders that she has met are 'deeply flawed in one way or another'. Robin Harper does not see himself as a leader and he points out that the Green party is 'not structured in that way'. Nonetheless, as Co-convener of the party and high profile parliamentarian he realises the influence he can have. As an example of this, he mentions that if he nominates someone for a particular party position they are almost 'certain to get the nod', which puts him off putting people forward.

In general, Chay Blyth has seen two types of leaders. The first is an organised and confident leader, such as Mirabel Topham who invited him and John Ridgway to the 1967 Grand National. She made sure that everything ran like clockwork, including 1st class train travel and a car to collect them at Liverpool Station. Sir Chay notes that her staff adored her and he describes her as a 'quiet leader', who led by being very well organised and exuding confidence. The second type of leader he has seen is a charismatic leader, which he witnessed when he attended a performance of 'Hello Dolly'. The show 'was a bit dull' until the leading female injected a high tempo that energised the audience through her enthusiasm. This brought the whole cast to life and made the performance a triumph. Sir Chay describes her leadership as charismatic from the magnetism of her presence.

In addition, a common and key aspect of leadership is given by Lewis Robertson as making decisions and then being firm in implementing those decisions.

'Grasp the nettle'

Decision making

George Robertson states that 'a government department requires you to make decisions', and Lewis Robertson believes that a common reason for company problems is a failure to reach decisions and 'grasp the nettle' on difficult or fundamental issues. Sir Lewis stresses the need for clear decision making, with the decision written down so as to minimise misinterpretation. Calum Colvin emphasises that the decision taken must be credible and not, for example, be 'misguided political correctness'. Professor Colvin adds that if the decision is 'nonsenical people laugh at it and there is a problem'.

Norman Drummond suggests that an inclusive leadership approach works best and he considers it crucial to build a consensus of opinion in the early stages of decision making. George Mathewson advises that a dictatorial approach is seen less and less although, he adds, many great businesses have been built on an authoritarian approach because there is 'more than one way to skin a cat'. Sir George thinks the effectiveness of the approach will depend on the leader's personality traits and choice of attitude. In addition, as part of decision making, Sir George encourages people to play to their strengths. This is something that John Crofton also does. Sir John does not consider himself 'bossy' and always tried to make decisions that allowed people to do tasks which interested them and played to their strengths. However, he notes that one of his successors was 'terribly bossy', which upset staff and led to a less effective team. Lewis Robertson advises that initial uncertainty is 'wise and right' when trying to reach a decision, as people must 'struggle to see the right way forward'. However, Sir Lewis believes that once the decision is made it must be followed through vigorously. This is something that Robin Harper sees difficulties with when a decision is taken and then not controlled. He thinks that was an issue when he worked on the Children's Panel, work that he describes as 'exhausting'. This was due to him making decisions on a child's welfare but not being able to supervise these decisions and only getting involved again if there was a problem. In addition, he thinks that to make a good decision people require confidence derived from having analysed all relevant information. Chay Blyth considers it proper to have challenge and debate in the initial stages of decision making, although he thinks there comes a time when the decision must be made and adhered to. When making a decision, Sir Chay recommends 'always taking the bolder, never the easier path', a quote he takes from Field Marshall William Slim the former Allied Commander of South East Asia during the Second World War and Governor General of Australia from 1952 until 1960.

In the Children's Hearing System, Alan Finlayson was called upon to make what could be 'life or death' decisions for children because the result might mean the return of a child to the parents or could lead directly to the child being received into care. To demonstrate the critical nature of this work, he recalls a case where, along with a colleague, they decided that an infant should not be referred to a Hearing as they concluded there was insufficient factual information to substantiate grounds for a referral. Social workers had expressed grave concerns about the child and had a referral been made it is highly likely that she would have been placed in care. While he was satisfied the decision was correct based on the information available, he did feel uncomfortable with this and can still remember the day in 1977 when he was informed that the child had died, at home, in 'mysterious cot death circumstances'. Even although it is 'purely speculation' that something more malicious was done to the child, this is a case that he has reflected back on a number of times. He advises that, more importantly than sharing the burden of responsibility for 'critical' cases, the practice of joint decision making recognised the potential impact of all Reporter decisions on a child's future and that these decisions merited optimum consideration,

In business, Ron Hamilton does not believe in making decisions by committee because he believes that produces weak conclusions through the need to make compromises. This, he thinks, gives mediocre results and he would prefer the decision to be more polarised thus giving either 'a right roaring success or a blinding failure'. He contends that a failure can be rectified by applying learning, although he tries to minimise the possibility of failure by upfront research that looks to stack the odds of success in his favour.

There may be some uncertainty when coming to a decision but once the decision has been made it is recommended that it is followed through on robustly. This is thought to require control and certainty.

'Occasionally wrong, always certain'

Certainty

A high level of certainty is something George Robertson purports, saying that once you have come to a decision 'stick with it'. Calum Colvin takes a similar view when using the word 'stubborn' to describe himself, and Lewis Robertson considers that once a decision has been taken it must be applied strongly. Sir Lewis believes that, in business, you must have a strong will and display a commanding and convincing approach which can force people to change whilst retaining their confidence and trust. This allows the leading person to drive forward a process and dispel uncertainty through demonstrating a determination and confidence that takes other people along and gains their buy-in. Norman Drummond considers that courage is also required to drive forward decisions because there will be some 'knee knocking moments'. When making and then implementing a decision, Reverend Drummond recommends that you 'look, listen, be brave and know in your heart what is true and right'.

Certainty, displayed through confidence, assists a leader to retain credibility and remain in control of any given situation. Examples of that are provided by William Stewart and John Crofton from when they had a responsibility to university students.

Sir John was Dean of the Faculty of Medicine between 1963 and 1967 and Vice Principal of Edinburgh University during 1969 and 1970. This was a period of student militancy and, while he felt that the student leaders were reasonable, there were some extremists in their ranks. Although he avoided the personal attacks which the University Principal, Michael Swan, was subjected to. On one occasion a mob of close to 400 students descended on the Medical School causing alarm to the point that the police were called. Sir John met them on the stairs of the building and they were surprised that he was not upset by their actions but instead referred to them as 'basically decent people' and persuaded them to attend a formal meeting in one of the lecture theatres. The students were 'rife with conspiracy theories', which he was able to alleviate, and he defused the tense situation by joking 'as Vice Principal I demand to be hanged with a silken cord!'. He continued to hold regular meetings with the students and he took a 'Machiavellian' approach in order to ensure that he was in control of the situation. This was often as simple as chairing meetings at 9 am because the 'more extreme elements' were rarely up in time, so it was the 'more reasonable and representative' students that attended.

Sir William would always ensure that he remained in control of his lectures, which often up to 300 students attended. If he received a 'difficult question' he would prefer to see the student separately if he did not have a clear response at hand, or discuss it with them in smaller groups, or promise to come back to the class in the next lecture on the points raised. If he allowed all 300 students to participate at once he was unlikely to be able to retain control of the debate, particularly as there were likely to be some in the 300 'who are brighter than you!'.

Ron Hamilton reiterates that strong decision making and clear direction are prerequisites in business, with his wife, Moya Hamilton, referring to him as 'occasionally wrong, always certain'.

'Polishing a kernel'

Learning

Some people are thought to have a natural aptitude for leadership, although both John Crofton and Lewis Robertson think that it is experience which allows leadership qualities to flourish. Sir John considers that it was his experience in the Army that taught him leadership and Sir Lewis thinks that leadership is 'difficult to teach' because it is 'learnt by experience', a view that led him to decline a student proposal to conduct an academic study to teach leadership. This view is taken by George Robertson, who advises that 'nobody taught me how to make decisions', and George Mathewson, who states that he would 'like to say that you can learn leadership but when you see someone who has it, it is pretty apparent'. Irvine Laidlaw also doubts that leadership can be taught but he does believe that you can improve certain aspects, something he describes as akin to 'polishing a kernel'. Lord Laidlaw thinks that leadership courses are in reality teaching, or trying to develop, interpersonal skills through instilling confidence and enthusiasm. Alan Finlayson also thinks that leadership is difficult to teach, although he considers that elements of management can be taught to help people develop their existing management skills. This, thinks Robin Harper, gives leadership with a 'small l', for example when someone is taught how to lead an outward bound course. Sheila McLean also believes that leadership is difficult to teach, especially aspects of charisma or popularity. In particular, Professor McLean thinks that teaching can only provide a veneer that other people will eventually see through. Chay Blyth agrees that certain leadership elements cannot be taught, such as the charisma that leaders often display. However, he thinks that other elements, like the ability to project yourself through an improved self-awareness, can be taught.

While leadership can be enhanced by learning from others, a leading person may also inspire other people. For example, Tom Farmer, George Mathewson, Lewis Robertson and William Stewart all hope that they have inspired those around them and have received feedback of some success. Calum Colvin was inspired by those artists that came before him and he hopes that others are inspired by the artists who are now living and working in Scotland, something that he saw as 'rare' when he commenced his career. Similarly, Evelyn Glennie hopes that she can inspire the next generation of musicians by sharing knowledge and through her music.

In addition, review is described as a key method of learning and as an important part of leadership.

'Keep it in its place'

Review

On a daily basis, Evelyn Glennie evaluates any critiques of her performances alongside her own take on how the day has gone. From that review she identifies areas in her attitude and approach that she could improve upon. Sheila McLean takes a structured approach to review in her professional life but less so in her personal life. This is because she considers that events in her personal life are less likely to happen again. Professor McLean advises that this review helps her to 'keep a sense of self' and enables her to 'keep it in its place', rather than letting go of something. Alan Finlayson also makes a point of reviewing his work and, for example, advises that he does not view a speech as finished until after he has reviewed it following its delivery to see what he could improve upon. From a conscious effort to improve and do 'what is right', Jonathan Long tries to be a 'better person' on a day-to-day basis as he strives for purer thinking through his spirituality. As part of this, he reviews his approach to see what he might have done better. This allows him to 'recognise the red flags' that warn him against repeating unsuitable behaviour and that direct him to more appropriate actions. Dr Long uses this strategy to improve and deal with the day-to-day issues and ambiguities that life brings, rather than a method of meeting any future targeted ambition.

Jackie Stewart considers that review may be more prevalent in people who are dyslexic because dyslexia forces you 'to look hard at yourself to identify what is good and how best to develop your attributes'. In addition, Norman Drummond contends that review informs and stretches ambition and, assuming that errors are learnt from and not repeated, he maintains that 'the more mistakes you make the wiser you become'.

Lewis Robertson reiterates that once a decision has been made it should be followed through vigorously and that ongoing doubts are debilitating. Sir Lewis does though believe that review is important if crucial new information comes to light. He sees this as a conscious part of the process because he considers that 'nobody is infallible'. Sir Lewis has rescued seven large companies from severe financial problems, with Stakis plc typical of these in that it had heavily over borrowed. Under his guidance borrowings were controlled and profits restored through his leadership approach of strong decision making, firm implementation of decisions and appropriate review. Similarly, George Robertson considers review to be a proper part of the implementation process because it allows new information or changing circumstances to be taken into account. Thus, Lord Robertson advises that by ensuring there is a place for review in whatever he is doing he hopes to avoid persevering in the wrong direction. Tom Farmer takes the same approach when advising that he is willing to adapt to new circumstances to ensure that he does not go down the 'wrong road', and Lord Robertson adds an old military adage that 'no plan survives the first engagement with the enemy'.

Leadership: Summary

'At the top of the mountains, not in the valleys'

A leader is described as providing guidance and influence over other people through an ability to absorb the bigger picture and, from that, provide meaningful actions. Key components of leadership are given as an ability to take decisions and a certainty that dispels any doubts that may have been rightly present when coming to the decision. Such certainty is seen to assist a leader in retaining control of any given situation. These qualities are thought to be supported by a wide range of skills, including: motivating others to improve, facilitating learning, providing encouragement, setting high standards, developing ideas, taking appropriate risks, displaying confidence, persevering, giving a structure in which people can work, relating to others, and communicating effectively.

Some people are thought to have more natural leadership abilities, which may be improved by learning from experience, and it seen as difficult to teach leadership in a more formal setting. In addition, within leadership, as in other areas, review is given as a method of improvement.

CHAPTER XI

Respect

'It is not how you behave in the company of kings'

The contributors referred to what they believe gives respect and their views on the recognition that they have received. Finally, the choices that are made throughout life are discussed.

'Do things that would be respected by people that you admire'

Respect

Norman Drummond believes that when people gain seniority and wealth they can forget the shared values of common humanity that, he thinks, are attained by 'being grounded'. Reverend Drummond describes these values as being 'good, kind, thoughtful and truthful'. Jonathan Long sees these attributes forming a moral character that is 'mainly caught' from the habitual influences of upbringing and experience. Dr Long likens values to fruits that ripen over time if proper attention is paid to the roots, the unseen part of a tree which the farmer must invest time in whilst retaining faith that the tree will grow and produce fruit. He does add that the farmer can 'hot house' his crop but the end product does not 'taste the same'. From giving this analogy, Dr Long purports a shift in emphasis from dealing with the problems and difficulties of behaviour after they are apparent, to 'cultivation' and ingraining positive approaches from the earliest stage. He reiterates that it is these early influences that will shape values. Also, Dr Long argues that psychologist Abraham Maslow's much quoted 'hierarchy of needs' is in fact 'upside down'. Dr Long contends that people have an underlying morality, lack of prejudice and acceptance of facts, rather than attaining these through eventual 'self-actualisation'. He points out that Abraham Maslow's work was a theoretical socioeconomic model and that research has shown 'that theory to be wrong'.

Dr Long is concerned that people tend to value what is measured which, he thinks, may cause 'a fear of ambiguity and unpredictability' and could lead to mediocrity. However, ultimately he believes that respect comes from the value you place on human life. William Stewart adds to this when saying that the 'most important things to human beings are the desire to stay alive and for their gene pool to prosper'. For that reason, Sir William believes that government can never neglect health and education.

Ron Hamilton believes in promoting honesty, integrity and pragmatism through trust and goodwill. In business, he generally does not have contracts in place with those he supplies because he believes that encourages these virtues. In addition, he thinks this ensures that his business keeps a strong commercial edge as it has to be good at what it does because people are not obliged to use it for purely contractual reasons. Generating and having goodwill is something which Tom Devine also values. He assumes that if you do a job properly and behave equably with people, in effect doing as you would want someone to do unto you, then 'everything should be fine'.

In academia, Michael Atiyah thinks that respect comes from your contribution and your achievements. More widely, he sees respect derived from honesty, being helpful and being friendly. Sir Michael likes to see people setting a good example and being thoughtful towards other people, as 'a good man may get respect'. He adds that, 'in the old days', respect came from being 'a gentleman' and was afforded to those who were in senior positions or were more experienced. Alan Finlayson values people who show understanding towards others and he respects imagination, reliability, sensitivity and honesty. George Mathewson also values honesty and believes that people can gain respect from 'being likeable', although he adds that 'you do not have to like someone to respect them'. In contrast, Sir George does not respect dishonesty or people who 'don't live up to their own promises'. Tam Dalyell respects the ambition 'to achieve something, rather than be somebody', and Chay Blyth values hard work, honesty, integrity and manners but does not subscribe to vanity. Vanity is also avoided by Ron Hamilton who dislikes 'entrepreneurial self-glorification', which he has seen at entrepreneurial 'gatherings' where showing off and ostentation were very evident. William Stewart dislikes pomposity, likes modesty, respects excellence and believes that people gain respect from showing sound judgment, while Irvine Laidlaw believes that respect is gained from what you have done and is maintained by 'always being a winner'. To illustrate this point he refers to Napoleon Bonaparte who, he argues, commanded less respect when living in exile 'than when winning battles'. In a similar way, Jackie Stewart believes that reputation is based on recent performance so 'you have to keep going' and 'you can't rest on your laurels'. Also, Sir Jackie respects honesty and if someone tells a lie 'that is pretty much it'. In addition, he likes good behaviour because there is 'no reason to be bad'. Sir Jackie also has equal respect for people regardless of their background or position in life. For example, he mentions that when taking time to speak to those who attended a book signing, it was suggested 'why are you speaking to them?', or when he is in the garden 'why are you picking up weeds?'. To these comments he responds 'what, am I above speaking to them?', 'am I above picking up weeds?'. Such equality in respect is something that Sir Jackie is very firm on and he thinks 'society is wrong' in the respect or value it can place on people, which, he contends, is often related to someone's occupation. Sheila McLean recounts that when she was at school you were considered second rate if, for example, you studied domestic science rather than languages. She saw little effort being made to evaluate those who had non-academic skills, something she thinks is very wrong as people deserve respect from being 'good at what they do'. Robin Harper also considers it wrong that society can view people who want to learn to be 'a plumber, dancer, musician or draughtsman' as 'second class' and he thinks that such skills are often 'undervalued'. He believes that respect comes 'from being yourself' and if you are not then you will soon be 'caught out', he thinks that is particularly true in politics. In addition, Professor McLean respects people that make decisions with regard to others, rather than themselves, and who are decent, able to relate their experiences and want to make a positive contribution.

Lewis Robertson tries to follow the proverb 'love thy neighbour' and remember that people can need help as, like everyone else, 'they may have problems'. In doing this, Sir Lewis tries to be polite and considerate towards others although, he adds, 'inevitably sometimes we fail'. In showing respect, Brian Gill thinks that 'it is not how you behave in the company of kings' but how you behave with 'everyone doing everyday jobs' which is important. He takes the view that everyone should be treated as 'an absolute equal', through being afford the same degree of respect, 'even the worst criminal'. Calum Colvin believes that you show respect by praising somebody on their achievements, and Evelyn Glennie considers that respect takes time to cultivate and is made or broken by actions. She can become frustrated by laziness because she views somebody who is not trying as 'showing a lack of respect'. Dame Evelyn applies this thinking in her own approach which means that she does 'clamp down' on herself 'pretty hard'. Margo MacDonald advises that respect can come from 'the oddest of reasons' and she considers that resisting temptation, even such as 'resisting that piece of chocolate', can help to build strength of character or 'mask doubts'. As part of this 'self-appreciation', she recommends that 'you look after and value your health'.

By having respect, Evelyn Glennie contends that people can influence others, and she gives the example of being 'proud to be in the room' with percussionist James Blades. Despite not being able to play due to arthritis, she advises that he was still able to influence others through the sincerity he showed and the equal respect he gave 'to both good and bad players'. This ability to influence can be viewed as a responsibility to spread knowledge or may be used more directly for the benefit of others. For instance, Lewis Robertson is happy to use his profile to support a number of organisations and charities, as is Tom Farmer who advises that 'it is not always about money, but can be about using my position'. Sir Tom adds that through building and keeping a good reputation he has more scope to have a positive influence. George Robertson also takes this view and describes his involvement in Maggie's Centre, The John Smith Memorial Fund, British Forces Foundation and the Commission on Global Road Safety as both 'good fun' and, far more importantly, allowing him to 'make a difference'. His ability to influence was shown when he telephoned an American donor on behalf of an Alzheimer research organisation, following his call the donor pledged US $1.9 million that cause.

Brian Gill believes that 'everyone has the right to dignity', which comes from having a right to work. Lord Gill argues that 'personality is corroded' if people do not gain an education and become unemployed. This right to work is echoed by Ron Hamilton when saying that 'the best thing you can give someone is a job'. He explains that his motivation for investing in a bakery which was on the point of closure, was his concern at the loss of 80 jobs which could potentially be secured by, what was to him at that time, a comparatively modest six figure investment. He retained his share for a year and then sold it to the management team who had helped turn the business around.

When considering respect, John Crofton recommends that you 'do things that would be respected by people you admire'. Calum Colvin does not worry about how celebrated someone is and he considers 'forelock tugging' unhealthy. Instead, he makes a judgment on how that person interacts with him, although Professor Colvin does find that people who lack respect for others are more often than not driven by competition or jealousy. George Robertson takes people for 'what they are' and he is unimpressed by ostentation, something he sees as a Scottish trait. Lord Robertson gives the example of attending a cattle market outside Aberdeen when a lady came over to say 'hello' because she said that he had appeared in her living room more than her relations, due to him being on television. Also, he was stopped in the street by a man who said 'you look bigger on the telly', he thought 'how do I answer that?', and he responded 'I'll try and do better next time', to which the man replied 'don't worry, I'll get a bigger telly!'. Lord Robertson gives these examples to show that 'people are people' and that you are the same person regardless of titles. In particular, he believes that respect comes from what you have done and not the trappings you have received. When meeting the President of the United States of America, George Bush, Lord Robertson did not sit and think 'look at me in the Oval office', as he stresses that if you think you have made it or boast about where you have reached 'you are lost'. Instead, Lord Robertson looks to do a good job and treat people properly and equally.

'Helps my ego'

Recognition

Evelyn Glennie takes satisfaction in the plaudits she receives and, in particular, she feels honoured to have been bracketed with James Black when they were named as The Scotsman people of the decade for the 1980s. James Black was jointly awarded the Nobel Prize in Medicine in 1988 for his work on drug treatments. Similarly, Lewis Robertson advises that he enjoys the recognition that he receives, in particular when he was awarded a CBE (Commander, Order of the British Empire) in 1969 and when he was Knighted in 1991. Jackie Stewart is proud of the awards that he has received and, out of respect for those who gave them, he takes care to use them appropriately. William Stewart thinks it is a privilege to receive recognition as he feels that he 'must have done something good'. Irvine Laidlaw also takes pleasure in his efforts being recognised, whether that is his peerage, an honorary degree or winning races (he is a keen sailing and racing car competitor). He goes on to describe them as 'all good'. When Sheila McLean started working in medical ethics she thinks she was viewed as a 'jumped up lawyer' and therefore she takes particular pride in the medical associations that she has been made a Fellow of. Professor McLean also mentions the recognition she feels on having work published and from the honorary degrees that she has been awarded, plus the 'real honour' of being made a Fellow of the Royal Society of Edinburgh. Chay Blyth was delighted to be made a Companion of Honour of the Institute of Marketing in 2000 and he describes both his CBE and Knighthood as feeling 'pretty good'. Sir Chay does add that these awards are really recognition 'for the whole team'. Likewise, Alan Finlayson describes being awarded the OBE (Officer, Order of the British Empire) as recognition for the whole of the Children's Hearing System. In addition to receiving the OBE, he took particular pleasure in being given the Freedom of the City of Cleveland, Ohio for his work on developing the Children's Hearing System there, and being made an Honorary Sheriff in recognition of his work as a Sheriff from 1991 to 2004. George Mathewson takes pride in the awards that he receives and he highlights the United Kingdom National Business Lifetime Award that he was awarded in 2003, although Sir George quips that 'it is a bit worrying when you win lifetime awards'. Tom Devine appreciates the recognition of his peers and the students that he has taught. In particular, he mentions that when he left his first Professorship, at the University of Strathclyde in 1998, he went for a drink with about 60 students. He enjoyed that the students had written a 'McGonagall-esq' poem about him which concluded with a skit on his marking style, 'good in parts, 58 per cent!'.

Recognition adds to the pride that people take in the work they have completed. For example, George Mathewson is proud of his contribution to the Scottish Development Agency, a project he describes as 'difficult' and that took the agency 'from poor to high public esteem'. Sheila McLean takes pride in her work to set up the Scottish Criminal Cases Review Commission and the Legal Medical School at the University of Glasgow, especially as she was the first female Professor of Law since the University's inception in 1451. An enjoyment and pride in business achievements is seen with Irvine Laidlaw who 'got a big kick' out of launching events. He gives special mention to City Scope, which within three years became the biggest conference in Dubai. Tom Farmer takes great pleasure in the recognition he receives, particularly compliments such as 'you changed the face of the motor industry', while Calum Colvin is 'surprised' but pleased when people recognise his work.

George Robertson gives the achievement that he takes most pride in as raising a family of 'good kids who are well motivated'. Also, he finds amusing the change in recognition in Islay where he used to be known as the son of George Robertson, the local policeman, which altered to people referring to his father as the father of George Robertson, the politician.

When discussing recognition, Alan Finlayson advises that he likes to think that he took on new roles for their challenge but that there may also have been an element of wanting to be in the 'limelight' or making a name for himself. Lewis Robertson notes that 'we all have a self-image to contend with', and Tom Farmer says that recognition 'helps my ego'. Sir Tom does though make a strong distinction between ego and being egotistical, where someone is self-centred. He goes on to add 'that when you try your best the vast majority of people recognise your efforts'. This recognition extends to Sir Tom being asked to speak at events and he does not differentiate between the awards he receives as 'they all felt good'.

Such recognition does not necessarily change approach or thinking as, for example, George Robertson says 'I am the same person I was 10 years ago, still George'. He gives the instance of when he was Secretary General of NATO and his Belgian bodyguards asked why everyone in Scotland called him 'George', they had been used to his predecessor using titles. He replied 'because George is my name'. Similarly, Calum Colvin and Noreen Murray are not put off if titles are not used. Professor Colvin is 'not in the least upset if not referred to as 'Professor'', and Noreen Murray says that titles can get confusing and that she is still 'Noreen Murray'.

'You are where you are'

Choices

Jackie Stewart sees choices being made from childhood as he thinks children are swayed towards the example of either their mother or father. When making choices in adult life sacrifices are perhaps made, although that does not necessarily equate to having regrets. For example, Irvine Laidlaw gives the apocryphal story of a concert pianist being approached and told that 'it would take half my life to learn to play the piano like that', to which the pianist replied 'it did'. Lord Laidlaw believes that to be really good at something the great majority of people have to focus, which means they have 'sacrificed everything'. Sheila McLean sacrificed a lot of spare time as she would work into the night and at weekends, plus rarely takes a holiday. Professor McLean would hear people outside 'enjoying themselves', which at times she 'resented' but felt that what she was doing 'had to be done'. George Mathewson advises that he was away from home a lot during his career and did not have much 'personal time'. However, in hindsight he says it is 'debatable' whether he regrets that choice. Sacrifices in her social time mean that Evelyn Glennie has 'a lot of acquaintances but not so many close friends'. She adds, rather tellingly, that given the same decisions again she would make the same choices.

Kenneth Murray and Noreen Murray mention the choice of not having children. In particular, they feel that the long hours they worked would have been unfair on children. Evelyn Glennie also gives the choice of not having children as she considers that due to the structure of her life it would be difficult to bring up children. Likewise, Irvine Laidlaw says that he 'might have liked to have children', although he jokes that he is not so sure about that 'having met some other people's children'.

Lewis Robertson does voice some regrets and he describes the death of his son and that of his wife as 'difficult times'. Calum Colvin feels that it is 'impossible to go through life without regrets', and he sees that as part of the options that people have on how they wish to conduct their lives, the ambitions that they follow and how far they are willing to go to meet those ambitions. Professor Colvin finds that, in most instances, people are 'just getting on with life' and he believes that people should 'live as they wish'. Although he does add that that there is a choice 'not to work for a faceless corporation'.

Michael Atiyah stresses the need to balance family and work time and considers himself 'fortunate that has worked out'. However, he advises that retaining that balance becomes more difficult at times of crises in personal or professional life. Sir Michael takes the view that it boils down to a choice of lifestyle and he thinks that everyone has a choice, for example, whether to have a 'quiet life' or try to 'improve society', something Sir Michael believes was perhaps more prevalent amongst previous generations. Choices are something that Jonathan Long believes everybody has in education. He emphasises that there is too much knowledge in the world for someone to learn everything so decisions have to be made on what to learn and who or where to learn it from. However, such choices need not mean that sacrifices are made. Dr Long gives the example of when he was offered the position of Headmaster at Aiglon College in Switzerland but felt that the school 'was in crisis'. He was concerned, that if he took the post, his own personal reputation may be tarnished by being so closely associated with the difficulties the school was experiencing. Nonetheless, he decided to 'sacrifice' his career and accept the position. However, in hindsight, he realises that he was not making a sacrifice but was in fact 'following my bliss'.

Tom Farmer has never felt that he was making sacrifices because he has never felt guilty about working. He attributes this to the tremendous support of his family, which meant that family life did not stop, or as he puts it 'you should marry the girl next door and she should be called Anne'. In addition, when considering the people he has met and the experiences that he has had, Sir Tom thinks that it would 'selfish of me to have regrets' because it has been 'like a dream, a fairytale'.

Everyone has choices but ultimately, rather pragmatically, Irvine Laidlaw says 'you are where you are'.

Biographies of the Contributors

MICHAEL ATIYAH: MATHEMATICIAN

Michael Atiyah was born in London on 22 April 1929 and spent his formative years in Egypt where he attended Victoria College. He completed his schooling at Manchester Grammar School and after his military service studied at Trinity College, Cambridge, where he followed his Master of Arts with a Postgraduate Doctorate. Sir Michael is an Honorary Professor of the University of Edinburgh and is a Fellow of the Royal Society of Edinburgh, which he has been President of since 2005.

From 1954 until 1958 Sir Michael worked as a Research Fellow at Cambridge University, during which time he became a member of the Institute for Advanced Study at Princeton, having attended Princeton as the Commonwealth Fund Fellow. In 1957 he started work as an assistant lecturer at Cambridge University and continued as a lecturer from 1958 until 1961, when he became a Reader in Mathematics and Professorial Fellow of St Catherine's College, Oxford. In 1963 he gained the Savilian Chair at Oxford University which he retained until 1969 when he was appointed Professor of Mathematics at the Institute of Advanced Study, Princeton. From 1973 up until 1990 Sir Michael was the Royal Society Resident Professor of the Mathematical Institute and Professorial Fellow of St Catherine's College, Oxford. Following that, he was Master of Trinity College, Cambridge and Director of the Isaac Newton Institute for Mathematical Sciences in Cambridge, which he was instrumental in establishing.

Sir Michael has contributed to the development and solution of many complex problems focusing on geometry, topology and synergies across mathematics. A major contribution culminated in 1966 when he was awarded the Fields Prize for outstanding mathematical achievement for 'joint work with Hirzebruch in K-theory; proved jointly with Singer the index theorem of elliptic operators on complex manifolds; worked in collaboration with Bott to prove fixed point theorem related to the Leftschetz formula'.

The many forums and committees that Sir Michael has led or participated in include: Executive Committee of the International Mathematical Union; London Mathematical Society; Science and Engineering Research Council; Advisory Council on Science and Technology; Chairman of the European Mathematical Council; Chancellor of the University of Leicester; President of the Pugwash Conferences on Science and World Affairs; and Fellow and President of the Royal Society. Sir Michael has received many honorary degrees, is a Freeman of the City of London, was Knighted in 1983 and made Order of Merit in 1992. Further recognition came in 2004 when Sir Michael and Isadore Singer were awarded the Abel Prize 'for their discovery and proof of index theorem bringing together topology, geometry and analysis, and their outstanding role in building new bridges between mathematics and theoretical physics'.

CHAY BLYTH: MAVERICK YACHTSMAN

The youngest of a family of five girls and two boys, Chay Blyth was born in Hawick on the 14 May 1940. He was educated at Hawick High School and left at age 15 to take up an apprenticeship as a frame worker with a local knitwear company. He joined the Parachute Regiment in 1958 and, at age 21, he became that regiment's youngest ever platoon sergeant.

Sir Chay and Captain John Ridgway, also of the Parachute Regiment, were the first people to row the Atlantic Ocean. They achieved this between June and September 1966 in a 20 ft dory, *English Rose III*, having set off from Cape Cod and completing their journey on arrival at the Island of Aran off the west coast of Ireland. In recognition of this Sir Chay received the British Empire Medal. He left the Army in 1967 and joined Cadbury Schweppes.

In October 1970 he set out on a circumnavigation of the globe westwards in yacht *British Steel*. He returned 292 days later on 6 August 1971 as the first person to sail round the world nonstop solo against the prevailing currents and winds. This was recognised when he was made Commander, Order of the British Empire in 1972. The many other sailing feats that Sir Chay has completed include: winner of the Elapsed Time Prize Whitbread Round the World Race 1973–74, as skipper to a crew of paratroopers; Atlantic Sailing record Cape Verde to Antigua in 1977; winner of Round Britain Race of 1978 with Robert James; winner of the double handed

Observer/Europe I transatlantic race in record time with Robert James in 1981; and he was Number One on the successful Blue Riband attempt by Virgin Atlantic Challenge II in 1986. In addition, he was mentor to Dee Caffari in her successful bid to be the first woman to sail around the world westwards in 2005–6. In 1971 Sir Chay was awarded the Chichester Trophy by the Royal Yacht Squadron and voted Yachtsman of the Year. This was followed in 1994 with a special award for outstanding services to yachting from the Yachting Journalists Association.

Sir Chay founded the Challenge Business in 1989 to organise the British Steel Round World Challenge of 1992–93 and he went on to organise the BT Global Challenge races of 1996–97 and 2000–1. He has held a number of company Directorships and he heads the Board of Directors of train company First Great Western.

The books that he has written include: *A Fighting Chance* in 1966, which details his transatlantic row; *The Impossible Voyage* in 1971, which tells the story of his solo circumnavigation of the globe; and *The Challenge* in 1993, which details the British Steel Round World Challenge of 1992–93. Sir Chay was made a Freeman of Hawick in 1972, Knighted in 1997 and received the Companion of Honour from the Chartered Institute of Marketing in 2000.

CALUM COLVIN: ARTIST

Born in Glasgow on 26 October 1961, Calum Colvin attended North Berwick High School before gaining a Diploma in Sculpture from Duncan of Jordanstone College of Art, Dundee in 1983. He then attended the Royal College of Art, London where he obtained a Masters of Art in Photography, graduating in 1985.

Professor Colvin received the Scottish Education Department Travelling Fellowship in 1983; the KJP Photographic Award in 1985; Young European Photographer of the Year prize winner in 1986; The Photographers Gallery Brandt Award in 1987; 13th Higashikawa Overseas Photographer Prize of 1997; the 2000 Leverhulme Trust Research Fellowship; the Carnegie Trust Award for 2002; University of Dundee Interdisciplinary Research Award in 2003; and that same year the Critics Award for Theatre in Scotland. Further recognition of his work and contribution came in 1989 when he was awarded the Royal Photographic Society Gold Medal. He was made Officer, Order of the British Empire in 2001 for his contribution to the visual arts, and in 2004 he was elected Associate Member of the Royal Scottish Academy.

By assembling a tableaux of objects, which he then paints and photographs, Professor Colvin explores ideas and narratives concerned with national identity, sexuality and contemporary culture. His work often references historical works of art and is sometimes referred to as 'constructed photography'. His first major exhibition *Constructed Narratives* was held jointly with Ron O'Donnell and toured a number of United Kingdom venues plus Helsinki between 1986 and 1988. This was soon followed by a solo touring exhibition, *Calum Colvin*, which toured Germany, the Netherlands, Spain, the United Kingdom and the United States of America from 1987 to 1990. Since then, Professor Colvin has exhibited in many group as well as solo exhibitions including, *The Two Ways of Life*, 1991; *The Seven Deadly Sins and the Four Last Things*, toured 1993–2000; *Ornithology*, 1996; *Pseudologica Fantastica*, toured 1996–2000; *Sacred and Profane*, toured 1998–2003; *Narcissus – 20th Century Self Portraits*, 2001; and *Ossian, Fragments of Ancient Poetry*, toured 2002–2007. This has seen his work displayed in many countries across the world and held in numerous private and public collections including those of the Art Institute of Chicago; Deutsche Bank; Metropolitan Museum of Modern Art, New York; Museum of Fine Arts, Houston; Royal Photographic Society, Bath; Scottish National Portrait Gallery, Edinburgh; and the Victoria and Albert Museum, London.

Professor Colvin was a Senior Research Fellow in Digital Imaging during 1995 at the University of Northumbria and he was a lecturer in fine art at the University of Dundee from 1993 until 2001 when he was made Professor of Fine Art Photography.

JOHN CROFTON: PHYSICIAN

John Crofton was born in Dublin on 27 March 1912 and educated at Tonbridge School before gaining a place at Cambridge University where he attained a Bachelor of Arts in 1933 plus Bachelor of Medicine and Bachelor of Surgery in 1937. He joined the Royal Army Medical Corps Reserve in 1939 and his Second World War service included posting to France, Egypt (where he played a key role in the diagnosis of tropical diseases), Eritrea, Greece, Malta and Germany.

In 1947 he completed his Doctor of Medicine, working at St Thomas's Hospital in London. That same year he gained a position part-time at the Tuberculosis Unit, Medical Research Council, Brompton Hospital as well as a part-time lectureship at the Postgraduate Medical School of London. Following that, he became Professor of Respiratory Diseases and Tuberculosis at the University of Edinburgh from 1952 until 1977. During this period he initiated controlled trials which established and then introduced an effective treatment against tuberculosis based on the simultaneous use of three antibiotics which provided close to 100 per cent total cure. The effectiveness of this protocol was confirmed following a 23 country trial held in 1963 and became known as the 'Edinburgh Method', which is still used to this day and has saved millions of lives worldwide. Also, Sir John carried out extensive research and work into other non-tuberculosis respiratory diseases especially the prognosis, treatment and immunology of bronchitis. In addition, he has written and contributed to many publications on tuberculosis and respiratory diseases.

In 1945 Sir John married Eileen Mercer (who was made Member, Order of the British Empire in 1984) and they are both leading figures in the fight against pulmonary disease, particularly through their early and ongoing involvement in ASH (Action on Smoking and Health).

Sir John was a lecturer at the Royal Postgraduate Medical School of London from 1947–51, and after moving to Edinburgh he was made Dean of the Faculty of Medicine in 1963 and Vice Principal of the University of Edinburgh in 1969. He was admitted as a Fellow of the Royal College of Physicians London in 1951 and of the Royal College of Physicians Edinburgh in 1957, where he went on to be Vice President in 1972 and then President from 1973–76. He is an Honorary Fellow of the Royal College of Physicians of Ireland; Royal Australasian College of Physicians; American College of Physicians; Faculty of Community Medicine; Royal College of Physicians Edinburgh; Royal Society of Edinburgh; Royal Society of Medicine, Kings College London University; and of the Medical Academies of Argentina, Catalonia and Singapore. Sir John holds honorary degrees from the University of Bordeaux and Imperial College London. He received the Wever-Parkes prize from the Royal College of Physicians in 1966, the Edinburgh Medal for Science and Society in 1995, the Galen Medal from the Society of Apothecaries in 2001, the Union Medal of the International Union against Tuberculosis and Lung Disease in 2005, and the Edwin Chadwick Medal for Contributions to Public Health in 2008. Sir John was Knighted in 1977.

TAM DALYELL: POLITICIAN

Tam Dalyell was born on 9 August 1932 and went to Eton College before attending King's College Cambridge and then studying at Moray House Teacher Training School in Edinburgh. His studies were interrupted by National Service between 1950 and 1952 when he served as a Trooper with the Royal Scots Greys. From teacher training he went on to teach at Bo'ness Academy from 1956–60 and then became Deputy Director of Studies at the British India Ship School, Dunera during 1961–62.

In the by-election of 1962, he stood for Parliament and held the constituency of West Lothian for the Labour Party. He retained this seat until 1983, when boundary changes created the constituency of Linlithgow which he represented until his retirement from the House of Commons in 2005. He was a Member of the Public Accounts Committee (1962–66) and Secretary to the Labour Party Standing Conference on the Sciences (1962–64). He served on the Parliamentary Labour Party Sports Group (1964–74) and as Chairman of the Foreign Affairs Group (1967–70). He was Vice-Chairman of the Defence and Foreign Affairs Groups (1972–74), Scottish Labour Group of MPs (1973–75) and of the Parliamentary Labour Party (1974–76). He was chosen as a Member of the European Parliament by the Labour Party in 1975 until 1979, during which time he served on its Budget and Energy Committees. Also, he was Chairman of the All Party Latin America Group (1997–2005) and Leader of the Inter Parliamentary Union Delegation to Brazil in 1976, Peru in 1999, Bolivia in 2000 and Libya in 2001. In 1998 he chaired the ad hoc committee against war in Iraq. From 1980 until 1982 he was opposition spokesman on science, with his long standing interest in science including Member of the House of Commons Select Committee on Science and Technology (1967–9) and political columnist for the New Scientist from 1967 until 2005. For six years, from 1964, he was Parliamentary Private Secretary to Richard Crossman who was Minister of Housing, Leader of the House of Commons and Secretary of State for the Social Services.

Amongst the many issues that he has raised during his parliamentary career are questions on the 1982 Falklands War and 2003 invasion of Iraq plus, in 1977, he raised the West Lothian Question, which considers the practicalities of Members of Parliament from areas with devolved powers voting on matters concerning other constituencies, but their counterparts in these constituencies not having the same rights. He has written a number of books including *Devolution: the End of Britain?* (Jonathan Cape), *Misrule* (Hamish Hamilton) and *Dick Crossman: a portrait* (Weidenfield and Nicholson).

In 2003 he was made a Fellow of the Royal Society of Edinburgh, was Rector of the University of Edinburgh from 2003–6 and he has honorary degrees from Edinburgh, London City, Napier, Northumbria, St Andrews and Stirling Universities, and from The Open University.

TOM DEVINE: HISTORIAN

Born in Motherwell on 30 July 1945, Tom Devine was educated at Our Lady's RC High School in Motherwell and then attended Strathclyde University where he attained a Bachelor of Arts with 1st Class Honours in 1968; this was to be the last 1st in history awarded by that institution for the next 10 years. He then went on to complete a Postgraduate Doctorate in 1972.

From 1969 to 1978 he was a lecturer in history at the University of Strathclyde, then senior lecturer up until 1983, becoming a Reader in Scottish History until 1988 and then a Professor of Scottish History until 1998. During 1993 and 1994 he was Dean of the Faculty of Arts and Social Studies and then Deputy Principal from 1994 until 1997. He is an Adjunct Professor of History at the University of North Carolina and University of Guelph in Ontario. From 1998 to 2003 he was Professor in Scottish History, Gluckman Research Chair in Irish and Scottish Studies, and Director of the AHRC Research Centre of Irish and Scottish Studies at the University of Aberdeen. In addition, he holds the Sir William Fraser Chair of Scottish History at the University of Edinburgh.

Professor Devine was a Governor of St Andrews College of Education (1990–94); Convenor of Council to the Scottish Catholic Historical Association (1990–95); Trustee and Chairman of the European Ethnology Research Centre, National Museums of Scotland (1995–2002); Convenor of the Irish-Scottish Academic Initiative (1998–2001); British Academy Member of Council (1998– 2001); member of the Secretary of State for Scotland's Advisory Committee (2001–2004); and from 2002 member of the Advisory Committee of the Economic and Social Research Council on Devolution.

Professor Devine has written many publications and books on Scottish history, starting with *The Tobacco Lords* in 1975 (a second edition was published in 1990) through to *The Scottish Nation 1700–2000* (new edition, taking the book to 2007), and in 2003 *Scotland's Empire*, which formed the basis of a six part BBC television series.

From 1980 he has been a Fellow of the Royal Historical Society and was awarded the Hume Brown Prize in Scottish History in 1976, Saltire Prize in 1992, Henry Duncan Prize in 1994, and the Royal Medal, Scotland's supreme academic accolade, from the Royal Society of Edinburgh in 2001. He was awarded the 1st John Aikenhead Medal for services to Scottish education and Membership of the Academy of Merit, received an Honorary Fellowship from Bell College (now the University of the West of Scotland) for contributions to Scottish culture, and holds honorary degrees from Queen's College Belfast, the University of Abertay and the University of Strathclyde. Professor Devine was made Fellow of the Royal Society of Edinburgh in 1992, Fellow of the British Academy in 1994 and Honorary Member of the Royal Irish Academy in 2001. He is the only United Kingdom based historian elected to all three of the national learned societies in the British Isles and he was made Officer, Order of the British Empire in 2005.

NORMAN DRUMMOND: EDUCATOR

Norman Drummond was born on 1 April 1952 and was educated at Merchiston Castle School in Edinburgh and then attained a Masters of Arts in Law from Fitzwilliam College, Cambridge University. From there he attended New College at the University of Edinburgh where he graduated as a Bachelor of Divinity and was ordained as a minister in the Church of Scotland. Reverend Drummond was commissioned to serve as chaplain to the Parachute Regiment and Airborne forces over 1977 and 1978, then chaplain to the 1st Battalion The Black Watch (Royal Highland Regiment) from 1978 until 1982. He was a Cambridge Rugby Blue in 1971 and Captain of the Scottish Universities Rugby XV in 1974 plus Captain of the Army XV and Combined Services XV over 1976 and 1977.

Reverend Drummond was minister of Kilmuir and Stenscholl Church on the Isle of Skye from 1996 to 1998, chaplain to the Governor of Edinburgh Castle from 1991 to 1993 and has been a chaplain to The Queen in Scotland since 1993. From 1982 to 1984 he was chaplain at Fettes College, Edinburgh and then Headmaster of Loretto School, Musselburgh from 1984 until 1995. He was a Governor of Gordonstoun School between 1995 and 2000, Member of Court of Heriot-Watt University in Edinburgh from 1986 to 1992 and was Chairman of the Board of Governors of Aiglon College, Switzerland from 1999 to 2005.

The many committees and forums he has served on include: BBC National Governor and Chairman of the Broadcasting Council for Scotland 1994–99; Chairman Musselburgh and District Council of Social Service 1984–94, of Community and Action Network Scotland 2001–3, and of the Lloyds TSB Charitable Foundation for Scotland since 2003. In 1997 he founded Columba 1400, the world's first prototype Community and International Leadership Centre, on the Isle of Skye of which he is Chairman.

In 1999 Reverend Drummond set up The Change Partnership Scotland. This provided facilitation, mediation, presentation and media management coaching to senior executives and he was its Chairman until 2003. Also in 1999, he established and remains Chairman of Drummond International which offers inspirational professional, business and personal development services. In addition, he is a non-executive Director of family owned shipping company J & J Denholm Ltd.

He is a former President of the Edinburgh Battalion of the Boys' Brigade and of the Victoria League in Scotland; and a former Trustee of the Arthur Smith Memorial Trust and of the Foundation for Skin Research; he is a member of The Queen's Bodyguard for Scotland, The Royal Company of Archers. Reverend Drummond has written a number of books including the bestseller *The Spirit of Success, how to connect your heart to your head in work and life* which was published in 2004.

TOM FARMER: BUSINESSMAN

Tom Farmer was born on 10 July 1940, the youngest of seven children. He attended St Mary's Primary School and Holy Cross Academy in Edinburgh which he left at age 15 to become a store boy with an Edinburgh based tyre distributor.

In 1964 he established his own business selling tyres and car accessories which he built into 15 outlets and sold in 1968. He then moved with his family to California but returned to Edinburgh and established car autocare company Kwik-Fit in 1971. He built Kwik-Fit into an operation comprising over 800 outlets in the United Kingdom and a further 500 in mainland Europe that employed over 4,000 people. He was Chairman and Chief Executive of Kwik-Fit until 1999 when he sold it to the Ford Motor Company. He now invests in start up companies across the United Kingdom and in Farmer Auto-Care, which operates a franchise where he takes part ownership in garage outlets.

Sir Tom was named Scottish Businessman of the year in 1989, was a member of the Board of Scottish Enterprise from 1990 until 1996 and Chairman of Investors in People Scotland from 1991 to 1997. Sir Tom bought Hibernian Football Club in 1991 and remains its owner and Chairman. He has been Chairman of Scottish Business in the Community since 1990, Chaired the Government sponsored Action Against Drugs, is a Trustee of the Duke of Edinburgh Award Scheme and has received the Carnegie Medal of Philanthropy. Also, he established the Farmer Foundation to provide support to local communities with the aim of encouraging self-development.

In 1998 he received the Institute of Management Gold Medal, was Scotland's Elite Leader of the Year for 1999, and received the Golden Plate Award from the American Academy of Achievement in 2000. He is a Companion of the Royal College of Surgeons and was made Deputy Lieutenant of Edinburgh in 1996. He received The Knight Cross of the Order of Merit of the Republic of Poland in 1993 and was made Officer in de Orde van Oranje-Nassau of The Netherlands in 1996. In 1990 he was made Commander, Order of the British Empire and he was Knighted in 1997. He is a strong supporter of inter-faith activities and in 1997 he was recognised by the Roman Catholic Church when he was made Knight Commander, Order of St Gregory the Great.

Sir Tom received honorary degrees in 1996 from the University of Edinburgh and Glasgow Caledonian University. In 2002 he received an honorary degree from Queen Margaret University, Edinburgh, and in 2007 became its Chancellor.

ALAN FINLAYSON: CHILD LAW CONSULTANT

Alan Finlayson was born in Dumfries on 19 December 1934 and attended Dalswinton Primary School followed by Dumfries Academy and then one year at George Watson's College in Edinburgh. From school, in 1952, he attended Edinburgh University from which he graduated as a Master of Arts in 1958 and with a degree in law in 1960. In 1955 he was called up for National Service, which he completed in 1957.

Between 1960 and 1963 he worked part-time as a school teacher in Ayrshire and part-time as an unqualified solicitor in Edinburgh and Haddington. From 1964 he worked in legal practice with Ranken & Reid SSC in Edinburgh, dealing with that firm's Court of Session and Sheriff Court business. In 1965 he was made a partner in the firm and established its court department where work concentrated on criminal and family law.

In 1970 he resigned from legal practice to become first Reporter to the Children's Panel for the City of Edinburgh as part of the new Children's Hearing System. He was the first Chairman for the Association of Reporters, served as a member of the Secretary of State's Advisory Council on Social Work, and the Study Group established by Lancaster University on *Secure Accommodation of Children in England and Wales, Scotland, Northern Ireland, and Eire*. In 1987 he was made Officer, Order of the British Empire for services to the Children's Hearing System in Scotland and retired as a Reporter to the Children's Panel in 1990.

In his still continuing role as a Child Law Consultant, he worked part-time for the Scottish Office, focusing on the establishment of the National Scottish Children's Reporter Administration and thereafter on what became the Children (Scotland) Act 1995. In 1991 he was appointed as a temporary, later part-time, Sheriff and in these roles sat in all 49 of Scotland's Sheriff Courts. He completed his term of office in 2004 on his 70th birthday and was appointed Honorary Sheriff of the Lothian and Borders at Edinburgh. In 1998 he acted for the Scottish Executive as first Chair of the Accreditation Panel for Programmes in a Community Setting to address Offending Behaviour. He was commissioned by the Scottish Executive in 2004 to write a *Parenting Agreement* that accompanied the Family Law (Scotland) Act 2005. In addition, he continues to act as court reporter in disputed cases of residence and contact of children with regard to adoption.

The numerous committees he has served on include: Board Member of the Royal Scottish Society for Prevention of Cruelty to Children (now Children 1st); and as Chairman of Scotland's first Family Mediation Service, of the Lothian Association of Boys' Clubs, and of the Legal Rights and Protection Committee Alzheimer's Scotland, Action on Dementia.

BRIAN GILL: LAWYER

Brian Gill was born in Glasgow in 1942. He was educated at St Aloysius' College, Glasgow and Glasgow University where he attained the degrees of MA (1962) and LL B (1964).

Lord Gill lectured in the Faculty of Law at Edinburgh University from 1964 to 1969 and 1972 to 1977. In 1975 he was awarded the degree of PhD by Edinburgh University. In 1967 he was called to the Scottish Bar and became a QC in 1981. He was Keeper of the Advocates Library from 1987 to 1994.

In 1991 he was called to the English Bar (Lincoln's Inn) and is an Honorary Bencher of Lincoln's Inn (2002). During his years in practice he served on the Scottish Legal Aid Board and the Scottish Valuation Advisory Council. From 1989 to 1994 he was Deputy Chairman of the Copyright Tribunal.

He was appointed a Senator of the College of Justice in 1994. Lord Gill was Chairman of the Scottish Law Commission from 1996 until 2001 when he was appointed to his present position of Lord Justice Clerk and President of the Second Division of the Court of Session.

Lord Gill is the author of *The Law of Agricultural Holdings in Scotland* (3rd ed, 1997) and is founder and General Editor of *The Scottish Planning Encyclopedia*. From 1999 to 2006 Lord Gill was Chairman of the Royal Scottish Academy of Music and Drama. Lord Gill is a Fellow of the Royal Society of Edinburgh (2004) and a Fellow of the Royal Scottish Academy of Music and Drama (2002). He holds the honorary degree of LLD from the Universities of Glasgow (1998), Strathclyde (2003), St Andrews (2006) and Edinburgh (2007).

EVELYN GLENNIE: MUSICIAN

Evelyn Glennie was born in Aberdeen and attended Cairnorrie Primary School, Ellon Academy and then the Royal Academy of Music. She is the first person in musical history to successfully create and sustain a full-time career as a solo percussionist. Dame Evelyn gives more than 100 performances a year worldwide, performing with the greatest conductors, orchestras and artists. For the first 10 years of her career virtually every performance she gave was in some way a first. Her diversity of collaborations have included performances with artists such as Nana Vasoncelos, Kodo, Bela Fleck, Bjork, Bobby McFerrin, Sting, Emmanuel Ax, Kings Singers, Mormon Tabernacle Choir and Fred Frith.

Dame Evelyn has commissioned 150 new works for solo percussion from many of the world's most eminent composers and she also composes and records music for film and television (EG Composer). Her first high quality drama produced a score that was nominated for a British Academy of Film and Television Arts awards (BAFTA's); the UK equivalent of the Oscars. Out of the 25 recordings made so far, her first CD, Bartok's Sonata for two Pianos and Percussion won her a Grammy in 1988. A further two Grammy nominations followed, one of which she won for a collaboration with Bela Fleck.

The Evelyn Glennie brand is constantly exploring other areas of creativity. From writing a best selling autobiography, Good Vibrations, to collaborating with the renowned film director Thomas Riedelsheimer on a film called Touch the Sound, to presenting two series of her own television programmes for the BBC, to regularly appearing on television across the world, including The David Letterman Show (USA), Sesame Street (USA), The South Bank Show (UK), presenting and performing on Songs of Praise (UK), Commonwealth Games Festival Concert, This is Your Life (UK), 60 minutes (USA), PBS Profile (USA), and many more.

Dame Evelyn's activities include lobbying the Government on issues as diverse as music education and parking rights for motorbikes (she is a keen biker). Other aspects include EG Images, which supplies photographs from her vast image library; EG Jewellery, which is a range of jewellery designed and made by EG based on Dame Evelyn's influences as a solo percussionist; EG Merchandise; and EG 21st Guidance, her work as a motivational speaker to a diverse range of corporate companies and events. In addition, she teaches music privately which allows her to explore the art of teaching and the world of sound therapy as a means of communication.

Dame Evelyn has received numerous awards, including in 1993 an OBE (Officer, Order of the British Empire). This was extended in 2007 to Dame Commander for her services to music.

RON HAMILTON: ENGINEER

Ron Hamilton was born in Bellshill on 13 November 1941 and attended Uddingston Grammar School. In 1963 he gained an Associateship of the Royal College of Science and Technology (ASCST) through a four year student apprenticeship funded by Hoover Ltd. Following a year in industry, he returned to study at Strathclyde University (the name adopted by the Royal College following its re-organisation) where he completed a Masters Degree in Engineering in 1966. In addition, he undertook a correspondence course and evening classes from which he obtained a Diploma in Management Studies from the University of Strathclyde in 1968.

In 1988 he left his role as Vice President of healthcare company CooperVision (along with Technical Manager Bill Seden) to set up Award, a company dedicated to the development and manufacture of disposable contact lenses. This had involved an initial £4 million of venture capital which was withdrawn. It was decided, under legal scrutiny, that was a breach of contract and the financial redress this gave provided enough funding to set up some development work and pay for the initial patent application. Through their process improvements and developments, the cost of disposable lenses was reduced from about £150 a pair to approximately £1 per pair, making this type of lens a commercial reality. They went public with their results in 1992 but were unable to raise any private sector funding and with no interest from eye care providers they raised funds mainly from Scottish Enterprise, augmented by regional assistance grants. This allowed small scale production to be established at a factory in Livingston in 1994. Boots Opticians became their major customer, which encouraged expansion and the start of large scale production. In 1995 they were approached by Bausch & Lomb for distribution rights but with demand running ahead of capacity they saw no need for a distributor but floated the idea of selling the business. In 1996 Award was sold to Bausch & Lomb. Approximately 35 per cent to 40 per cent of contact lens wearers in the United Kingdom wear lenses produced using the processes which he established with about 1.5 billion of these lenses manufactured and sold worldwide.

From 1996 he developed a new lens with ultra violet inhibitor and a direct to customer distribution process through an Internet based ordering system. In 2001 he commenced manufacturer and distribution at

Hamilton Technology Park in Blantyre, using the brand names daysoft in the United Kingdom and daylens for the rest of the world.

In 1996 he was awarded the United Kingdom Entrepreneur of the Year Award by the British Venture Capital Association and he is a John Logie Baird Award winner. He received an Honorary Doctorate in Business Studies from Strathclyde University in 2007.

ROBIN HARPER: POLITICIAN

Robin Harper was born on 4 August 1940 in Thurso and attended St Marylebone Grammar School in London and then Elgin Academy before graduating in History and Natural Sciences from Aberdeen University. In addition, he gained a Diploma in Guidance and Curriculum from Edinburgh University in 1992.

On graduating from Aberdeen University in 1962, he attained a place as a temporary teacher at Crookston Castle Secondary School in Glasgow, from where he went on to a full-time teaching role at Braehead School in Fife. He left that position in 1968 to teach at Kolanya and Amukara schools in Kenya, returning to Braehead School in 1970. He then left teaching for one year to work as an actor and stage manager at the Ayr Civic Theatre but returned to teach English at Newbattle High School and, from 1972, taught modern studies at Boroughmuir High School in Edinburgh. He continued working there until he was elected to the Scottish Parliament.

Since 1986 he has stood for the Green Party in European and local elections, and in 1999 was elected to the Scottish Parliament as a Member for the Lothians and thus became the first Green Party member to be elected to Parliament in the United Kingdom. During his time in office the bills and debates he has introduced include those on organic food, renewable energy, job creation, pollution, land value taxation, transport, and housing. Also, he was Convenor of the Scottish Parliament's Cross Party Group on Architecture and the Built Environment; Renewable Energy Group; and the Cross Party Group on Children and Young People. He is Co-convener of the Scottish Green Party.

In addition, he serves on the board of several theatre companies, is member of Equity and a Fellow of the Educational Institute of Scotland and of the Royal Society of Arts. He was a member of the Lothian Health Council 1993–98; Lothian Children's Panel 1985–88, Rector of Edinburgh University 2000–3 and was elected Rector of Aberdeen University in 2005.

IRVINE LAIDLAW: BUSINESSMAN

Born in Keith, Banffshire on 22 December 1942, Irvine Laidlaw attended Blairmore Preparatory School in Huntly and then Merchiston Castle School in Edinburgh before going to the University of Leeds to study textiles. He switched course to Economics in which he graduated as a Bachelor of Arts. He went on to gain a Masters of Business Administration from Columbia University in New York.

In 1974 Lord Laidlaw established the Institute of International Research, IIR Holdings, in New York as an international newspaper publisher and in 1978 undertook two conferences in the United Kingdom. Following the success of those conferences, the company focused on that market. Growth in this field was swift and by 1980 offices had been established across South East Asia, with further expansion until IIR had offices throughout the world. In 1984 IIR diversified into exhibitions and it went on to become the largest business of its type, comprising of 48 companies and over 100 operating units. This included conferences for the life sciences industry and for financial services, such as for those involved in private equity markets and hedge funds. In addition, IIR held the rights to the Adam Smith Institute name in Russia, which it leveraged to organise economic related events. The company also provided training for government departments in the United States of America and for over half of America's Fortune 500 companies. Furthermore, it provided special events such as motivational talks by high profile individuals.

Following an aborted listing on the New York Stock Exchange in 2002, due to falling stock exchange values at that time, Lord Laidlaw sold the Institute of International Research to T&F Informa in 2005.

In 2003 Lord Laidlaw established the Laidlaw Youth Project, which aims to support vulnerable young people in Scotland and has funded a number of education causes and mentoring schemes. This gives particular focus to encouraging charities to work together.

Lord Laidlaw received an honorary degree from the University of St Andrews in 2003 and was created Baron, life peer, Lord Laidlaw of Rothiemay in Banffshire in 2004.

JONATHAN LONG: THEOLOGIAN AND PHILOSOPHER

Jonathan Long was born in Plymouth, England on 3 April 1958 and spent his formative years in west, central and southern Africa, particularly Zambia, and he attended Maritzburg College in Pietermaritzburg, South Africa.

Dr Long gained degrees in theology, ethics and education from universities in South Africa and the United Kingdom. He was ordained into the Church of England and conducted youth and pastoral work in South Africa as well lecturing in theology and moral philosophy. Following this, he undertook a position as chaplain and teacher at a school in Oxford and became involved in the development of approaches to personal and social education in independent schools at a national level.

In 1995 he won an Economic and Social Research Council award to study the moral and spiritual development of children at Oxford University's Department of Educational Studies. After completing that study he joined Aiglon College in Switzerland as chaplain in 1998 and then as College Principal from 2000, where he promoted the College's mantra of holistic education through academic study and outdoor education which brings together children from diverse cultural, religious, national and socioeconomic backgrounds. In 2002, Dr Long was appointed European Director of the Round Square Organisation. This is an association of over 50 schools from around the world that share a commitment to personal development and responsibility through service, challenge, adventure and international understanding.

Dr Long is interested in the challenges facing schools and the development of relevant and meaningful learning approaches. This led him, at the end of 2006, to leave Aiglon College and take up a position as Associate Director with Columba 1400. He believes that this charity, based on the Isle of Skye, is providing a new and radical approach to education and leadership that releases the potential of young people. His role at Columba 1400 is to develop these education programmes further and expand them internationally. Dr Long is also currently completing postgraduate work in psychotherapy at Sheffield University's Faculty of Medicine.

MARGO MACDONALD: POLITICIAN

Born Margo Aitken in Hamilton on 19 April 1943, she attended Hamilton Academy and then Dunfermline College from where she graduated with a Diploma of Physical Education.

From 1963 until 1965 she taught physical education before becoming a freelance journalist and broadcaster. She contested the Paisley constituency on behalf of the Scottish National Party (SNP) in the 1970 General Election but the seat was held by the Labour Party. She won the Govan by election of November 1973 for the SNP and represented that constituency at Westminster until she was beaten by the Labour Party candidate in the February 1974 General Election. She contested the Govan seat again in the October 1974 General Election and Hamilton in the May 1978 by-election; both seats were retained by the Labour Party.

From 1981–3 she continued her work in journalism and was a broadcaster for Radio Forth, then from 1983–5 its editor of topical programmes and from 1985–91 a reporter on political and current affairs. She has presented on various television and radio programmes and is a columnist for the *Edinburgh Evening News* and *The Sunday Post*.

In 1972 she was voted Vice-Chairman of the SNP, a post that she retained until 1979, and was Senior Vice-Chairman of the Party from 1974–9. Over 1980 and 1981 she was a member of the SNP National Executive and from 1978–81 she was Chairman of the SNP '79 Group. Following the proscription of the '79 Group by the SNP she left the party in 1982. She returned to the SNP and was elected as a SNP member for the Lothians in the Scottish Parliament of 1999. Following the SNPs decision to lower her position on the Lothian list for the 2003 elections, she stood as an independent candidate and was re-elected as a member for the Lothians. She retained her seat in the 2007 Scottish Parliamentary elections and is currently the only independent member of the Scottish Parliament.

In the Scottish Parliament she is Vice-Chair of the Cross Party Group on Sport plus a member of the Cross Party Group on Culture and Media, and of the Cross Party Group for Survivors of Childhood Sexual Abuse. She is a campaigner for improved wheelchair provision; support for those with celiac disease; community health services designed to help people manage their own care and treatment supported by specialist assistance; more effective laws to manage street prostitution; improved physical education facilities in schools; and 'Capital City' status to be given to Edinburgh to take account of that city providing services for the whole of

Scotland. She was a Director of Shelter (Scotland) from 1978 to 1981 and is patron of the Edinburgh Cricket Club and of the Scottish Breast Cancer Campaign.

SHEILA MCLEAN: EDUCATOR AND LAWYER

Sheila McLean was born on 20 June 1951 and attended Glasgow High School for Girls and then Glasgow University from where she qualified as a Bachelor of Law in 1972, Master of Letters in 1978 and Doctor of Philosophy in 1987.

During 1972–5 she was an Area Reporter to the Children's Panel in Scotland and from 1975–85 a lecturer, then senior lecturer until 1990 at the School of Law at Glasgow University. She has been the Director of the Institute of Law and Ethics in Medicine since 1985 and became the first International Bar Association Professor of Law and Ethics in Medicine at Glasgow University in 1990. She has acted as a consultant in medical law and ethics to the World Health Organisation, the Council of Europe and to the United Kingdom Government. In addition, she is an expert reviewer for many of the major grant awarding bodies in the United Kingdom and is regularly consulted by the media on medical law and ethics.

Professor McLean's research includes all aspects of medical law but with a focus on consent to treatment, end of life issues, human rights, genetics and reproduction. In addition, Professor McLean has undertaken a number of research projects that focus on the implications of legal, ethical and social science methodologies for public policy in healthcare delivery. She has published extensively in the area of medical law and is on the editorial board of a number of national and international journals. Her present activities include United Kingdom Advisor to the World Health Organisation Europe on revision of Health for All, and Policy and Specialist Advisor to the House of Commons Select Committee on Science and Technology. She is a member of the British Medical Association Ethics Committee; Nuffield Trust Policy and Evaluation Committee; Selection Panel of the Broadcasting Council for Scotland; Audit Committee of World Association for Medical Law; American Society for Bioethics and Humanities; Force on Ethics Consultation College; Arts and Humanities Research Board Peer Review College; and Ethics Committee of the International Federation of Obstetrics and Gynaecology. Professor McLean has chaired the Scottish Criminal Cases Review Commission; Review of consent provisions of Human Fertilisation and Embryology Act; Inter-agency Forum on Female Offenders; Review of the Professions Supplementary to Medicine Act; and the Independent Review Group on Organ Retention at Post Mortem. She was Vice-Chair of the Multi-Centre Research Ethics Committee for Scotland and has been a member of various other groups and committees.

In 1996 she was made a Fellow of the Royal Society of Arts and of the Royal Society of Edinburgh, and an Honorary Fellow of the Royal College of General Practitioners in 2003. She received honorary degrees from the University of Abertay and the University of Edinburgh in 2002. In 2005 she was awarded the first ever Lifetime Achievement Award at the Scottish Legal Awards.

GEORGE MATHEWSON: BUSINESSMAN

George Mathewson was born on the 14 May 1940 and attended Perth Academy before attaining a Bachelor of Science in Mathematics and Applied Physics followed by a Doctor of Philosophy in Electrical Engineering from the University of St Andrews. He was an assistant lecturer at the University of St Andrews from 1964 until 1967.

From 1967 to 1972 he undertook and managed research and development programmes in avionics engineering with Bell Aerospace in United States of America. During this time he completed a Masters of Business Administration at Caisius College, Buffalo. In 1972 he returned to Scotland to take up a role with the Industrial and Commercial Finance Corporation (now 3i) in Edinburgh. From 1974 he was its Area Manager in Aberdeen before being made Assistant General Manager and Director in 1979. From 1981 to 1987 he was Director of the Scottish Development Agency.

In 1987 Sir George joined the Royal Bank of Scotland as Director of Strategic Planning and Development, becoming Deputy Group Chief Executive in 1990 and then Group Chief Executive in 1992. In 2000 he was made Deputy Chairman followed by Chairman in 2001 until 2006. In addition, he was a Director of Santander Central Hispano from 2001 until 2004. During this period the Royal Bank of Scotland established itself in the leading group of world banks, grew Citizens Bank from the 7th largest in the state of Rhode Island to the 8th largest in the United States of America, purchased the National Westminster Bank and in 1998 became the first Scottish company to deliver a £1 billion annual profit.

From 2002 to 2004 Sir George was President of the British Bankers Association; is President of the International Monetary Conference; a Director of the Institute of International Finance; and is Chair of the Council of Economic Advisers, which aims to improve the rate of sustainable economic growth in Scotland. He is Chairman of the campaign board of the Royal Botanic Gardens in Edinburgh, and is a Director of Scottish Investment Trust, Cheviot Asset Management and of Stagecoach.

Sir George is a Chartered Engineer, member of the Institute of Electrical Engineers, and companion of the Chartered Management Institute. Sir George was made Companion of the British Institute of Management in 1985, Fellow of the Royal Society of Edinburgh in 1988 and Fellow of the Chartered Institute of Bankers in Scotland in 1994. He holds honorary degrees from the Universities of Dundee (1983), St Andrews (2000), Glasgow (2001), Edinburgh (2002) and City University, London (2005). He received the United Kingdom National Business Lifetime Achievement Award in 2003, was made Commander, Order of the British Empire in 1985 and was Knighted in 1999 for services to Scottish banking and to economic development in Scotland.

KENNETH MURRAY: MOLECULAR BIOLOGIST

Born on 30 December 1930 in Yorkshire and raised in Nottingham, Kenneth Murray left school at age 16 to take up a position at Boots the Chemist as a laboratory technician. Gaining sufficient qualifications to secure a place at Birmingham University he graduated with a 1st Class Honours Degree in Chemistry and then a PhD in Chemistry. In 1958 he married Noreen Parker with whom he has collaborated on many projects.

Sir Kenneth continued his research on nulceohistones at Stanford University, California from 1960 until 1964, and then at the MRC Laboratory of Molecular Biology at Cambridge in Sanger's group, where he began working on nucleotide sequence analysis of DNA. In 1967 he accepted a position at the recently constituted Department of Molecular Biology at the University of Edinburgh, where he was senior lecturer then a reader between 1973 and 1976, and from 1976 onwards Professor of Molecular Biology. Between 1976 and 1978 he joined Werner Arber and others in producing the European Molecular Biology Organisation Recombinant DNA Courses in Basel, Switzerland. In 1979, with his research focusing on the hepatitis B virus, he progressed his research at the European Molecular Biology Laboratory in Heidelberg, returning to Edinburgh in 1982.

As an early worker in DNA, Sir Kenneth was a pioneer in developing DNA sequencing and recombinant DNA technology. In 1978 he was one of a small group of scientists involved in the formation of the international biotechnology company, Biogen, NV, and served on the Scientific and Directors Boards for 25 years. Recalling the deaths of carers of patients with hepatitis B in discussions and collaborations with Biogen colleagues, he developed reliable diagnostics for that virus and then produced a vaccine through cloned parts of the viral DNA. This has saved countless lives across the world. Patents on this work brought large royalty payments to Biogen and the University of Edinburgh. Sir Kenneth donated his share to the Darwin Trust of Edinburgh, which he established in 1983 to support education and research in natural science. The Darwin Trust of Edinburgh also endowed the Royal Society, Darwin Trust of Edinburgh Research Professorship.

Sir Kenneth is a member of the Biochemical Society, the European Molecular Biology Organisation (EMBO), the Academia Europaea, the Academy of Medical Sciences, and remains Chairman of the Darwin Trust of Edinburgh. Sir Kenneth's awards include the Willem Meindart de Hoop Prize in 1983, and the Saltire Society (Edinburgh) Scientific Award in 1992. He has written many papers on DNA, genetic engineering and viral hepatitis.

In 1975 he became a member of EMBO, a Fellow of the Royal Society in 1979, Fellow of the Royal Society of Edinburgh in 1989, Fellow of the Royal College of Pathologists in 1991, was Knighted in 1993, and is Emeritus Professor of Molecular Biology at the University of Edinburgh. Sir Kenneth has received honorary degrees from the Universities of Birmingham, Dundee, Edinburgh and University of Manchester Institute of Science and Technology (UMIST), and in 2000 was awarded the Royal Medal of the Royal Society of Edinburgh.

NOREEN MURRAY: MOLECULAR BIOLOGIST

Noreen Murray was born on 26 February 1935 and went from Lancaster Girls' Grammar School to King's College London in 1953 to study botany, from which she graduated in 1956. From King's College she went to the University of Birmingham where she gained a Postgraduate Doctorate. Her postgraduate thesis on neurospora crassa initially looked for linkage between methionine loci but eventually focused on polarised gene conversion. In 1958 she married Kenneth Murray with whom she has collaborated on many projects.

From 1960 to 1964 she was a Research Associate at Stanford University, California and then undertook a Fellowship at Cambridge University from 1964 to 1967. In 1967 she moved to the University of Edinburgh as a member of the Medical Research Council Microbial Genetics Unit located in the United Kingdom's first Department of Molecular Biology. From 1974 she was a lecturer, then senior lecturer and a reader from 1978 until 1988 when she became a Professor of Molecular Genetics. From 1976 to 1978 she joined Werner Arber and others in producing the European Molecular Biology Organisation Recombinant DNA Courses in Basel, Switzerland. In 1980 she moved to the European Molecular Biology Laboratory in Heidelberg as a Group Leader. She returned to Edinburgh in 1982 to continue her research programme and the training of postgraduate students and research associates.

Along with her colleagues in Edinburgh, and as an early worker in genetic engineering, she was at the forefront of recombinant DNA research. Her contributions have included fundamental studies of restriction enzymes and the development of cloning vectors based on the bacteriophage lambda along with their use to develop efficient expression systems for several of the enzymes that are now used in every molecular biology laboratory around the world. These contributions were recognised by the Royal Society (Gabor Medal) and the Biochemical Society's AstraZeneca Award. She has written and contributed to many research papers on genetics and molecular biology.

From 1994 to 1997 she was a Member of the Biotechnology and Biological Sciences Research Council, President Genetical Society between 1987 and 1990, and Member European Molecular Biology Organisation in 1981. In addition, she has been a Member of Council of the Royal Society and is a Trustee of the Darwin Trust of Edinburgh. She was made a Fellow of The Royal Society in 1982, Fellow of the Royal Society of Edinburgh in 1989 and Commander, Order of the British Empire in 2002. She is Emeritus Professor of Molecular Biology at the University of Edinburgh and holds honorary degrees from the University of Warwick, University of Manchester Institute of Science and Technology (UMIST), and the University of Birmingham, and is a Fellow of King's College London.

GEORGE ROBERTSON: POLITICIAN

George Robertson was born on 12 April 1946 on the Isle of Islay. He attended Dunoon Grammar School and from there went to study economics at the University of Dundee where he was heavily involved in student politics, graduating with as a Master of Arts in 1968.

From university he took up a full-time position with the General, Municipal and Boilermakers' Union (GMB) where he had responsibility for a 9,000 membership in the Scotch whisky industry. Over 1977 and 1978 he was Chairman of the Scottish Labour Party and in 1978 he stood for the Labour Party in the Hamilton by-election and won that seat, which he retained until 1999. In opposition he was spokesman on Scottish Affairs (1979–80), Defence (1980–1), Foreign and Commonwealth Affairs (1981–93), European Affairs (1984–93) and Principal opposition front bench spokesman on Scotland (1993–97). When Labour won power in the 1997 General election he was made Secretary of State for Defence and during that time he implemented the Strategic Defence Review. In 1999 he relinquished his Hamilton seat, becoming Lord Robertson of Port Ellen, and took up the role of Secretary General of NATO. His four year tenure as Secretary General of NATO included NATO forces being deployed in Kosovo, expansion of the alliance and the modernisation of its capabilities, as well as the 11 September attacks on the United States of America in 2001.

On leaving NATO in 2004 he accepted a position as Deputy Chairman of Cable and Wireless and he is Deputy Chairman of TNK–BP. Lord Robertson was a non-executive Director of the Smiths Group and is on the board of the Weir Group. He is also an advisor to the Cohen Group (USA) and Engelfield Capital.

From 1985 to 1994 he was Vice-Chairman of the Board to British Council and, from 1984 to 1991, Member of Council of the Royal Institute of International Affairs. He is Chairman of the John Smith Memorial Trust, Deputy Chairman of the Ditchley Foundation, Honorary Regimental Colonel of the London Scottish (Volunteers), Elder Brother of Trinity House, and Honorary Guild Brother of the Guildry of Stirling.

Lord Robertson was made a Honorary Fellow of the Royal Society of Edinburgh in 2003. He became a Honorary Senior Fellow of the Foreign Policy Association (USA) in 2000 and holds honorary degrees from the Universities of Dundee, Bradford, Baku (Azerbajan), Romanian National School, European University of Armenia and the Royal Military College of Science, Cranfield. He has been awarded Orders of Merit from Italy, the Netherlands, Germany, Poland, Luxemburg, Hungary, Spain, Portugal, Lithuania, Bulgaria, Croatia, Ukraine, Belgium, United States of America, Estonia and Slovakia. He was made Privy Councillor in 1997, Knight Grand Cross Order of St Michael and St George in 2004 and Knight, Order of the Thistle in 2004.

LEWIS ROBERTSON: INDUSTRIALIST AND ADMINISTRATOR

Born on 28 November 1922 in Dundee, Lewis Robertson attended Dundee High School, Ardvreck Preparatory School and Trinity College, Glenalmond. Prior to his war service, Sir Lewis was an apprentice Chartered Accountant with Moody, Stuart & Robertson in Dundee.

Sir Lewis started his war service in 1942 as a Royal Air Force photographer but was transferred to Government Code and Cipher School, Bletchley Park where he worked on breaking enemy codes. On demobilisation he joined the family textile business, rather than completing his accountancy training, because his elder brother was killed during the war. Sir Lewis became Managing Director and undertook extensive trade association work, including Chairman and leading witness for the industry's Restrictive Practices court case. In 1965, Robertson Industrial Textiles merged to form Scott & Robertson Ltd, with Sir Lewis appointed Managing Director and Chairman until his resignation in 1970. He then became Chief Executive of Grampian Holdings where profits were trebled during his five year tenure.

From 1981 Sir Lewis followed a career as a Specialist Rescue Chairman, Policy Consultant, and Part-time plc Chairman. The companies whose fortunes he revived included steel manufacturer F.H. Lloyd Holdings plc, light engineer Triplex plc, food processor Borthwicks plc, construction group Lilley plc, furniture manufacturer Havelock Europa plc and leisure group Stakis plc. Other appointments included member and then Chairman of the Eastern Regional Hospital Board, where he was involved in the construction of Ninewells Hospital, Dundee; the Monopolies Commission, where he considered items such as fire insurance, Boots/ House of Fraser merger, contraceptive sheaths and electric cables; he was appointed to the steering Committee of the Scottish Development Agency then accepted the role of Deputy Chairman and first Chief Executive; was the first Chairman of Girobank Scotland; and he has held numerous non-executive Directorships.

In recognition of his contribution to the Carnegie Trust for the Universities of Scotland the Robertson Medal is awarded annually. He has served on many other committees, including those of the Scottish Episcopal Church, and one of his longest contributions was as Trustee to the Dundee Disabled Children's Association from 1960–2002. As a Fellow of the Royal Society of Edinburgh, since 1978, he has been a Council Member, Treasurer, Chairman of Trustees and was awarded the 2001 Bicentenary Medal. Sir Lewis was recognised as Commander, Order of the British Empire in 1969 and was Knighted in 1991. He was elected Fellow of the British Institute of Management, 1976; Honorary Fellow, The Royal College of Surgeons of Edinburgh, 1999; received the Lifetime Achievement Award, Society of Turnaround Practitioners, 2004; and has honorary degrees from the Universities of Dundee, Napier, Stirling, Aberdeen and Glasgow.

JACKIE STEWART: RACING DRIVER AND BUSINESSMAN

Jackie Stewart was born in Milton, Dumbarton on 11 June 1939 and attended Dumbarton Academy which he left at age 15 to work at the family garage. From his mid-teens until 1962 he shot competitively, during which time he won the British Grand Prix of Shooting twice plus the English, Irish, Scottish and Welsh championships and he was named first reserve for the 1960 British Olympic Shooting team. Sir Jackie signed his first professional driving contract with Ecurie Ecosse in 1963 and in 1964 drove for Ken Tyrell in Formula Three and also drove Formula Two from 1964 until 1970. He married Helen McGregor in 1961 and they have two children, Paul and Mark.

In 1965 he commenced his Formula One career driving for BRM. His first victory coming that year in the non-championship Daily Express International Trophy, followed by his first World Championship win at the Italian Grand Prix in Monza. After a crash during the 1966 Belgian Grand Prix he became a leading campaigner to introduce improved safety to Formula One. Sir Jackie drove for BRM until 1967 and then joined the new Tyrell Formula One team with which he drove until 1973. He clinched the Formula One World Championship in 1969, following another first place at Monza, and was again World Champion in 1971, following the Austrian Grand Prix despite retiring from that race. He achieved a third World Championship in 1973 after a fourth place finish at Monza, having trailed the field for much of the race. Sir Jackie retired from Formula One at the end of the 1973 season with a record of 27 victories from 99 starts.

Along with his son Paul, in 1998 he established Paul Stewart Racing, which achieved 136 race wins in the formative racing classes. In 1996 they formed Formula One Stewart Grand Prix, which recorded a win at the Grand Prix of Europe in 1999. Stewart Grand Prix was bought by Ford in 2000. Sir Jackie worked as a commentator and expert motor racing television summariser for the American Broadcasting Company (ABC) from 1971 until 1986. From 1964 until 2004 he was contracted to the Ford Motor Company; first as a racing driver, then a public affairs representative, sales and marketing spokesman, vehicle assessor, concept design consultant and, finally, as a strategic adviser. In addition, he has commercial relationships with, amongst others, Moet & Chandon and Rolex, and he is a global ambassador for the Royal Bank of Scotland. Sir Jackie also developed the Gleneagles Jackie Stewart Shooting School and he published his autobiography *Winning Is Not Enough* in 2007.

Sir Jackie holds honorary degrees from the Lawrence Institute of Technology in Michigan, Glasgow Caledonian University and Heriot-Watt University in Edinburgh. In 1973 he was named BBC Sports Personality of the Year, made Officer, Order of the British Empire in 1972 and he was Knighted in 2001.

WILLIAM STEWART: SCIENTIST

William Stewart was born in Glasgow on 7 June 1935. He spent his entire childhood on the island of Islay and went on to study at Glasgow University. He was appointed, at the age of 32, the foundation Professor of Biological Sciences at the University of Dundee on its establishment in 1968 and he chaired the Independent Scientific Advisory Group which oversaw the decontamination of Gruinard Island of anthrax. Sir William became Chief Executive of the Agricultural and Food Research Council and set in place a structure which saw its development in to the Biotechnology and Biological Sciences Research Council. He was Chief Scientific Adviser to the United Kingdom Government from 1990-95, during which time the Government published its first White Paper on Science and Technology for over 20 years, and was the architect of the Government's first Technology Foresight programme (Government Foresight programme has continued ever since).

Sir William was President of the Royal Society of Edinburgh from 2000-03 and is currently Chairman of the Health Protection Agency, the first one-stop shop in the world dealing with public health hazards from radiation, chemicals and infectious diseases. The 3,000 strong Agency now includes the Centre for Applied Microbiological Research at Porton Down and the National Radiological Protection Board (both of which he had previously chaired) and the Public Health Laboratory Service at Colindale. He is also a Trustee of the Royal Botanic Gardens Kew. Sir William has held numerous other posts including President of the British Association for the Advancement of Science, Chairman of the Government sponsored Independent Expert Group on Mobile Phones, and President of the Scottish Marine Biological Association (now Scottish Association for Marine Science).

He has been awarded 24 honorary degrees and fellowships, including honorary degrees from eight Scottish universities (Aberdeen, Abertay, Edinburgh, Dundee, Glasgow, Napier, Stirling and Paisley). Sir William is particularly proud that he received the Presidents Medal from the Royal Academy of Engineering in 1995, the only biologist ever to be so awarded, and to be the first person in the history of the University of Glasgow to receive two honorary doctorates from it. He was Knighted in 1994, has lived in Dundee for the past 40 years and lists his clubs as the New Club, Edinburgh; the Farmers Club, London; and Dundee United.

Luath Press Limited
committed to publishing well written books worth reading

LUATH PRESS takes its name from Robert Burns, whose little collie Luath (*Gael.*, swift or nimble) tripped up Jean Armour at a wedding and gave him the chance to speak to the woman who was to be his wife and the abiding love of his life. Burns called one of 'The Twa Dogs' Luath after Cuchullin's hunting dog in Ossian's *Fingal*. Luath Press was established in 1981 in the heart of Burns country, and now resides a few steps up the road from Burns' first lodgings on Edinburgh's Royal Mile.

Luath offers you distinctive writing with a hint of unexpected pleasures.

Most bookshops in the UK, the US, Canada, Australia, New Zealand and parts of Europe either carry our books in stock or can order them for you. To order direct from us, please send a £sterling cheque, postal order, international money order or your credit card details (number, address of cardholder and expiry date) to us at the address below. Please add post and packing as follows: UK – £1.00 per delivery address; overseas surface mail – £2.50 per delivery address; overseas airmail – £3.50 for the first book to each delivery address, plus £1.00 for each additional book by airmail to the same address. If your order is a gift, we will happily enclose your card or message at no extra charge.

ILLUSTRATION: IAN KELLAS

Luath Press Limited
543/2 Castlehill
The Royal Mile
Edinburgh EH1 2ND
Scotland
Telephone: 0131 225 4326 (24 hours)
Fax: 0131 225 4324
email: sales@luath.co.uk
Website: www.luath.co.uk